Dr. Clarence Shuler

Contributing Editor
Myrna Gutierrez

BUILDING LASTING RELATIONSHIPS PUBLISHING

www.clarenceshuler.com

www.clarencefs@gmail.com

Twitter: @clarenceshuler

Facebook: Building Lasting Relationships Community Page

Gary Chapman, *New York Times* Best-selling author of *The Five Love Languages* says, "In *Single and Free to Be Me*, Clarence Shuler challenges single adults not to spend their lives 'waiting,' but to invest their lives in meaningful pursuits every day. The decisions we make each day affect the rest of our lives. Make wise decisions and you assure yourself of the best possible life. I highly recommend this book."

Building Lasting Relationships Publishing House
Colorado Springs
Single and Free to Be Me, © 2012 by Dr. Clarence Shuler
with Contributing Editor Myrna Gutierrez
and Guest Editor Glynese Northam

Cover Idea: Brenda Shuler and Myrna Gutierrez

Cover Design: Clarianne Medina

ISBN- 13: 978-1480280038

Third Printing

Dr. Clarence Shuler's (a.k.a. The Love Doctor*) Contact Information:*
E-mail Address:clarencefs@gmail.com
Website:www.clarenceshuler.com
Facebook: Building Lasting Relationships Community Page
Twitter: @clarenceshuler

Contents

DEDICATED TO

My beautiful daughters, Christina, Michelle, and Andrea, and my beautiful nieces, Angela, Dee Dee, Jasmine, Jennifer, Jessica, and Leah, all single at the time of the writing of this book.

Dr. Suzanne Mayo's Webinar Class at Southern University at New Orleans (now Vice President for Institutional Advancement at Wiley College)

Fellowship of Christian Athletes at Wake Forest University and their chaplain, Joe Haynes

And a Special Dedication to the men on the eleventh floor of Culbertson Hall (Fall of 2011), Moody Bible Institute, Chicago, IL

Luke Aubrey	Eddie Cuevas
Adam Noone	James Black
Hyun Jun Kim	Ben Anderson
Minha Ha	Johnny Oehler
Danny Garnett	Jeremy Warren
Eric Larson	Brandon Fenner
Trevor Jamieson	Jonathan Huang
'Lil' Jake Ocha	Aaron Wright
Aidan Lane	Sam Amis
David MacKay	

ACKNOWLEDGMENTS

Thank you so much to Andrea Shuler, Becca Friesen, Connor Neignfind, Dale Collins, Jean Shuler, Leah Holder, Patrick Walker, Paul Saunders, Steve Angevine, and Walter Brown. These singles—ranging from early twenties to sixties—provided a vast range of perspective: some have never been married, some are divorced, some are virgins and some not, and some are single parents. All graciously sacrificed their time to read this book and give insightful feedback. All readers of this book are indebted to you for your time, input and prayers for this book. May God richly bless you for your service to many!

To Daniel, Luke, Catrina, Connor, Jean, Patrick, Hillary, Paul, Hephzibah, Adam, Heidi, Rachid and Steve, Myrna and I can never repay you for writing the last chapter of this book, *What the Church Can Do for Singles*. Hopefully, pastors and other church leaders will learn from you and bless other singles with your wisdom.

David Reyes, "Thank You" for making my *Building Lasting Relationships (BLR) Community* Facebook page a reality and teaching me how to be the administrator. I'll never forget your kindness and patience.

Ian Westermann, I'm so grateful to you for the improvements you made to the *BLR* website with the videos and well as other invaluable ideas. Thank you for forcing me to overcome many of my fears about being technically challenged. And I also appreciate your patience with me.

Steve Sicola and Kenneth Bates, "Thank You" both for selflessly using your computer genius skills to revive my Mac, so I could finish writing this book.

Thank you to my Prayer Warriors for your words of encouragement, especially for interceding for our provision while writing this book and for praying for all the sometimes difficult steps involved in publishing *Single and Free to Be Me*.

Glynese Northam, thank you for your additional edits that were so helpful.

David Malone, your generous and gracious offer to help blessed me so much! Thank you for the gift of your friendship.

Myrna White and Yvonne Wolf, thank you two wonderful ladies for your comfort, encouragement and words of wisdom during a time of disappointment while trying to get this book published.

Patti and Jacob Unger, thank you so much for working so hard to help me get this book ready at the last minute.

Janie McGee, thank you for making it possible for me to self-publish books on CreateSpace.com. I wouldn't be able to do it without your skill. I continue to be blown away by your gifting and your passion for the ministry God has given me. Thank you for being a channel in which I can get God's word out to so many, so quickly!

And to Clarianne Medina, Janie, Myrna, and Brenda, thank you so much for all of your amazing contributions to this book's final cover. Each of you provided rich creativity. And thank you for your incredible patience with me during this very long process.

Clarianne, thank you for taking these cover ideas, plus your own and creating our final front and back covers.

To Walter White, former Alumni Association Executive Director for giving me my first opportunity to speak in a Moody Bible Institute Chapel and giving me the topic of relationships, which revealed singles need for such a book as this. Your allowing me to speak in this chapel was an answer to a forty year-plus dream as a Moody student.

To Nancy Hastings, Moody Bible Institute's Alumni Association Executive Director for more chapel opportunities to speak to students about relationships on the Chicago and Spokane campuses, confirming the necessity for this book.

Myrna, as I have said to others, the same is true of you. There is no way I could write this quality of a book without you. Your walk with God truly inspires everyone who interacts with you. I've learned much from you about God. Your spiritual gifts are simply amazing! Thank you for all of your research, challenging questions, edits, thoroughness, etc.

And last, but never least is you, Brenda: Thank you for the original front cover idea! As soon as I saw it, I knew it was from God! Thank you for allowing me to write this book and believing in me. You are so patient, especially with this book, which took longer to write than any of my previous ones. Sorry for becoming such an airhead when writing. Yet, you love me anyway. I'm so blessed having you in my life!

INTRODUCTION

Just between you and me: are there times when you are a little frustrated with the way our society treats you as a single teenager, college student, divorcee, widowed or a never-been-married single? Are there situations in which you feel you aren't free to be yourself because you are experiencing pressure to be someone else? And if you are really honest with yourself, you're not sure or possibly fearful to discover who you really are?

This pressure, especially to be in romantic relationships, comes from both the secular and religious communities. They say if you aren't in a relationship, something must be wrong with you or you're slightly abnormal. Do you feel the pressure of not being in a dating relationship? Do you sometimes feel you are not worthy to be in a relationship? Throughout this book, I want to show you how to be free from most of these pressures.

What does a nearly sixty-year-old man, who has been married for almost thirty years know about today's singles world? That's what I asked myself until a series of events compelled me to write this book.

After speaking to athletes at Wake Forest University about relationships, I was shocked that these eighteen-twenty something year old single students were buying my marriage book, *Keeping Your Wife Your Best Friend*. I imagine some of the guys addicted to pornography wanted to see in detail how I was able to defeat my addiction and how I've been able to remain clean for nearly twenty years.

Single girls said they bought my book because they wanted to see how a guy should treat a girl and they wanted more insight into the mind of a man (this could be a scary place to go!).

Then I spoke at a religious school, Moody Bible Institute in Chicago and Spokane about relationships. After speaking in the chapels, students lined up to talk with me right then or to schedule a relationship counseling session. Students often said, "No one is speaking to us about relationships the way you are."

My "For Men Only" sessions on college campuses revealed the epidemic that includes even Christian guys' daily struggle with pornography and related addictions.

And after I conducted a relationship webinar at Southern University at New Orleans, the students requested that I come down for a week to speak more about relationships, fathering, sex, and to my surprise, God's perspective on all of this!

The positive responses of these college students and comments from counseling sessions with teenagers, young adults, and divorcees (young and old) made me feel that writing this book wasn't optional.

You, like me, may be wondering what all these singles want to learn from an old married man. One of the most precious compliments I've received from high school students, college students, and young adults is, "You're *real.*" This is why they say I'm able to connect with people much younger than me. Hopefully, this book will relate to what you're experiencing as a single, regardless of your age.

I didn't marry until I was in my thirties, which in the 80s, was really *late* to be getting married. That age today, would have been like being single well into my forties. For me, being single was difficult because I didn't seem to fit anywhere. So, I've always had a passion for singles. After hearing about the relationship plight of many singles and even married couples, I felt a need to try to share some principles with which teenagers, college students, young and older adults and divorcees all seem to resonate. This is a broad group, so as you read, realize that every situation may not apply directly to you, but the principles usually will be applicable to some degree.

Most singles books focus on a particular facet of being single, especially dating. However, singlehood consists of much more than dating. Singlehood involves discovering who you are, feeling lonely, healing and for some, discerning the right one. Since singlehood has different cycles, this book is divided into major sections that you can reference depending on which stage you are in. You can either read the entire book all at once or focus on one particular section. *Single and Free to Be Me* will be your handy companion as you walk through your entire singlehood journey!

Regardless of what stage of singlehood you are in right now, I urge you to read the first section: *The Art of Flying Solo.* A primary goal of this book is to help you know yourself better and appreciate yourself more as a single. I want you to understand and embrace your self-worth. I don't want you worshiping yourself, but you do need to understand that you have value just the way you are.

If you are widowed, hopefully, this book's title doesn't in any way make you feel that you are disrespecting your late spouse. Even though you were not rejected, you have experienced the loss of a relationship. You may find Chapter Four: *Healing a Broken Heart* comforting and helpful.

Yes, everyone needs some tweaking which is why there is an entire chapter on healing, but you are still priceless in value! And if you begin living out this principle, you will naturally make yourself more attractive and desirable to *those* people who are good for you. I don't want you to value yourself just to impress people, get a date, or get married, but because it will free you to fulfill your purpose, find peace with yourself, and experience the best that life has to offer!

Another goal of this book is for you as a single teenager, college student, a never-been-married single adult, or divorcee to get off the *I've got to be in a relationship merry-go-round.* If this is where you are, it has got to be wearing you out. Freedom, *your* freedom, is a priority of this book! I want you free from the pressure of feeling you have to be a certain way in order to get into a relationship. I want you free from thinking and feeling you have to *be in a relationship, and if you aren't, something is terribly wrong with you!* You may be a little crazy or rough around the edges, but so are most people. Basically, you are probably fine. I'm not sure if anyone is completely normal.

Freedom to be *you* is another motivating factor for this book. Some of you struggle with impressing others by attempting to be something or someone you are not. A friend once told me, "No one can be a better you than you." I was trying to impress a crowd by speaking in a certain way and failing terribly, rather than being myself! I was afraid the crowd wouldn't like the real me. And I hated the way I was speaking in pretense. I was so wrong. Don't be like me. I want you to be free to be you. You are unique and have a lot to offer. If you are struggling with this issue, then this book may just set you free!

In this book, we also explore freedom (not totally) from loneliness, a paramount issue with most singles. Sound interesting?

In *Section II: Confused About Relationships?* you'll discover biblical and practical principles for healthy relationships with the opposite sex. We live in a culture where dating is evolving and increasingly confusing to singles of all ages.

For those of you who have been seriously dating and considering taking it to the next step, check out the third section, *Before You Say "I Do".* You'll learn about practical resources, questions and clues that will help you cultivate a healthy marriage while you're still single. After all, a healthy marriage begins with being a confident and whole single. Even if you aren't in a serious relationship, this section will give you a preview of how to identify Mr. or Mrs. Right and arm you with confidence to enter compatible relationships that could lead you to the altar.

If you are looking for a book with steps guaranteeing to put you in a relationship, this ain't the book for you. But embracing some of the principles found in the following pages will most likely help you become more attractive to potential partners. This really isn't the goal of *Single and Free to Be Me,* but it may become a by-product.

Since I am married, I reached out to a dear sister friend, Myrna Gutierrez, an Emmy award-winning TV producer, writer, and businesswoman who has consulted for Fortune 500 companies, nonprofit organizations, government, and media. Her communications strategies have helped shape the messages in this book to make it more relevant to singles of all ages, particularly since she has been through most of those stages.

You see, Myrna in her early fifties, remains happily single and has navigated the dating world with all the ups and downs that many of you face. As my contributing editor, working from her sick bed (after suffering a work injury), she has given me tremendous insight into the evolving world of Christian singles living under the dating pressures of our culture.

Hopefully, this book will provide the best of several worlds: Myrna's insight on singlehood, my thirty plus years of experience as a relationship counselor for singles and married couples, as well as my nearly thirty years of marriage to the same woman, Brenda.

Additionally, we invited a diverse group of singles (some virgins, some not; some never married; some divorced; and some single parents) from the ages of fifteen to sixty to provide input on this book. Myrna and I found their insights invaluable. You will also see incredible research throughout each chapter due to her journalism background.

My prayer for you as you read this book is that each chapter will be a Blessing for you and help you recognize your value as a single, regardless of your age or relationship status.

Clarence Shuler, President/CEO
BLR: Building Lasting Relationships
"Taking the BLuR out of Relationships"

Chapter One

I Can Be Single, Complete, and Content —Really?

"I've learned by now to be quite content whatever my circumstances. I'm just as happy with little as with much, with much as with little. I've found the recipe for being happy whether full or hungry, hands full or hands empty. Whatever I have, wherever I am, I can make it through anything in the One who makes me who I am."

Philippians 4:11-13, The Message

After graduating college and being semi-employed, being single initially presented me with some problems. Unlike college, where I was a basketball star at one school (even though barely on the team at another), dating wasn't an issue. But being in the workplace and getting older, I erroneously allowed my singleness to dominate my thoughts and my self-image. When no other thoughts were occupying my mind, I was obsessed with being single. Imagine a barely audible voice, consistently reminding you, "You're single. If you just had someone—you'd have it going on." Incompleteness, sometimes accompanied with inadequacy was the implication of this voice. Buying into this voice's message also made me selfish because I focused on what someone could do for me, not thinking at all about what I might need to do for a girl.

Having a lot of married friends didn't really help either. As honorable as their intentions were, their matchmaking attempts also made me feel pressured. Their well-meaning efforts even seemed to imply that I was incomplete without a spouse. To be fair to them, they just wanted me to be as happy as they appeared to be and they knew I was lonely. But I also knew that every married person wasn't happy and some were lonely despite being married.

When there were no girls around with whom to be friends, I viewed girls more as sex objects than people, which increased my sex drive. Guys often joke about taking a LOT of cold showers, but I had to do something to control my sex drive. I noticed that having girls as friends actually lowered my sex drive!

Having girls who were my friends, but not girlfriends, allowed me to see them as people because talking with them reminded me that they had issues just like me. Also, these girls became more like my sisters.

Going to grad school was helpful because the majority of this community was single, so I felt more normal again.

Learning to Embrace My Singleness

Grad school helped me mature a little, but after graduation, I repeated my single crisis cycle. Praying with one of my adopted grandmothers, the late Anne Wenger, forever changed my life. Taking me to the book of Philippians in the Bible, she showed me where Paul's imprisonment didn't prevent him from accomplishing his mission. My grandmother wanted me to learn that no situation should limit me or make me feel inferior. She wanted me to figure out a way to be victorious regardless of my circumstances. Grandmother was pretty smart. She knew that developing such a mindset for life would keep me from using my circumstances as excuses for feeling sorry for myself or for quitting. So her prayer for me was to learn to experience the best of life when life isn't the best. This experience radically changed my perspective on being single. And for the first time, I began embracing my singleness. Feeling less out of place was the result of my time with my grandmother. I began to change my attitude to that of "I probably won't get married and I'll be fine." Getting married was my preference, but I removed the pressure from myself by not thinking that I had to get married or that something was wrong with me because I wasn't married. Years later—I can't remember if I was married or not—my former grad school friend, Herb Brisbane, the singles pastor at a mega church, made this statement, "If you are not content being single, you won't be content being married." Herb's quote initially caught me by surprise. It kept bombarding my thoughts and the more it did, the more profound it became to me. Here's what I've added to Herb's quote, "If you are not content being single, you won't be content in a friendship or dating relationship or being married."

Why do Herb and I say such a thing? If you are not content as singles, you usually have an inaccurate, poor self-image, often resulting in seeing yourself as inferior or lacking in some respect. Taking such a perspective of yourself into a relationship on any level almost certainly will result in some form of dysfunction and create baggage.

If You Aren't a Follower of Christ

Now for those of you, who aren't followers of Christ, I just want to give you a heads-up that I will be making some references from the Bible. This isn't an attempt to persuade you to subscribe to my spiritual beliefs. I do believe regardless of where you are in relating to spiritual issues, what you are about to read won't hurt you and can actually help you. Several successful NBA and college basketball coaches have used biblical principles with their teams and won championships. And several of these coaches aren't religious. So if you don't believe in Jesus Christ, then determine if you can apply any of the following principles. Keep an open mind—a key to any education.

I will do my best to be sensitive, but please be patient with me if I get a little preachy. When preachy, I'll be challenging those who are following Christ. I'm so glad you are reading this book!

God Values You Just As You Are

For those of us who are followers of Christ, an inaccurate biblical perspective of ourselves often and unfortunately can have us erroneously believing we have nothing to offer in relationships. We may even feel unworthy, inferior, or insecure.

Julie Morris' book, *Worthless to Worthy: A 30-Day Guide to Overcoming Inferiority* is an excellent resource if you struggle with this issue. If you feel inferior due to abuse, Dr. Garry C. James' book and workbook, *Drying Silent Tears* are incredible!

Let me encourage you. You need to like you for who you are. God certainly does. Read Psalm 139:13-16 (The Message).

"Oh yes, you shaped me first inside, then out; You formed me in my mother's womb.

I thank you, High God—you're breathtaking! Body and soul, I am marvelously made!

I worship in adoration—what a creation! You know me inside and out,

You know every bone in my body;

You know exactly how I was made, bit by bit, how I was sculpted from nothing into something.

Like an open book, you watched me grow from conception to birth;

all the stages of my life were spread out before you,

The days of my life all prepared before I'd even lived one day."

Think about these verses. God is saying you are neither an accident nor unwanted. He purposely planned for you! So you aren't too short, too tall, the wrong complexion, too skinny, the wrong gender, nor whatever you think your shortcomings are. God has even created days specifically for your use! Now, this is the God of all creation doing this for you and me! I don't know about you, but His actions before I was born make me feel so special now! He isn't talking about us here in the context of being in a relationship. He is speaking to you as singles—as individuals!! You are a SPECIAL individual!!!

You may not know or realize it, but when you don't like yourself or you criticize yourself, you're unintentionally criticizing God. You should know that God considers you special and that He obviously wants you! Most of you would never want to criticize Him about how He created you, dwelling on whatever you think is wrong with you. It is one thing to discuss any situation you are in, get counsel, and even ask God to change your circumstances; but it's quite another to criticize God. Some of you do intentionally criticize God because you are angry with Him, feeling He has let you down in one way or another. These are legitimate feelings, which will be addressed later in this book. I'm not implying nor demanding that you like any of your circumstances. But you may need to learn how to see God's Big Picture for you.

So what does seeing God's Big Picture look like? Great question! Seeing God's Big Picture often, but not always, requires waiting (yeah, I dislike waiting too), preparation, discipline, and faith; but it also requires getting into position to see His Big Picture. Compare seeing God's Big Picture to preparing for and taking the SAT, GRE, GMAT, LSAT, or other big exam. Or it could be waiting in line for tickets for a concert, then waiting in line again to actually get into the concert, and finally, waiting for the concert to begin. In sports, it is waiting for a play to develop so you can make the pass to a teammate. Often you have to make the pass before your teammate is open. Discipline and faith are huge components in business, sports, and academics, just as they are in singlehood. Complaining about circumstances and yourself usually communicates to God, "God, you blew it." Or "God, you really can't handle my situation. You really don't have my best interest at heart." Such thinking can be disheartening and lead to desperation. Reading Romans 9:20-21 (The Message) hopefully gives you a better perspective.

"Who in the world do you think you are to second-guess God? Do you for one moment suppose any of us knows enough to call God into question? Clay doesn't talk back to the fingers that mold it, saying, "Why did you shape me like this?" Isn't it obvious that a potter has a perfect right to shape one lump of clay into a vase for holding flowers and another into a pot for cooking beans?"

See if you can embrace this principle: "God's best for me is Always Right Now, not yesterday and not tomorrow!" For example, while single and in grad school, I tore my anterior cruciate ligament (ACL) in my right knee playing basketball. Initially, it was humbling as my buddies had to help me dress until I became limber enough to dress myself because of the ankle to thigh cast I was in.

Here are a few things I learned from my injury:

- I was meeting people I probably never would have met because my normal routine was changed, so I spoke with more people who tried to help me because I was on crutches.

- I no longer take my body and health, especially walking, for granted.

- I learned to be more grateful for what seems to be insignificant abilities like being able to dress myself, being able to walk without help, and being able to get places quickly.

- I gained a better appreciation for interdependency, enriching the value of my friendships.

- My physical recovery provided me with a better understanding of faith, of facing my fears, and working through pain in order to experience healing.

- I learned to swim as part of my recovery and it helped alleviate many years of my fear of water.

- I learned the priceless lesson of learning not to quit when there were setbacks in my recovery. It increased my patience and perseverance.

- I learned the value of physical fitness aided by lifting weights with a cardiovascular emphasis, which serves me to this day to stay in shape helping my body and my heart.

- I learned to receive, as people were so gracious to give while I was on crutches.

- God's power through prayer changed my life forever as my church prayed for my healing. God miraculously healed my knee without surgery. There was no need to place a needle in my leg to drain the fluids on my knee.

- I learned that delay isn't always denial. My injury was inconvenient, with a long recovery process. At times, I wondered if I'd ever be able to play again. But God had a much bigger plan to change my life for the better.

- God exposed me to His principle that when He allows or causes what seems like a problem, His goal is to draw me closer to Him and make me better than before my problem or situation occurred.

- I learned that God will often heal you, usually spiritually first, then physically. Within 10 months after my injury, I was playing basketball in Brazil against its Olympic basketball team at full speed. In the early 80's, it normally took a year or more to recover.

I realize reading all those bullet points may have been a little much for some of you, but I want you to see how much we can learn from what may initially seem like bad luck, injustice, or a painful waste of time.

After experiencing all these physical and spiritual lessons from a torn ACL, it was easy for me to realize: God always has my best interest in mind and He knows what is best for me, more than I do. That principle took a lot of pressure off me to try to make things happen, especially in the area of relationships.

Think about it: if you are not content being single, there is a tendency to put tremendous pressure on the person who wants to be your friend, boyfriend, girlfriend, or spouse. You intentionally or unintentionally put them on a performance track to please you. And the relationship becomes all about what they can do for you—resulting in a one-sided relationship instead of one that is mutually beneficial. This once-attractive relationship becomes dysfunctional, destructive, and painful. And no one wants that!

If you are a follower of Christ, you are complete according to Colossians 2:10, which says, *"and in Him you have been made complete..."* (NASB). This verse is spoken to people as singles, as individuals. You don't have to be in a relationship of any kind—friendship, dating, or married—to be complete as far as God is concerned. Thinking that you do may leave you feeling empty, forsaken, and sometimes even depressed.

So if God isn't putting this pressure on you to be in a relationship, then don't put pressure on yourself.

Consider, if you haven't already, processing, understanding, and then embracing the concept of self-worth, not self-worship. Self-worth is the understanding that you have value as an individual person and that you are made in the image (likeness) of God. Genesis 1:27 says, *"And God created man in His own image, in the image of God He created him; male and female He created them."*

God also created man and woman after all of His other creations, because humans are His crowning achievement! So you are special and have value! Embrace the fact that you are made in God's image. Simple translation is that God has made us like Him—reflecting His nature.

Some of you may not totally eradicate your inferiority complex. You may have been wounded and wounds take time to heal. But hopefully implementing a mindset of self-worth will do serious damage to this complex and be a positive step in your emotional healing.

You have a Godly destiny; so don't wish your time away on tomorrow or wanting things to be different. Matthew 6:34, says, *"Therefore do not worry about tomorrow, for tomorrow will worry about itself. Each day has enough trouble of its own."*

Myrna says that she's asked many of her married friends, "Knowing what you know about marriage now, what would you have done differently as a single person?" Unanimously, they echoed, "I wouldn't have worried so much about when I'd get married." So learn to embrace today! Ask God what is it He may be trying to teach you in the midst of your singleness.

"Because of the Lord's great love we are not consumed, for His compassions never fail. They are new every morning; great is Your faithfulness. I say to myself, "The Lord is my portion; therefore I will wait for Him." Lamentations 3:22-24 (NIV)

If we focus on yesterday or tomorrow, we may miss God's Blessings for us today! It is all about trusting God.

Singleness' Benefits

Don't be in a hurry to be in a relationship (and then have to rush to get out).

If we are going to focus on the way things are now, exactly what are the benefits of being single? Since many of you have never been married, I am going to compare the benefits of being single with being married so that you can appreciate what you have now as a single.

As a guy when I was single, I loved . . .

- Being able to make quick decisions about money or purchases. As a married man, my wife Brenda and I make financial decisions together which usually takes longer.

- My general sense of freedom, like going anywhere when I wanted to without having to ask or tell anyone when I was returning home. When married, your time is not your own. You have to share it with your spouse and kids.

- Not making my bed if the sheets were clean. Now, I make our bed much more often as an expression of love to Brenda.

- No spring cleaning in my apartment. Brenda likes to vacuum once a week.

- Eating what I wanted, when I wanted. In our house, what you are eating is usually discussed ahead of time. Family dinnertime is critical to see how kids' day at school went, problem-solve, and have family devotions.

- Wearing my favorite old t-shirts with holes in them while relaxing. As a guy, I found my wife wanting to get rid of these favorite t-shirts and wanting me to dress better.

- Playing basketball and tennis every day for as long as I wanted. When I got married, I voluntarily made a choice to play less, and earlier in the morning so I could be at home more.

- Living on much less money. We still live on little money, but, in marriage, you have to think how this will affect your spouse and kids.

These points may seem like overkill, but I want you to recognize your blessings as a single and have a more realistic understanding of some of the adjustments you may have to make in a marriage.

Other Benefits of Singleness:

- Self-Discovery. Having all this time with yourself allows you to explore interests and passions: what gives you joy individually and in relationships. It's an exciting time to learn who you are and why you feel or behave the way you do because, if you don't know who you are, it will catch up with you later in life, especially if you marry. How will you know who is a good match for you in a mutually beneficial and lasting relationship if you haven't discovered your identity?

- Being a single is not a waiting period. Appreciate the now and the gifts of singlehood. Myrna says that when she travelled with one of her female bosses on business, her boss was anxious to return home to be with her husband and children, while Myrna was eager to stay the weekend and go sightseeing. "Through my boss, I learned vicariously how difficult it is to juggle career and kids, so I learned to enjoy the gifts of my singlehood and the importance of living life to the fullest."

- It's a time to be adventurous! To celebrate being able to take off and do whatever they wanted to as singles, Myrna and her friends would do an annual "freedom ride" on the Fourth of July. "In the first year, we got in the car without any idea of where we were going and started driving along the California coast from Los Angeles. At 9:00 p.m. we arrived in Monterey, California, just in time for the fireworks show. It was fun to be single and free!"

- Pursuing God's purpose for you. As a single, you have ample time to seek God and pursue your purpose without the demands of marriage. My friend Walter says, "I am 100 percent sure that I could not have written two books, three-fourths of a third book and started on a fourth book with a wife, kids, work, and everything else going on in my life."

Myrna has found that her singlehood has allowed her to not only spend a lot of time with the Lord, but also dedicate years of her life serving Him in full-time ministry. She lived and ministered full-time among the poor in the Southside of Chicago for several years, something she couldn't have done with a husband and kids.

"Again, I would stress that the service of My followers must be ever one of Love, not of duty. Temptations can so easily overcome a resolution based on fear, on duty, but against Love temptation has no power. Live in My Spirit, rest in My Love. Remember, if you look to Me for everything, and trust Me for everything, and if I do not send the full measure you ask, it must not be thought that it is necessarily some sin or weakness that is hindering My Help from flowing into and through you. In some cases this may be so, but it may be simply My restraining Hand laid on you as I whisper, "Rest, step aside with Me. Come apart and rest a while."

From *God Calling 2: God at Eventide-a Companion to God Calling 1* edited by A.J. Russell.

The goal of being single is not to get married. Focus on being the right person and not finding the right person because God doesn't send His Best to Mess!

What's Next?

I hope this chapter has given you a better perspective of who you are and how special you are! Also, I hope you have been exposed to and encouraged about some more benefits of being single.

Don't stop reading. The next chapter will tackle some of the challenges of being single. Trust me. My goal in writing this book is to ultimately help you to experience your spiritual potential and find fulfillment, whether you get into a relationship or remain single. And for you to know that reaching your spiritual potential isn't determined by your relationship status. Think bigger! We think you'll find it liberating and for some even cleansing. This is critical before moving on to healthy relationships, whether they are friendships, dating, or a marriage.

SUMMARY POINTS

1. You are so special that God created you in His very image and likeness. And He created days for you to use.

2. When evaluating your singleness or any situation as a follower of Christ, it is imperative that you see God's Big Picture.

3. There are definite benefits to being single.

ACTION POINTS

1. How does it make you feel to know that the God of all creation specifically created you the way you are with your personality, looks, intelligence, likes, etc.?

2. Since God cares so much for you, how do you think you should feel about yourself?

3. Take a moment to think about a situation that you initially didn't like, but in walking it out, turned out to be an incredible experience?

4. What are some of the benefits of being single that you love? Why?

5. Are you set in your ways of doing things? Do you honestly think it will be easy for you to change if you get into a relationship? Why or why not?

6. What do you think might be God's Big Picture for you in your singleness?

Chapter Two

Singles' Issues and Thoughts

*"So we are not giving up. How could we! Even though on the outside
it often looks like things are falling apart on us, on the inside where
God is making us new life, not a day goes by without His unfolding
grace. These hard times are small potatoes compared to the coming
good times, the lavish celebration prepared for us. There's far more
here than meets the eye. The things we see now are here today, gone
tomorrow. But the things we can't see now will last forever."*
2 Corinthians 4:16-18, The Message

Over the years working as a relationship counselor and particularly more
recently while interviewing individuals for this book, I've heard countless
single men and women share their struggles with singlehood. Too many to
mention here! So, *Sally* with her loneliness, frustrations, and other issues,
embodies several of the concerns singles of both genders shared with me in
counseling sessions.

Sally, an attractive woman, pokes her head around the opened door of
my office, greets me, and after introductions, I ask her why she has come.

*Sally sighs, reluctantly preparing to explain. Her sigh suggests she has
explained numerous times before and probably with little or no satisfaction.
"I'm not sure where to begin," she says. "I'm in my forties and STILL
single. I've dated a lot, even been in a few serious relationships, but for
various reasons, they ended. It may sound vain, but I'm a successful
businesswoman and I don't feel I'm unattractive. I've done the church thing
and I'm a social animal. But, I'm still lonely. I'm so frustrated because by
now, I should have been married and should be driving my kids to their
soccer games. I desperately want a companion, affection, love, and
children. I am so ashamed and disappointed that I haven't been able to get
all of this by now. What's wrong with me? I feel like I don't belong—so
alone—and I don't know what to do or what I'm doing wrong."*

Simultaneously praying for wisdom as I say, hopefully to reassure and
relate, "Sally, I'm so sorry that you are experiencing this frustration and
loneliness. Even though I was single into my thirties, I don't know how you
feel, but I do care." I continue, "May I ask you some elementary questions
in order to get a feel for where you are, why you are where you are, possibly
where we go from here, and how to get there? Please don't be disappointed
if we don't get there today."

She gives an affirmative nod.

"Sally, of the issues you've shared, which one is eating at you the most and why?" I ask.

Without hesitation, she blurts, but recomposes herself; yet firmly states, "Loneliness!"

"Why loneliness? How does loneliness make you feel about you?" I inquire.

"Honestly? It makes me feel powerless and frustrated with myself—like a failure. I've been successful in sports in high school and college, and in business. So, I'm used to getting what I set my mind to do." She responds.

Though still frustrated and without any of her issues being resolved, Sally is visibly less tense. Just beginning to talk honestly about her loneliness, while having someone listen without condemning is allowing her to relax. Genuinely listening to her without trying to immediately *fix* her or her problems communicates to her that she is valued and not crazy. Such listening, especially for most women, can be interpreted as being loved. And everybody wants to be loved simply for who they are. My goal of creating a *safe place* for Sally is working.

Now that she is beginning to relax, I make statements attempting to reassure. "Sally, thank you so much for your transparency. Internalizing your issues often causes stress and can negatively impact your emotional and physical health. And your honesty allows me to be more effective in providing you with your best options."

I add, "You need to know that you aren't alone in your feelings about being single, so you are probably not crazier or more abnormal than most. I believe all of us are a little crazy or abnormal. Family, friends, schoolmates, and coworkers can see it. We seldom do because we are used to us. We tend to think everyone else is a little weird. Everyone has some *issues,* especially when it comes to relationships. A majority of single men and women are experiencing similar struggles with loneliness. Some aspects of relationships such as meeting Mr. or Mrs. Right are often beyond our understanding and our control. We typically can't force a relationship to happen according to our timeline because if we could, we would. Thus, you cannot fail in an area in which you have no control. So even though other singles, society, and you, yourself, might make you feel like a failure, you are not."

I continue by saying, "It's not unique to singles either. Even most divorced couples feel like failures when their marriages end, whether they have legitimate grounds for divorce, such as adultery, or not. Many divorced couples feel like they have failed because their relationship ended. They didn't live *happily ever after together.* So they have to face the reality that in most cases, both of them contributed to the demise of their marriage." I conclude with a request. "That was a lot to give at one time and seldom will I do that, but I want you to respond to what you have just heard."

*"Hearing that I can't control the timeline for a relationship helps. I think I know that, but actually hearing it, puts it more in perspective. I appreciate you saying that I'm not crazier or more abnormal than most people. Hearing that I'm not a failure with something I can't control is good and bad because, in one way, I'm powerless. I'll have to process all of what you have said some more, this concept of powerlessness more than anything else. Also I'm sorry that other singles are experiencing loneliness like me, but I'm glad I'm not the **only** one! That's a terrible thing to say isn't it?"* *She sheepishly asks, looking to see if my countenance condemns her.*

"No, it isn't a terrible thing to say. It is an incredibly honest statement to make!" I commend her for her courage. Sally has taken a key step in trusting me. "Sally, I'm not here to judge or condemn you. You are free to say whatever you want or as much or as little as you want. Everything you say is confidential. And I'm here to help, not hurt you," I state as reassuringly as possible.

"Sally, in reality there are some things we can't control, like the weather, our birth, our gender—whether we like it or not, who our parents are, and many other things. So let's focus on a few things you can control," I say in hopes of challenging her present way of viewing herself. And I don't know if I would consider myself powerless. I think that is a negative perspective that could become a place of defeat. Things, I can't control, I tend to give less energy and focus more on the things I can control. Does this make sense?

Affirmatively she nods, but her eyes are questioning where we are going.

"Since you have been successful in business and in sports, you know that not having your dream come true of being married doesn't make you a failure. Right? Look at all that you have accomplished in your life. Yes, you have lost some games, but you also won some games. Sometimes, no matter how much effort we put into something, we can't control the outcome. Other times, it may mean we need to be equipped or better equipped in some areas. Instead of focusing on what you don't have, focus on your blessings, successes, and accomplishments. You are not a failure."

Sally said, "I understand. I think I can buy into this."

Gently challenging her, I add, "I don't want you to *think* about buying in, I want you to live it. You have been successful in a man's world, correct? Women tell me that business is a male-dominated world, so you have learned to *play with the boys and win*—no easy feat. Write this down: '*I may occasionally fail at one thing or another, but I'm not a failure!*' Never again view yourself as a failure. You're in the game of life. You obviously haven't failed or else you wouldn't be here. Those who fail, quit."

Again, she nods affirmatively.

Her vulnerability emerges as this intelligent and successful leader is mentally recalibrating who she really is. She is seeing herself in a different light, possibly for the first time.

"Have you ever been discriminated against for being a woman?" I ask.

"Yes, I have been." She responds with a little fire.

"So in the midst of intentional opposition, you actually strived?" I continued. "Sally, that means you're emotionally tough and you don't quit. I want you to take the discipline of the businesswoman inside of you and apply it to your personal life."

"I don't understand," Sally replies.

I further explain, "You've been successful in stressful and unfavorable situations, yet you didn't quit, so you haven't been failing. Is this beginning to make sense now?"

"Yes, it is!" she responds with a smile on her face as she mentally embraces a new perspective of who she is, which is not defined by her circumstances of being single. Sally is beginning to see a glimpse of her freedom from the negative chain of pain she has been needlessly carrying for too many years!

"Tell me more about your gut feelings of loneliness," I ask pressing a little more this time hoping she will become more vulnerable, so we can get to her pain, an essential step before we can get to her healing.

"Okay, here goes. It is pretty raw," as she tries to brace me for her experience. She continues, "Most people don't understand our struggles as singles and belittle it. Maybe if I compare it to the plight of women who can't have children, it will make more sense. They ache for a child so much that they try to do everything in their power to have a child. Many spend thousands of dollars on fertility treatments or on adoption. The church, communities, and everyone seem to empathize with them." Sally pauses and bites her lip. "We singles also experience the sadness of not being able to

29

find the right 'one,' but we're told to not worry, wait on the Lord, or serve the church."

"Thank you again for your transparency and feeling safe enough to share your heart. I can't imagine this is easy for you," I say as reassuringly as possible.

She responds, "I feel like you are really listening to me without condemning me. So it makes it easier for me to share."

"Sally, we all have issues with which we struggle. I'm here to serve you," I respond. "Do you have a support system here in town, family or friends?"

She replies, "No, there is no real support system. My family lives out of town. And the church thing really didn't work for me. The church leadership didn't do much for singles except have some social functions. When churches tell singles, to put Jesus at the center of your life or that God is the only One who can fulfill your needs . . . *What does that mean when I'm in emotional pain, lonely, and have sexual desires? It sounds so high and lofty when my human needs are practical. In most churches, singles don't see this modeled or preached. We singles need this truth explained in practical terms with doable applications because we are asking, 'What does it look like?'"*

"I'm sorry to hear this. You sound alone—even at church," I say, attempting to console her. "Do you know people here who appear to be somewhat friendly either where you live or at work?" I inquire.

"Yes, there are a couple of girls in my apartment complex who seem very friendly," she responds. Then she continues, *"There is also a young couple with a baby in the apartment below."*

"What is the chance of you inviting those girls to your place for coffee and, another time, having that couple with the baby over for dinner?" I gently suggest. "I realize in today's culture, that everyone has to be extremely careful in initiating friendships with strangers, but if you have peace about it, it could be a good opportunity for you to create your community. Developing friendships creates community for you, which is one way of defeating some of the negative effects of loneliness. What do you think?"

"I like that idea," she says with excitement as her face lights up. But then asks, "What does that community or friendship look like?"

"May I tell you what my friend, Myrna shared with me?" I asked.

She nods.

"Myrna says, 'You can have a lot of friends, but during tough times you discover who your brothers and sisters are. With them, you feel safe being who you are and sharing about yourself. When one is down, the other lifts him or her up and vice versa. These special friends also let you know when you're going off track and encourage you when you're hitting the mark. Friends are even more special when they pray for you and with you. They're companions on this leg of the journey. So when you're going through those lonely seasons like New Year's Eve and Valentine's Day that emphasize having a boyfriend, girlfriend, husband, wife, or date, these friends become a comforting and even fun source of support."

"'We all accept each other without pressuring each other to be something we're not," comments Myrna. "'For these special days when everyone is supposed to be on a date, we have fun. Everybody brings food; I decorate a pretty table; we take pictures; and enjoy our special evening with great stories, laughter, and enjoy each other's company.'"

"That's what I have back home and I'd give almost anything to have such relationships here!" Sally responds, almost shouting.

"Initially, what I'm about to say may sound as though I'm judging you, but I'm not. Process what I'm saying, then see if you have unintentionally allowed yourself to experience this principle." I say this, hoping she trusts me enough to allow me to challenge her to more critically examine her own thoughts and consequent actions regarding her views of herself and her situation.

I begin by saying, "Some singles, certainly not all, can drive themselves into isolation because of frustration with the way the world and even their church treats them. Some do this in a proactive fashion, comforting themselves with the idea that they are controlling their own destiny, even if it leads to isolation because it's a way of exercising their choice! Since you mentioned the church thing, in the Bible, Proverbs 18:1 says, "'*A man (woman) who isolates himself seeks his own desires.'*"

I continue, "Often an unforeseen result of isolation is self- focus. And when that sets in, it can lead to depression. For singles, especially those without support, experiencing loneliness can grow into depression, resulting in withdrawing and isolating themselves." I pause and ask, "Sally, will you please respond to what I've just said?"

"Wow, I never thought about it from that perspective, but I must admit, I'm guilty at times. I felt that if I was calling the shots, then I could justify my loneliness as my choice and not rejection. But I guess I was just fooling myself and not realizing it. I was hurting myself simultaneously," she said thinking aloud without measuring her words.

Finally, we are beginning to peel back a thin layer of Sally's onion of pain and at the same time, providing options from which she can choose life and community over self-imposed isolation, which often leads to depression.

"The ache to be married is pretty intense," explained Sally. She told me about a call to a friend who sounded as if she had a cold. When Sally asked her what was wrong, her friend admitted she had been crying because she was depressed that she was unmarried.

I asked, "How did she deal with her depression?"

Sally replied, "Well, she got married."

"Do you think she really escaped depression by getting married, or do you think she self-medicated her emotions into thinking she escaped depression?" I probed.

Continuing, I question, "Sally, do you think if she wasn't happy single, she will be happy married? Do you think she, like all of us, needs to learn to be content as a single before getting into a relationship? If singles are depressed because they feel somehow they are lacking, and if this isn't resolved before entering a relationship, can you see how it can possibly create a dysfunctional relationship? You need to like *you*. You need to understand and embrace your *self-worth*. I'm not talking about *'self-worship.'"* As I gently continue to press Sally to linger on this train of thought, I ask, "What do you think about what I just said?"

"You are really forcing me to contemplate issues I never have before," *she replies.*

"Sally, I certainly hope your friend did escape her depression. But if she didn't, she will struggle with being alone, even in her marriage. She will also unintentionally put tremendous pressure on her husband—to meet all of her companionship needs, and may never effectively communicate those needs to him, which may create even more problems. A spouse's sole purpose can't be or shouldn't be to make the other spouse happy or content. So now, who do you think is primarily responsible to address your loneliness?" I ask. "Sally, your friend had what is called the *Fairytale Syndrome,* 'If I just get married, everything will fall perfectly into place."

"You've got my head spinning! Are you saying that I am responsible for creating and maintaining my own happiness apart from anyone else? Do you mean that I can't blame God, society, men, or my church for my loneliness?" she asks.

"Excellent questions, Sally. You would make an outstanding

counselor!" I respond with an encouraging smile. Putting the ball back in her court, I say, "But you must answer these questions, not me."

"I can see how I could take some responsibility for some of my frustration and my subsequent actions based on how I'm coping with my loneliness at a particular time," she pensively answers.

"Sally, I'm not asking you to agree with anything I'm saying, but I do want you to consider what I'm proposing to you," I interject. "Depression can also be inverted anger, and that's why addressing the anger issue is essential in helping the single individual to process it. Such processing allows singles to better understand where they are and why they are where they are, as well as where to go from here, and how to get there."

"Well," Sally pauses studying my eyes to see if she can really go there, "I have been angry at times. It just doesn't seem to be fair. And I've actually said this to God. 'Okay God, if it's not happening and I can't do anything about it, then I'm just going to live my life and do all the things that I can't do or won't be able to do if I were married.'"

"Sally, I don't want you to think of your singleness as settling, an abnormality, or that somehow for some reason that God is holding out on you." I respond.

"Why?" she asks.

"Embracing your singleness in this context consciously or subconsciously gives you a *less than* mindset which can result in anger or an inferiority complex or both. Both of which can be damaging personally and may sabotage any chances at a long-lasting and mutually beneficial relationship," I reply. Continuing I say, "Such an attitude can easily be interpreted as a defeatist one that exudes negative vibrations. Some people can actually sense these vibrations, which may keep relationship prospects from approaching you."

"Sally, we've covered a lot of ground here today, more than I anticipated," I say encouragingly. Why don't we stop here? If you would like to continue we can schedule it. How does this sound?" I inquire.

"Dr. Shuler, this has been thought provoking! I would like to continue. Next time, could we talk about the shame I occasionally experience as a single?" is her response.

"We certainly can!" I say.

The Shame Game

Sally confidently knocks on my opened office door, smiling as she sees me.

"Hello, Sally! You have quite a smile there," I say waving for her to come in.

"I've really been looking forward to meeting with you again," she responds with expectancy in her voice. "Having two weeks between our sessions gave me a lot of time to evaluate some of your suggestions regarding my singleness. I still have issues, but I also have a better perspective about myself and being single. I'm liking myself more. I'd still prefer being married. But I don't feel quite as desperate or depressed as before," she concludes.

"That is excellent news, Sally! Sounds like you are taking some critical first steps towards transforming yourself," I enthusiastically reply.

Before I can get another word out of my mouth, *Sally nearly jumps out of her chair simultaneously asking me, "Did you see Piers Morgan grill Condoleezza Rice for being single* on TV?" Again, before I can respond,

She states, "To me, he was really giving her a hard time for being single."

"He told her what a good catch she would be. Then, he asked her why she has never been married! Can you imagine such a question? It seems she wasn't expecting that question, but she made cool points with me the way she handled his questions. He asked her if she had been close to getting married and how many times had she been close. Does she still hold out hope? I don't think he would have asked her such personal questions if she had been married and divorced."

As she pauses to inhale, I quickly ask, "Why do you think he wouldn't have asked her so much about her personal life if she had been divorced?"

"To me, divorce is now accepted as normal. If you're divorced, at least once in your life somebody, no matter who they were, wanted you. Not being married and not being divorced is no longer normal and carries rejection baggage from the world's perspective. There was a time in my life when I thought it was preferable to say that I had been divorced instead of never having been married," she concludes.

I encourage her to continue with her story.

"Piers Morgan then asked Rice if she was romantic. How is she romantic—definitely a question I don't think he would have asked a man in political office or a man, period. When he asked her if she was high maintenance, it made my skin crawl! He said he thought she would be a tough wife. Please! Just because a woman is powerful and a leader, she is labeled as handful! Lastly, he asked her what she would cook for him if he

came over for dinner," she said with agitation.

"Okay, I think I know why you are frustrated with Piers Morgan's interview, but let me hear it from you" I request.

Raising her voice as she states, "I felt Piers put Condoleezza in a position of shame for being single and I resented that! Really? She's the first female African-American U.S. Secretary of State and he decides to drill her on being single?

Society, colleges, churches, friends—everybody, often intentionally or unintentionally attach a badge of shame to being single. Instilling this kind of thinking can begin as early as kindergarten, elementary or middle school! Rejecting that which is different from what is considered the norm is subtle in its teaching. Not only is it difficult enough being single, but if you keep true to your faith, there is added pressure and shame, especially when we're in secular circles." She bows her head, but continues relating her obvious pain, "As a woman, even going to my doctor can be embarrassing. When I told my doctor that I wasn't sexually active, he said that my lifestyle wasn't healthy! And, it doesn't end there. Work colleagues are always talking very casually about their sexual escapades. I keep quiet for fear of sounding like a freak. And the older you get, the weirder you feel. So whether it's at work or school, it seems everyone is doing "it" except you!" she concludes.

"Pain seems to be accompanying your shame. Is this an accurate observation?" I ask.

Dropping her head again, then raising it, she softly and dejectedly says, "Yes."

"Sally, remember our first session? You have to remember who you are," I say, trying to resurrect that previous spark. "Right now, you sound defeated and wounded."

"Sharing all this brought back so much pain from past experiences," she says.

I repeat my question, "What did you learn from our first session, Sally?"

"I'm complete as I am, a single. And I shouldn't let situations beyond my control dominate my thoughts. Also, I have some control as to how I respond to my loneliness and now, I guess, issues of shame or what I should no longer consider as shame for me—maybe refer to them as uncomfortable situations," *she utters almost as though she believes it.*

"Sally, that is an excellent way of processing and mentally working through some of your issues," I say, commending her. Feeling more of her trust, I challenge her saying, "Sally, write down this phrase. *Don't let the pain of your past punish your present, paralyze your future, or pervert your purpose because you have a godly destiny."*

"Sally, why do you allow people you don't know and who have no impact on your life control how you feel about yourself?" I question.

"I don't know," she responds. "I guess I feel I'm alone or the odd one or that everyone but me is happy."

"Who is *everyone*, Sally? Also, why are you trying to impress people you don't even know?" I ask to illustrate that what she *thinks* other people are thinking controls her thoughts about herself and her actions. Such thinking can make her feel powerless and may also lead to depression.

"As a businesswoman, you would never buy into this type of thinking, so don't think like this in your personal life," I encourage her with a more forceful tone in my voice. "This sounds like an over-simplification, but your perspective about yourself is everything. You need to develop an emotional balance," I tell her.

"How do I do this?" she innocently wonders aloud.

"Sally, it sounds like you are ashamed of being single," I say. "You shouldn't be. Unfortunately, our society often makes singles, whether they are teenagers or near retirement age, feel as though they are abnormal." I say as reassuringly as possible. I continue, "If you have bought into the mindset that you have to be in a relationship, you may have been wounded by one or all three of the following groups: society, well-meaning family or friends. If this is true for you, then you may be in *emotional slavery."*

"Let me explain emotional slavery. You are in emotional slavery when you've been hurt by people to the extent that just hearing their names, their voices, or seeing them, you lose it for a few moments, few hours, or a few days. Such a person owns you emotionally, which unfortunately for some people can lead to a physical ownership. Usually the only effective cure is forgiving that person.

Biblical forgiveness is totally separate from emotional healing. Forgiveness is actually treating the person who has offended you as though they haven't. For example, if I repeatedly borrowed money from you but never paid you back, you treat me as though I don't owe you money. And when I would ask you for more money, you would not give me more, but you would be kind and gracious about it.

Emotional healing takes time. It may take you some time to work through your disappointment with someone for a character flaw. As you get over this disappointment, you come to realize that the person is a friend who is worth keeping. Or you still come see that this person isn't all bad; but you may not want to continue a close friendship. Either way, in time, this person no longer dominates your thoughts as you have emotionally healed from your disappointments or wounds. This forgiveness doesn't eliminate that person's accountability or responsibility," I explain. For clarity, I ask, "Does this make sense to you?"

"It is definitely a different perspective for me. I've always attached emotion to forgiveness so I told people, 'I can't forgive you right now, or I will forgive you when I feel better about it and you,'" Sally answers.

"Sally, this may sound crazy, but you probably need to forgive our society as well as people you know who may have intentionally or unintentionally wounded you, causing you to feel ashamed of being single," I recommend to her.

"I think that is a good idea, a little strange when I think of trying to forgive society, but probably necessary so the next time I hear something hurtful, I won't take it personally." She responds.

"Sally, this is part of the church thing you mentioned earlier. What I've shared with you is biblical forgiveness. (*Biblical forgiveness will be discussed in chapter four, Healing A Broken Heart*) Forgiveness isn't an emotion, even though many people attach emotion to it," I share with her. "Well, we have come to the end of our time together. I hope it has been helpful to you to evaluate some other possibilities in regards to the shame issue," I reply.

"If you want to meet again, I'm going to give you some homework. Remember my quote which begins, "*Don't let the pain of your past, . . . ?* Put it on your mirror and read it daily until you are sure you are no longer in emotional slavery to former issues. Take your time with this," and finally I say to her, "and I want you to think of yourself as complete in your singleness and that you are not less."

"Thank you again for your time," Sally smiles as she leaves.

A Revolutionary Value

Maybe many of you can relate to Sally's feelings of shame and loneliness because of your singlehood. But, do you know that it was Christianity that gave a revolutionary value to singles? Prior to that, according to some Bible scholars, ancient societies viewed unmarried adults as prostitutes. Pagan widows were actually fined in Caesar Augustus' time if they didn't marry within two years, while Christian women were given choice and supported by the church.

In 1 Corinthians 7:8 (NIV), Paul says something outrageous for his time, *"Now to the unmarried and the widows I say: It is good for them to stay unmarried, as I do."* Can you imagine how outrageous that must have sounded to a culture that perceived single adults as prostitutes?

He goes on to say, in verses, 25-28:

"Now about virgins: I have no command from the Lord, but I give a judgment as one who by the Lord's mercy is trustworthy. Because of the present crisis, I think that it is good for a man to remain as he is. Are you pledged to a woman? Do not seek to be released. Are you free from such a commitment? Do not look for a wife. But if you do marry, you have not sinned; and if a virgin marries, she has not sinned. But those who marry will face many troubles in this life, and I want to spare you this."

Do you want to learn why you have value as a single? Then read on!

SUMMARY POINTS

1. If you are single, whether male or female, it is quite natural to experience feelings of loneliness and shame, resulting in frustration. These feelings reveal you are quite normal in the midst of a society that puts pressure on finding your one true love.

2. Realize that we cannot force a relationship to happen according to our timeline because, if we could, we would. And understanding that there are other circumstances or situations out of our control produce a healthy state of mind. Accepting this concept may help avoid some frustration and possible depression. So, we cannot fail in areas in which we have no control.

3. We may be able to create some communities for ourselves in order to combat our loneliness.

4. We have some responsibility in our loneliness and our response to it.

5. It is critical that you don't allow what others may negatively think of you as a single to influence who you are and how you respond.

6. You need to like yourself. You have worth and value. Some singles attach shame to being single in the workplace, church, parties, and even doctor visits.

7. Being temporarily frustrated with God about your singleness is okay. He isn't as concerned about your initial response as He is your end results.

8. If you are not content being single, there is a good possibility you won't be content in a relationship.

9. Click on this link and see how well Condoleezza Rice handled uncomfortable questions:

   http://www.popeater.com/2011/01/20/piers-morgan-condoleezza- rice/

10. Remember, you are complete as a single.

ACTION POINTS

1. If loneliness is an issue for you, how does it make you feel? Why?

2. If loneliness is an issue for you, how are you managing it? Is your method working for you? Why or why not?

3. When your loneliness is making you feel like a failure, think of your successes. Go back to elementary school and come forward to the present. If you are a follower of Jesus Christ, take time right now to thank God for those successes and for making you who you are today.

4. If you just prayed, thanking God for your lifetime of successes, how did that make you feel?

5. If your parent(s) live in the same city and you have a good relationship, her, or them, go see them and personally thank them for helping you to achieve your successes by the way you were raised.

6. How did that make you feel? How did it make your parent(s) feel?

7. So next time you are lonely, consider going for a walk, to the mall, the park, etc. Look for someone who may not be having a good day. Take a chance and say a positive word to this person. You just may make this person's day. And you will feel better too! Giving to others is a tremendous temporary cure for loneliness attacks.

8. Are you successful in business or other areas of your life, but not in relationships? If this is true of you, why do you think this is so?

9. Do you see yourself as incomplete or not perfect as a single? Why or why not?

10. How do you think your view of yourself impacts your relationships? And why?

11. Do you think you might be able to create a community of support in your neighborhood? Why or why not? If yes, what do you need to do and when will you begin?

12. Do you believe that you have some responsibility or role to play in coping with your loneliness if it is an issue for you? Why or why not?

13. If shame as a single is an issue for you, how can you overcome it?

14. If you aren't content being single, what does being content as a single look like for you? Why?

15. If you viewed the Morgan/Rice interview, did you like Miss Rice's responses? If so, why? Did the way she handled uncomfortable questions enlighten you as to how you can do the same. If so, how? What are some ways you can prepare for similar questions that might make you uncomfortable?

16. How do you feel about the fact that you have a unique destiny, just for you?

Chapter Three

When God Isn't Enough

*"At first I didn't think of it as a gift, and begged God to remove it.
Three times I did that, and then He told me, 'My grace is enough; it
is all you need. My strength comes into its own in your weakness.'"*
2 Corinthians 12:8-9, *The Message*

With few exceptions, almost all the singles interviewed for this book—
regardless of age—mentioned God. George Barna's research supports the
notion that four out of five single adults believe they are Christians.
However, the singles' references to God, that I interviewed was not always
positive. In fact, quite a few were more than just a *little* frustrated with God.

If God is supposed to be so good, why isn't He giving these Christian
singles, (whether in high school or college or older) who are in a
relationship with Him what they want-a boyfriend or girlfriend or a
marriage partner? I am consistently bombarded with questions like: *What
could possibly be good reasons as to why I'm not in a healthy relationship?
Why doesn't God have me hooked up by now? Is something wrong with me?
Is God punishing me?* And why doesn't God give these singles, who
confessed they are committed to following Him, a boyfriend, girlfriend, or
spouse, especially since He has said, *"It is not good for man (woman) to be
alone; I will make him a helper suitable (literally, corresponding) for him"*
in Genesis 2:18.

What Kind of God Is God?

If God doesn't seem to be all that good, why in the world are these singles
following Him? What do we really know about this God of the Bible? In
order to answer this question, let's examine the Bible to see what it says
about God.

In the first book of the Bible, we discover that God is THE CREATOR.
God creates something out of nothing. He creates the atmosphere and the
earth, then plants and animals. God's last creation is mankind, who God
says He created in His own image (Genesis 1:27). Adam is the first human
created. *Adam is the first single!* So the very first human is a single adult!

In the previous section, God says, *"It is not good for the Man to be
alone. I'll make him a helper, a companion for him."* So, God fashions a
woman out of one of Adam's rib. Adam probably says to her, "You're the

41

only woman in the world for me." Hence, God seems be into relationships. I know what you are thinking— "So where is my boyfriend, girlfriend, or spouse?" Hang on. Let's learn more about God, which may answer some of your questions.

Most Bible scholars say God created mankind last because He wanted to make the earth ready and inhabitable for His crowning achievement— *us*—mankind. The implications are powerful! Think about it. God values you and me so much that He made the earth for us! God's actions speak of intentionality! God wants you and me! Consequently, we're not here by accident. If we're not here by accident, then we each have a purpose—a destiny. Because God is involved, we have a godly destiny.

In this perfect environment called the Garden of Eden, man is given responsibility to work in and care for His creation. God tells the man he has the run of this garden, *but* that he is forbidden to eat from the tree of knowledge of good and evil or he will die! So man is hanging out with the God of the universe and has a spouse (without question—*the most beautiful woman on the earth*) who is a perfect corresponding match for him. Life is literally perfect!

When God Is Not Enough

Satan, disguised as a snake, begins questioning the woman as to what God actually said. When he sees that the woman in Genesis 3:3 adds to God's instruction when she says that God told them not to even *touch* the tree, Satan sees it as a sign of weakness or that his temptation is working. Then Satan says to the woman in Genesis 3:4, *"You will not surely die, for God knows that when you eat of it your eyes will be open and you will be like God, knowing good from evil."* Basically, Satan tells the woman that God is holding out on Adam and her. Consequently, they agree with Satan that God isn't giving them His best.

Let's process this. In Genesis 1:27, God creates man and woman in His image or likeness. Then Satan tells the woman that if she eats of the fruit of the tree of the knowledge of good and evil, she will be *like* God. So Satan is trying to trick the woman into believing he can give her something God has already given her! This is why he is called a deceiver because he can't deliver the good, only evil. He can't give us peace either through people or things. Only God can give us perfect peace and that is when we keep our minds on Him (Isaiah 26:3).

A key thought we cannot ignore is that God's very best for Adam and Eve wasn't enough for them even though all Satan could promise is what God had already given them.

We also need to be sure to observe that Adam was there with her (Genesis 3:6), but he didn't protect her. Could it be that since Adam didn't stop the seduction of his mate, that in general, men—and certainly not all men—have a natural tendency to be passive in relationships once they have achieved their conquest? Was this passed down from Adam? And did Adam feel guilty about not protecting his woman and decide to eat of the forbidden fruit so she wouldn't face the consequences of her actions alone? We don't know.

But this first couple disobeys God. After their disobedience, God doesn't kill them, even though God said they would surely die if they ate from the tree of knowledge. Is this act what some call God's grace? God kills animals, His beloved creations, in order to clothe this couple before putting them out of His garden. And God sets in motion a plan to restore the oneness relationship between Him and mankind, which was destroyed by Adam and Eve's sin. He did it by sacrificing the life of His own son, Jesus Christ.

WOW!! Sounds, like God loves you and me no matter what!

He really loves the humans He created. And it appears that God doesn't need us, but rather *wants* us. Now, it's up to you to decide if you want to receive God's love for you, a love that is so incredible, that you'll discover your true identity and how complete you are in Him.

Let's learn a little more about the God of the Bible.

God As Our Father

Examining God as father may be an emotional topic for many of us, but discussing it is essential because it not only affects our relationship with God, but with others as well. Often, how our fathers treated us will influence our ability to accept and trust God as our father.

I don't ever remember my Dad telling me he loved me. Hearing "I love you" from him would have been priceless!

In 1963 when I was nine, our family was driving to our grandparents' home in South Carolina when we stopped for gas. Three white men harassed Dad as he filled the gas tank, calling him every bad name imaginable. Dad never responded nor looked up at these men. I felt he could beat all three men with no problem. So I asked, "Mom, why is Dad letting them talk to him like that? He isn't scared is he?" She replied, "Honey, he is being as brave as he knows how to be. If he says anything to them or looks them in their eyes, there is no telling what they would do to him and to us. He is protecting us. He is being as brave as he knows how to be." From that time on, at least until my teenage years, my Dad was my hero!

Yet, at fifteen, I pulled a bowie knife with a five-inch blade on my Dad, not because he was abusive, but because I had decided to take matters into my own hands. He had hit me because he thought I was being lazy and conning my sister into more work, so that I had less to do. Ninety-nine percent of the time, he was right, but not this particular time; I was actually trying to help her. I thought, "I'm a man and I don't have to take this from anyone." I got my knife and confronted my father. Dad didn't approach me because he was trying to figure out how to get my knife from me without killing me. I regretted getting it, but in my stupidity— trying to prove my manhood, whatever that is—I couldn't retreat; I was frozen with fear. Fortunately, Mom let out a blood-curling yell and everything stopped.

At sixteen, I began following Christ. My lifestyle, language (away from home), and priorities radically changed. With Christ, I am never alone. This is huge for an incredibly insecure person like me. Some of my insecurity came from the uncertainty of my relationship with my Dad. At seventeen, I became a licensed minister. While I was home for the Thanksgiving holiday of my freshman year, my Dad began following Christ, too. He wrote me once while I was in Chicago in college. His note said, "Saw a young preacher today. He reminded me of you. Keep the faith." I read and reread that note until it literally fell apart. The last, time I was with my Dad, we prayed together. Two days later, he was robbed, shot, and killed. I was twenty years old when it happened. He was becoming my best friend and teaching me about life. Thinking of him always brings a smile to my face and sometimes a tear to my eye. But I'll see him again! As much as I loved and still love Dad, I decided to do some things differently as a father. For example, I made it a point to tell my girls early and often, "I love you." It is difficult to say how my relationship with Dad impacted my relationship with God as my father. When Gary Chapman shared John 3:16 with me, he quoted the first part of it like this, "For God so loves Clarence..." In John 3:16, when God talks about the world, He is talking about you and me. God started telling me through His Word (the Bible) and others that He loves me.

While my relationship with Dad ended as a good one, I realize that this might not be the case for many of you. Please forgive me if I unintentionally remind you of a painful past. Discussing fatherhood may be painful for some of you because your father may have been absent, resulting in you feeling abandoned or rejected. If your father was present, he may have been domineering. Your father may have been an alcoholic or unfaithful to your mother. Or he may have been abusive verbally and maybe even physically.

If this has been your experience, I'm very sorry that this happened to you. Please know that I wouldn't introduce such an emotional topic without intending to try to help in this area. So keep reading because you'll find tools that may help you heal from the pain of your past as well as break the cycle of pain in your life and in your family's lives.

I want you to know that God our father is nothing like our human fathers. Even if you have or had a wonderful father, he isn't perfect. But God is. Though I never heard my Dad say he loved me, God never stops telling us how much He loves us in the Bible, His love letter to us, and often through those who are followers of Christ.

So be encouraged. Whether your father was absent, abusive, or amazing, God the Father loves you. He sees you as His child. And knowing that you are loved no matter what makes it easier to love *yourself* as well as others.

Before healing a heart wounded from a relationship, it's crucial to explore the notion of God as a father. If you have had a negative experience with your earthly father, then it naturally affects your perspective of God as a father. Such experiences may result in you feeling that you are on your own and need to *make* things happen according to your terms and timetable.

That's what happened with Sarah and her husband Abraham. Abraham is well-known because of his great faith in God. At age, seventy-six, Sarah got tired of *waiting on God* to fulfill His promise of a child and took matters into her own hands. She demanded Abraham have sex with her maid, Hagar. Ishmael is the result of their union, but Sarah rejected him. It is fourteen more years, before Sarah gives birth to Isaac, the son God promised her.

Being single, regardless of your age, could be because God has your best interest in the center of His heart (just a thought?). Could it be that God isn't holding out on you, but holding His best for you? Maybe He sees what we can't see—hence could it be that our God who loves us is protecting us? And could it possibly be that you are so special to God that He doesn't want to share you with anyone? Or maybe He is growing your faith and setting the stage for a miracle as He did with Abraham and Sarah?

Have you ever thought of God as your father? Have you ever had a loving father, mother, or parent figure tell you, "no?" If your answer is "yes," why do you think this person said no to you? Consider this individual who loves you, saying "no," to you at a particular time in your life because he or she has your best interest at heart.

We've already seen God as Father do several things:

- Create life out of nothing as an expression of His love.

- Provide the best for His children in the Garden of Eden.

- Give direction so His children (Adam & Eve) could have options later.

- Create children with the ability and freedom to make either wise or poor choices.

- Discipline His disobedient children with the intent of restoration, yet not giving His children who disobey Him what they deserve. God demonstrates His grace and mercy.

- Sacrifice animals He created and loved in order to clothe His disobedient children who didn't need clothes before they disobeyed God.

- Set in motion a plan to restore His relationship with His disobedient children and their offspring by sacrificing His innocent and only Son.

Fatherhood, especially from absentee fathers, is probably a root issue for many singles. Numerous single women have said they have feelings of being abandoned, uncared for, and unprotected (men can have these same feelings, but seldom have a *safe place* to share them with anyone—so they keep their feelings to themselves). One single woman in her forties once said to me, *"A woman never recovers from losing or not having a good father."* She connects it to her promiscuity—looking for love and finding it in the wrong places. She felt she didn't have protection, nor a model or guide as to what a *good* man is.

Men have said that not having a father to model life for them resulted in their immaturity, insecurity, disdain for authority, and not knowing how to treat and keep a woman. These men say that getting sex isn't a problem, but they are clueless in developing a friendship, a companionship and commitment. Many of these men have said they feel guilty about the sex and it really isn't that fulfilling because it is not in the context of a relationship or marriage.

We've seen the love God has for us. Having Him as our Father may eliminate or at least minimize some of the feelings for those of us whose earthly father wasn't the best. When we don't have God as our father, we may, like Abraham and Sarah, resort to trying to manipulate relationships and our situations.

Think about it. With God as our Father, we should begin developing some of His traits. For example, as the father of three young adult single ladies, I can see some of my traits, strengths, and weaknesses in them: a good sense of humor, determination, athleticism, intelligence, English speaking (because their mother and I are), and they can struggle with insecurity.

One godly trait that is worth learning is biblical contentment. In Philippians 4:11-13, Paul says,

> *"I am not saying this because I am in need, for I have learned to be content whatever the circumstances. I know what it is to be in need, and I know what it is to have plenty. I have learned the **secret of being content** in any and every situation, whether well fed or hungry, whether living in plenty or in want. I can do everything through Him who gives me strength."* (NIV)

It seems God has shared the secret of being content with those of us who are following Him in our hearts and in our situations. But we have to get to know God to discover His secret. We can know we have a relationship with God because He says in Romans 8:15-16:

> *"For you did not receive a spirit that makes you a slave again to fear, but you received the Spirit of Sonship (daughtership). And by him we cry, 'Abba (Daddy), Father.' The Spirit (Holy Spirit) testifies with our spirit that we are God's children."* (NIV).

Our relationship with the Holy Spirit is a supernatural one. The way He interacts and communicates with one individual may be totally different from how He interacts and communicates with another.

We also see God as a father who gives us direction now, so we can have options later; but He doesn't force us to follow His direction. In fact, according to the Bible, the God of the universe consistently asks us to allow Him into our daily lives.

In practical terms, how can God be involved in the daily issues and struggles singles face? Good question. John 10:27 says, "My sheep listen to my voice. I know them and they follow me." In other words, He wants to have an interactive relationship with us.

Yes, God wants to hear our cries, disappointments, frustrations, fears, and in return, He wants to give us His strength, His wisdom, and those *aha* moments He gives us that help us navigate relationships.

Myrna tells how she does this in dealing with her relationships, even dating. "I seek God's counsel through His Word, elders with wisdom, godly friends, or I often sit still waiting for that quiet stirring in my spirit."

A friend once asked if she could set me up with a non- Christian friend. At first, I questioned the idea so; I sought the Lord. I sensed in my spirit that I was to go out only once with him. As it turned out, we had absolutely nothing in common, but I had a wonderful time. Why? Because the Lord had to show me how much He had healed me. Normally, I would have gotten into a debate about all of our differences. I gracefully accepted him, knowing my job was not to "fix" him. Then, I was able to enjoy discovering the new and improved me. Including God's counsel in your relationships can save you from a lot of heartache and it adds fun to your single life."

Myrna continues, "I always ask Him about dating. If a friend wants to set me up with someone, I first consult (pray) with the Lord. Sometimes, right up front, He'll tell me that this is not my husband, but to go out with Him three times. Why? He wanted me to heal from something through the experience of that casual dating. Another time, He led me into Internet dating and it was for the same reason: to discover things about myself and have fun with it."

Online dating may not be for some of you. You need to be led of the Lord as to what method He may use for you. Of course, whatever method you use, be sure it is of God and that you are not being driven more by culture and peer pressure than Him.

Myrna often speaks about God talking to her and her hearing Him. Now don't freak out about this or feel spiritually inferior. If this isn't your experience, don't worry. We didn't initially. If you want to begin hearing God communicate to your heart, try to get in a position to listen to Him. An excellent place is reading His love letter to us, the Bible, on a regular basis. If you want to hear from Him once a week, then read once a week. If you want to hear from Him daily, then read the Bible daily.

God doesn't make us robots for His control. He wants us to want Him! God says He will not withhold any good thing from those who walk uprightly and with integrity. Just ask Adam and Eve. But they sure paid a price for their disobedience and so did we as their descendants. God doesn't lie and He always wants to bless us with His best.

For men, God wants to train us up to be kings, just as He trained David in the shepherd's field (an entry-level position), so he would know how to treat and lead all people, the poor as well as the rich. David also learned to be responsible for a few seemingly unimportant things before becoming king of a nation. And David learned through adversity how to be king.

God often allows adversity (rejection, waiting, injustice, etc.) to build and shape our character. Our character determines what kind of man, leader, husband, and father we will be and thus impacts our destiny. Our character also determines if and what kind of women will be attracted to us. Furthermore, God also wants men to understand that being His sons makes us royalty. So it is not about striving to gain something like Adam and Eve did; but about learning how to embrace who we are as sons of a King. Sonship also teaches us about loyalty and commitment. This commitment and loyalty will help us to be monogamous.

For women, God wants to protect and provide for them as described in Psalm 91:1-2 and 11-12 (NIV).

> *"He who dwells in the shelter of the Most High will rest in the shadow of the Almighty. I will say of the Lord, "He is my refuge and my fortress, God, in whom I trust . . . For he will command his angels concerning you to guard you in all yours ways; they will lift you up in their hands, so that you will not strike your foot against a stone."*

It is interesting that God's desire is to protect and provide for you because these are also the core values for most men: to protect and provide. Ladies, think of yourselves as the daughter of a King, which makes you a princess. And He wants you to be trained to be queens. Therefore, appreciate who you are. You don't have to focus on and strive to get married, but instead, focus on "being." We need to be careful about trying to impress people to make them "like" us, because we run the risk of not being ourselves. When we are not ourselves, we are acting, and we can unintentionally deceive the person in whom we are interested. What if we were to get married but then got tired of *acting?* Our spouse may justifiably have serious issues with us. So be you—the best you can be. No longer see yourself in a negative light as being too tall or too short, too big or too skinny, the wrong complexion, and don't believe the enemy's lie that the size of your breasts defines your womanhood! If a man can't love you the way you are, he isn't worthy of your love and he has forfeited the gift of who you are!

According to Judges 1:12, a book in the Old Testament of the Bible, a man would often have to prove himself before the father would give away his daughter in marriage. Then, he gave her land, but she also asked for the water rights and the father gave her that too. What belongs to the Father is yours and He wants the best spouse and life for you.

Perhaps, it's difficult to believe He is our Father because our earthly father wasn't that kind of example. Or perhaps church taught us that He was a punitive God with rules and laws. Perhaps you believed that if you did something wrong, He would not want you anymore. According to the Word of God, He is a Father to the orphans. You have a heavenly Father who is always with you.

You may even blame God for all the things that have gone wrong in your life and ask how a loving God could allow that? Unresolved anger turns to bitterness. Sometimes we may unknowingly harbor this against God for not sending us a date or spouse. Then we may fall into calculating to make things happen on our own terms, like Sarah in the Old Testament.

You are not alone in your frustrations. In Psalms, another Old Testament book, David on numerous occasions is found pouring out his heart to God and communicating his frustrations with his circumstances. His expressions of his emotions are often raw. But once he gets it all out, then he praises God. God is big enough to hear all of our frustrations about our singleness and still love us. Remember, Jesus Christ, God's only son, was a single adult.

God: Our Comforter

What is God's role when you are grieving the loss of your friends as they get married while you remain single? School is one of the best times to meet close friends. Typically everyone in college is single, but soon after graduation, they get married. Then, a gap grows in the relationship between the single and now-married friend. The married friends now naturally focus more on their marriages than the friendships with the single friends, which they should. These chords of friendship often sever completely when kids are born. Imagine sitting with your married friends with kids discussing their children's school, soccer games, and other family related topics, which are foreign to you. Some of these married friends are even hiring coaches to help their kids get into the best preschool. And, there is all the talk about remodeling the home (which can be interesting if you're into interior design). All of this is foreign to a single person. When the conversation focuses on you, it's to ask, "So, any dates lately? As if you already didn't have anything to contribute, your answer is *"no"* or *"none."* You receive a sympathetic sigh or the reassuring, "You'll find somebody," which you've heard a million times!

Such previously mentioned conversations can make you feel like you don't belong anymore or even give you a sense of rejection. Perhaps a change of mindset is required for both singles and married friends. So singles need to have patience in this new relationship. Your married friends need to try to remember what it was like to be single and stop putting pressure on you to be just like them now. They need to appreciate singles for who they are in their singleness—which isn't a disease. But it may be your responsibility as a single to remind your married friends of this. But be gentle, not angry with them, realizing they might be unintentionally as insensitive as they seem to you if the roles were reversed. It's part of a cycle of life for singles and their married friends.

Maybe your relationship with your married friends will be resurrected later when their kids are grown, or it can become a new type of friendship. Some married friends embrace singles as part of their family and can provide a sense of stability and role modeling of healthy relationships.

Maintaining friendships with married couples may prove to be invaluable for singles. For instance, having married friends as mentioned in the previous paragraph could provide an inside look into a marriage relationship, the good, the bad, and sometimes the ugly. Such a view can provide a realistic perspective of marriage, helping to eliminate the "starry eyed" view of marriage. The married couple can assist in relationship accountability for the single, asking the single questions that other singles wouldn't know to ask simply because they wouldn't have the experience of marriage. If the couple has children, the single can also see how they impact a marriage. So maintaining a friendship with a married couple could better prepare a single for marriage or help some singles evaluate whether marriage is really for them. It is times like these that make having a personal growing relationship with Jesus Christ so wonderful and necessary. Jesus was single. He understands your struggles.

"For we do not have a high priest who is unable to sympathize with our weaknesses, but we have one who has been tempted in every way, just as we are—yet without sin" (Hebrews 4:15).

Jesus also understood grief. His friend, Lazarus had physically died. Jesus wept when He saw Lazarus' grave. Some Bible scholars say that Jesus wept because He had to bring Lazarus back from heaven to earth to eventually die again. And I think that is a very real possibility, but I would include that it appears that Lazarus was also single. So he could understand Jesus in His singleness more than most. Nowhere does Scripture seem to indicate Lazarus was married. And if Lazarus wasn't married, it wouldn't have been uncommon for Jesus and him to talk about the temptation of maintaining sexual purity—Jesus was *tempted* in *every* way, yet didn't sin. Jesus was fully human and fully God.

Jesus can relate to your grief of not being married and the loss of friends more than you may realize. He is more than able to bring new friends and relationships into your life. As Jesus cried out while dying on the cross for us, "Why have you forsaken me?" God, the Father must have hurt too! But He allowed His Son to endure this suffering for a greater good, which was creating a channel for us to be restored to oneness with Him. It cost God His only Son. So God understands your grief, loss, and sacrifice.

I Love God—I'm Not Sleeping Around, So Why Am I Still Single?

At times like these we must be careful not to be so desperate that we'll do anything to end our singleness. Don't get married in order to escape your singleness, loneliness, boredom, parent(s), etc. Please **don't ignore God's warning** that you shouldn't get married. If you don't have a peace about it, don't get married. Please don't ignore certain reoccurring behaviors, any kind of abuse, fear of your significant other, etc.—don't do it. If your parents or close friends who love you don't approve, they may be seeing a blind spot that you don't. Seriously consider their concerns or objections before entering a marriage you may regret. Love gives; it doesn't demand.

I've counseled too many people who rushed into marriage, ignoring God's warning that they shouldn't marry a particular person. Some married because they are people pleasers and didn't want to offend anyone. For example, I've heard statements such as, "I liked a guy, and I didn't want to hurt his feelings," or "I sent the wedding invitations out already so it is too late to cancel the wedding." Then after they are married, they want to rush out of the marriage, wishing they had never gotten married. Don't let this happen to you.

Possible Reasons You May Still Be Single

But what about my dreams of marriage being shattered? Didn't God say it was not good for us to be single and that He would give us the desires of our hearts? So why am I still single? Many of our single friends thought they'd have a girlfriend by now, or would be a dad by now, teaching his child how to play basketball, or a soccer mom driving a van, or be remarried, but instead they are single living with only their dog or cat.

As we discovered earlier in this book, God loves us and wants the BEST for us! Do you remember the following principles from chapter one?

- "God's Best for me is *Always Right Now*, not yesterday and not tomorrow!"

- Realizing God always has my best interest in mind, and, He knows what's best for me more than I do, took a lot of pressure off me to try to make things happen.

- You have a *Godly Destiny*, so don't wish your time away on tomorrow or wanting things to be different. Learn to embrace today (Lamentations 3:22-24)!

- If we focus on tomorrow, we may miss God's Blessings for us *today*!

- Ask God what He may be trying to teach you in the midst of your singleness.

- It is all about trusting God.

- We are made in the image of God (Genesis 1:27).

- So we should focus not on **self-worship**, but on gaining a better understanding of *self-worth*. So we need to see ourselves as God does.

- **If we aren't content being single**, usually when we finally do get into a relationship, we can unintentionally push with tremendous pressure our friend, boyfriend, girlfriend, or spouse toward a performance track of "pleasing me."

Or we can have an inferiority complex and constantly degrade ourselves, which can become destructive in a relationship. Some of the symptoms can be public self-humiliation or jealousy or other destructive behaviors.

If God Loves Me So Much, Why Am I Still Single?

- You may not be emotionally ready, which may cause you to be dependent and needy, creating a co-dependent relationship.

- The person God wants to connect you with isn't ready.

- God doesn't want to compete for our affection with anyone. If your desire to be married is greater than your love for Christ, then God may not allow this because it could destroy your marriage, your spouse, and your children.

- There could be spiritual lessons God wants you to learn before allowing you to be in a relationship.

- God may be allowing you to see whom or what you love most—Him or being in a relationship.

- Maybe God wants you to determine if you will continue living for Him if you *never* get into a relationship.

- Maybe God wants you to understand that life's ultimate goal isn't getting married, it is a relationship with Him.

- Maybe singlehood is also a time to get to know God personally and individually before being in a relationship. Getting to know God better would also allow you to get to know yourself even better. Myrna says, "The best thing about being single is all the time I get to spend with Him in prayer."

What if none of the above is an issue for you? I've often told women who have had miscarriages that often some babies are so special that God wants the privilege of raising them Himself. I'm wondering if the same principle of God is true for those of you in your twenties, thirties, forties, fifties, sixties, and older as well. That you are so special to God, that He doesn't share you with anyone! He wants you all to Himself. In heaven, marriage won't exist. God could be giving you one of His greatest honors, so don't reject it. Embrace it!

Just before the release of this book, my pastor was preaching from the book of Daniel (an Old Testament book in the Bible). Shadrach, Meshach and Abednego, Jews, were in trouble with the Babylonian king, Nebuchadnezzar because they wouldn't worship his ninety-foot idol of himself. This king taunted them by asking the question, ". . . . *Then what god will be able to rescue you from my hand?"* These Jewish single young men responded,

> *"O Nebuchadnezzar, we do not need to defend ourselves before you in this matter. If we are thrown into the blazing furnace, the God we serve is able to save us from it, and he will rescue us from your hand, O king. But even if he does not, we want you to know, O king, that we will not serve your gods or worship the image of gold you have set up."* Daniel 3:16-18 (NIV)

Is there a principle here that as a single who is following Christ that it is quite natural to want to be in a relationship or even married, but if that doesn't happen, you are committed to continue following Christ, no matter what?

Lecrae, the Christ-following, Grammy Award winning, rapper says in his song, *God Is Enough.* You may want to hear his perspective as to why God is enough for him.

Another reason for singleness may be a broken heart that has not yet been healed. To learn how to deal with this issue, read the next chapter.

SUMMARY POINTS

1. God created us last because He first prepared all of creation for us.

2. God loves us even when we disobey Him.

3. God has provided His best for us. Look around you.

4. God demonstrated His grace and mercy after Adam and Eve rejected Him.

5. Some of us had good fathers and some of us didn't. None of them were perfect. God is a perfect Father. He wants to protect, provide, counsel, and have you experience His love. He wants an interactive relationship with you.

6. It's okay to cry out from the pain in your heart from your frustration of being single. He wants you to honestly express yourself to Him, even if it's raw. He can handle it (Jeremiah 20:7-18 and Habakkuk 1:1-17).

7. Your singleness is not an indication that God doesn't love you. In fact, it may be a sign that He does, more than we realize.

8. Your life's primary goal as singles shouldn't be getting married, but to become whom God created you to be. Certainly, marriage should be one of your goals, but your life isn't a failure or a success due to your marital status.

9. God is your comforter during your singleness, especially as friends transition into marriage and family life while you grieve for not having a spouse by the time you expected.

10. There are various reasons why some singles aren't married, and many of them are good reasons.

11. Jesus Christ was single and thoroughly understands your struggles as singles.

12. Your singleness may be God's highest form of honor for you.

ACTION POINTS

1. Whether you are a follower of Christ or not, how does it make you feel knowing that God loves you? Why?

2. Why do you think God's best wasn't enough for Adam and Eve? If you are a follower of Christ, are there times when God's best is not enough for you? If "yes," why do you think that is?

3. How do you feel knowing that God provides His best for us? Why?

4. What do you think about God not putting Adam and Eve to death for disobeying Him, but instead clothing them and giving them another shot at eternal life?

5. Before reading this chapter, how did you view your singleness? Why? After reading this chapter, how do you now view your singleness? Why?

6. Why do you think you are still single? Do you think God is preventing you from getting married? Why might He allow this?

7. How has your relationship with your earthly father affected your view of God as Father? Your relationships with the opposite sex?

8. If you are a follower of Christ, will you continue to love God if you never marry? Why or why not?

9. So whether you believe in God or not, what if such a God loves you and me, and not because of anything we have done to earn His love? How does this make you feel?

10. How does it make you feel to know that God loves us even when we feel unlovable?

Chapter Four

Healing a Broken Heart

"The Lord is close to the brokenhearted and saves (delivers/rescues) those who are crushed in spirit." Psalm 34:18

My theme song in junior high was **What Becomes of the Brokenhearted**, made famous by Jimmy Ruffin in 1966.

> *What becomes of the brokenhearted*
> *Who had love that's now departed?*
> *I know I've got to find,*
> *Some kind of peace of mind.*
> *Help me.*

Some of you can probably relate to these lyrics. These words epitomized the state of my romantic life during my years in junior and senior high school.

Have you ever been dumped in a relationship? Whether it is in elementary or secondary school, college, or divorce, it results in hurt and painful thoughts of being a failure or not good enough. Sometimes we feel as though we are the *only* person that no one wants. Questions such as, *Why? What happened? I thought we were doing so well. What did I do wrong? Can I get her back? Who else is going to want me?"* plague our minds.

I asked girls plenty of times to be my girlfriend in junior high school and they very politely said, "no." It happened so frequently I didn't even have the opportunity to be in a relationship to get dumped. I felt unwanted by girls for most of junior and senior high school. Obviously, it seemed that I didn't have whatever other boys had that attracted girls. Some of the girls who were interested in me had dated my homeboys. Unfortunately, the unwritten "man-code" of the time didn't allow you to date girls who dated your friends.

Of course, only growing one inch each year in junior high, from 4'7 to 4'9 didn't help either. And even though I shot up over the summer to a towering 5'1 as a sophomore, my social life wasn't much better. From fourteen to eighteen years old, I was extremely desperate to be in a relationship because I was so lonely. Maybe I was in love with being in love, but the wounds of rejection were so great that I stopped asking girls out by the time I was fifteen. Much of my time during those years was spent on fantasyland, imagining I was in a relationship with the girl of my dreams. The funny thing is, if one of these beautiful girls had said yes, I wouldn't have known what to do with her. This intense, long-term rejection resulted in feelings of inadequacy. "Just My Imagination" by the Temptations was another theme song that described my situation.

College for the most part was better because I became a basketball star as a freshman for a small predominately white Chicago Christian college and the dating doors opened up. Basketball made me *cool*. Girls like *cool*. It is funny and sad how sports can transcend both fear and prejudice.

But even in college as a popular basketball player, I experienced rejection from two girls that I dated: one at the Chicago school and another in a smaller Christian school in Tennessee. In both instances my girlfriends' fathers forced them to stop seeing me because of the color of my skin. I was devastated because the girl in Tennessee was the first girl I ever loved and wanted to marry. Even though these fathers discriminated against me, I couldn't discriminate against beautiful girls no matter what color they were. I definitely maintained my equal opportunity dating policy, but I was much more guarded and cautious dating cross-culturally.

In Chicago, I didn't have anyone with whom to process the pain after my father was shot, robbed, and killed during spring break of my junior year. My girlfriend in Chicago had been the one with whom I talked about everything. I desperately needed to talk with her about Dad's death. I wasn't in love with her. We were just good friends. So having her father abruptly terminate our relationship and all communication was beyond my comprehension. I didn't handle the situation well. I didn't curse her out, but I did give her evil stares for a while. I didn't understand my emotions and I certainly didn't know how to control them or heal from them. I just survived this terrible experience, stuffing it somewhere in my brain, but never having closure. Time eventually numbed my pain. Not sure when I healed from it, but now I only want the best for her. Time doesn't heal all wounds, but in this case it did.

Later in Tennessee, I fortunately had close roommates, professors, and administrators who cared and helped me heal from my broken relationship. In fact, I wrote the father of the girl from the Tennessee school, telling him he was disobeying God by his actions. He was a well-known pastor and writer for a denomination. After a year of praying for a chance to talk with him face to face, God provided the opportunity and, to my amazement, this father apologized. I felt he was genuine, so I accepted his apology. I never forgot the pain, but my pain subsided as I realized that she had never really loved me. Right or wrong, I felt her ending our relationship because we were facing adversity meant she would have had a difficult time in a cross- cultural marriage. She would not have been a bad choice, but she was not God's best for me, which also meant I wasn't God's best for her either. This allowed me to move on and become wiser and healthier for the *next* relationship.

Years later, I learned of some unfortunate situations regarding the young lady at the Tennessee school and her family. By allowing her father to break up our relationship, God was actually protecting me even when I didn't know I needed protection. So, not all break ups are bad. Some are actually good, even though they are initially painful.

If we don't work through our rejections, broken relationships, or bad experiences with the opposite sex, it can close our hearts to ever seeking a healthy, mutually beneficial, and Godly relationship. And if we feel unwanted, unattractive, unworthy, or unappreciated, these feelings can cause us to become demoralized. Relationship wounds often become our baggage, which we will carry into all of our future relationships. Therefore, this chapter, which is about healing a broken heart and being able to discern if we are emotionally healthy, is incredibly critical.

So even though I'm happily married now, I know what it's like to have my heart broken, more than once. And over the years, as I've counseled numerous others with hearts wounded by relationships. I've practiced and shared biblical principles that have helped their hearts mend. Maybe these principles can help you navigate through the healing process.

God so cares for you. He feels the pain of the brokenhearted. Here is what He says about the brokenhearted: *"The Lord is close to the brokenhearted and saves* (delivers, rescues) *those who are crushed in spirit,"* Psalm 34:18. In Psalm 147:3, He says, *"He* (God) *heals the brokenhearted and binds up their wounds."*

As you read this chapter, invite Him to search your heart for any brokenness and ask Him to bind up your wounds.

After the Break Up:

But what do I do after the break up?

Some Women

Many women tell me that they cry for days. Then their anger takes over and many begin demeaning all men. For example, *"What a jerk! I deserve better than that! Why does he have to be that way? What's wrong with guys! Why don't they know how to treat women? Men are flaky! Men can't be trusted."* For some women, a break up gnaws at their fear that they'll never get married before their biological clock stops ticking, or worse, that there will never be anyone out there ever again. Single women sometimes sedate their pain by overeating, overworking, shopping, reliving the break up over and over, or through other distractions. Some women will go pick up a guy just to prove she is attractive to at least one guy. And of course, there is the nagging hope that he'll call and say he was crazy for breaking up with the woman of his dreams!

Some Men

Typically, most men don't cry or at least we don't let anyone see us crying. Like women with their girlfriends, men seek guy friends for support, and it can turn into a pity party bashing women, especially toward the one who just dumped them. They may even ask their moms to explain women— these strange, yet desirable creatures. Some may go to a bar or church to find a woman who shows interest in them. Usually she is someone they would not normally date, but he may use as an immediate and short-term remedy (making out or a one-night stand) to mend his damaged ego. The problem with this is that an innocent and unsuspecting young lady can be needlessly wounded. Other guys may get drunk. Unfortunately, some who don't have a good support system may turn to pornography or masturbation, further negatively impacting their future relationships.

Singles tend to struggle with the opposite sex, particularly when, from their perspective, the opposite sex does seemingly irrational things. Singles also wrestle with feelings of rejection and unworthiness, causing them to want to get rid of all reminders of their former relationship, such as gifts and pictures for example.

And it is quite common for men and women to adopt, for a period of time, an *I don't want to go out anymore. I'm giving up on the opposite sex—they're all the same,* attitude due to disappointment and disillusionment. The flipside of this attitude is getting busy with parties and activities, dating with no commitment, or drinking to numb the pain.

Some singles force themselves to move on by attempting to bury the past. Often you think you've done this. But when you see your ex, hear his or her name or voice, your wounds resurface and you lose it for a few moments, hours, or days. This is your indication that you don't have healing or closure. If you are experiencing this, you are in the emotional slavery that we discussed in the previous chapter. You are allowing someone who has wounded you intentionally or unintentionally to control you. Usually this person isn't even thinking about you anymore. They are free, but you aren't. You may have deceived yourself into thinking you were over your ex, but retaining bitterness and placing a wall of self-protection reveal you aren't.

Your response to a break up involves many factors, including the length of the relationship, its intensity, how intimate you were, remorse if you lowered your standards, devastation if you felt he or she was the *One,* what role God did or didn't play. Nonetheless, a break up can trigger some of the reactions described above. It's part of the grieving process explained (not in a particular order) below:

- Shock/pain at the loss, with varying emotions, especially if termination of the relationship was unexpected.

- Anger – Why? This isn't fair!

- Depression – not wanting to do anything, go out, etc.; but wanting anything to numb the pain.

- Denial – going out to ignore the loss; wishing and secretly expecting to get back together again.

- Acceptance and tolerance – learning to live with *it.*

Dr. Suzanne Mayo-Theus, Vice President for Institutional Advancement at Wiley College and author of *Learning & Healing from Bad Relationships: Solutions for Survival & Success,* says, "Some people experience *disruption of attachment* in relationships. This disruption occurs when an attachment figure is unavailable. Insecurity in attachment may occur due to earlier interactions. And the stages to attachment separation and stages of reactions to attachment separation or disruption are protest (distress, fear, desperation, despair, and hopelessness about attachment figure); and detachment (acceptance of new attachment figure)." She also says, "Change requires commitment. It's not where you are today that counts; it's where you are headed."

Creating and Finding a *"Safe Place"* for Healing

All of us need to have or create a safe place for healing from wounds and from life in general. If you have a family or close friends that love you enough to tell you what you may not want to hear, but need to hear, then you have a safe place for healing. If you don't have this support base, then you can possibly create one by finding one or two people you can help, even though you are struggling yourself. This is exactly what Joseph did in the Bible after he was unjustly imprisoned. Instead of having a pity party, he helped two other inmates, one of whom returned the favor years later.

Another possible support candidate could be another single at church, that you've seen and maybe know, who could be an excellent person with whom to share a cup of coffee. Just approach them and say, "I've recently gotten out of a relationship and I just need to process it. Would you allow me to buy you a coffee and be a confidential sounding board for me please?" For some of you, this is totally out of your comfort zone and I hear you. If this is true of you, consider reaching out to a married couple from church and do the same with them.

And whether or not we have a human support base, God can always touch our spirit if we put ourselves in position to fellowship with Him. Malachi 4:2 says, *"But to you who fear My name, the Sun of Righteousness shall arise with healing in His wings."*

Those who fear His name are believers trusting God even when it isn't easy to trust. The Sun of Righteousness is the source of a new day of hope and deliverance, combined with healing. The wings refer to God's moving swiftly—in His time, not necessarily ours. We need to meditate on God's magnificence. His safety and love create an atmosphere for healing. Psalm 91:4 reads, *"He shall cover you with His feathers and under His wings you shall take refuge."* God will protect us.

Assess and Learn

After a break up, it's helpful to begin your healing process to get clarity as to why it happened. Think of it as a relational exit interview, just as many employers do with their employees. Discussing the break up over a dinner or cup of coffee could actually help speed up the healing process. It isn't always possible, but talking civilly with your ex to hear his or her perspective could be incredibly helpful, not only for the immediate need of healing; but also for the success of your future relationships. Frustration in relationships frequently comes from not knowing exactly what or why something happened. We may not agree with the reasoning, but at least having some kind of explanation can keep you from going crazy wondering *why?*

Many singles (including divorcees) frequently go from one relationship to another believing that they have emotionally moved on—that they *are over* their previous relationship. Too often, this isn't true. In fact, some singles actually rush into a new relationship because for whatever reason, being single is unbearable for them. Many singles' next relationship is built upon the rebound phenomenon.

Having family, and a few close friends you trust, to help you process what happened in your relationship that just ended may prove helpful. This is your first step toward legitimate closure of your previous relationship. Try with the help of family and close friends to evaluate this relationship and its demise objectively. Where did you meet: church, work, or a bar (it usually makes a difference)? Some of you may ask, *"What possible difference does it make where we met?"* Whether you realize it or not, you are advertising. So where you frequent is saying something about who you are and your character. Remember, when you are advertising, you can't always control who answers your ad.

What initially attracted you to this particular person? Did this individual possess similar characteristics of others you have dated? Is this a good or bad pattern? What were his or her strengths and weaknesses? How did that compliment your strengths and weaknesses? Why or why not? What did being in this relationship do for you? Are you better or worse for having dated this person? Why or why not? Did this person influence you to be more Christ-like or not? Why or why not? Did you help your former significant other become more Christ-like or not? If your answer is *Yes,* how so? Did you lower standards to date this person? If you lowered your standards, why? Was it worth it? Did you part as friends or would you prefer not to see this person again? Why or why not? Did dating this person from your perspective better prepare you for marriage? Why or why not? Were you the dumper or the dumped? Why? What is your mindset about beginning a new relationship?

And another benefit of this process is that you will at least slow down a little before jumping into a new relationship and wait until you are emotionally healthier for your next relationship.

Possible Signs We Haven't Healed or Don't Have Closure

What are signs that we haven't healed nor have closure? Many singles, even after becoming aware that they still haven't overcome the pain of their previous relationship, still don't feel ready to let go. You know who they are. It's been ten years since their break up and they're still talking about that relationship.

Why can't they let go? They could be dealing with the fact that they don't believe they will ever find someone as good as this person. Perhaps, they wish to go back in time and make changes in themselves or their significant other to solve the problem. It wouldn't matter.

Typically, a relationship back then would be considered the "good old days." Frequently, the reason the good old days are so good is because we tend to forget or mentally block out the bad experiences concerning those *good old days*. If these singles could go back and honestly look at the relationship, they might remember that their old relationship wasn't perfect. They may also compare their new relationship to "the perfect one," resulting in all of their new relationships falling short of the "perfect one's" standard. This nostalgic illusion could completely turn off many singles to future relationships.

To still be in pain ten years later over a *perfect* boyfriend or girlfriend, especially if the other person terminated it, may be evidence of deeper abandonment and rejection issues, which need to be processed with the assistance of an effective counselor.

I wonder if these singles, as followers of Christ, don't believe God can or will find them a spouse who is better than their ex? I also wonder if getting married is more of a priority for them than their personal relationship with Jesus Christ? Could it be that God is not enough and may never be enough? For some, trusting God can be difficult when they project upon God the human traits of earthly fathers, men, or others who have wounded them. What is sad is that such singles are living unfulfilled lives—not being married, and not loving themselves or living the lives they have. They are allowing their past to punish their present. Equally as sad is that they may not realize that their desperation may be a turnoff to prospective candidates.

Other signs that some singles haven't healed or don't have closure are harboring angry or wounded emotions toward their ex. If this is how you feel, you aren't ready for a new relationship. Some people initiate new relationships as a cure for a wound from a previous relationship. If we are in some way emotionally hurting from a past relationship, then it is quite possible that we won't be thinking clearly when considering a new one.

Initiating a new relationship, just so you won't have the "single" status is actually a selfish motive. Selfishness kills relationships. Another sign you haven't healed from your past relationship is desiring to be in another one simply to prove that the problem in the relationship was your "ex" and not you. Such a relationship is also motivated by selfishness.

What Motivates Us to Closure?

How do you prepare *yourself to let go of a previous relationship?* This is an excellent question. The answer may be complicated because it frequently exposes deeper issues such as abandonment, rejection, or other issues from childhood. When I'm ready to let go, I prayerfully use the *Letting Go* principles. These principles helped me override my emotions so that I could make a choice as an act of my will. Hopefully, my reasons to let go, will also benefit you:

Letting go releases and frees you to move on to function more effectively for God in the present, instead of constantly living in the *past*. When you live in the past, you often find yourself constantly having self-pity parties. This is non-productive and retards your moving on. Don't let the pain of your past, punish your present, paralyze your future, and pervert your purpose because you have a godly destiny!

Letting go allows you to begin the process of understanding the rejection issue. God Himself was rejected by His own people. When the Israelites rejected God, wanting a human king instead, Samuel, the priest, became upset. But God told Samuel, *"They are not rejecting you, but they are rejecting ME."* Be careful not to continue rehearsing the hurt.

Letting go provides you with insight into God's incredible love and patience for you.

Letting go can also begin the process of emotional detachment. Be careful, though, not to allow your emotional detachment to lead to resentment and bitterness. The detachment is a critical step if God is in the process of releasing us from one relationship to another.

Letting go helps you begin understanding that your situation is bigger than you and not just about you! Let go of the self-pity. Therefore, in letting go, don't worry about what your situation looks like to anyone other than God. You may think you look like a failure to others, but concentrate on what your relationship with God IS!!

Letting go can lead to the *time of your life!* God wants to increase your intimacy with Him and to continue providing you with opportunities to grow spiritually. God desires to connect you with people who want to celebrate you, not just tolerate you.

Letting go requires an attitude of trust in God, a mental adjustment to see God's big picture, and not see the people who hurt you as your enemy. There is an evil spirit behind those people—some of whom may be Christians.

Letting go opens a door to more intimacy with God, more understanding, more freedom from depression, less stress, and less competition. My friend Johnny Parker shared with me his principle of **"Staying in My Lane."** He means don't be jealous about others' success. Instead, be happy for them, knowing that God has a specific and unique plan for you. It requires dependency on God's sovereignty, resulting in a calming spirit and a *"wait and see"* attitude. You gain more peace because you are in your proper and safe place of *following God* instead of trying to lead Him. Desiring to control or manipulate the situation lessens because having others recognize what a tremendous gift of God you are becomes less of an issue. (Be careful to understand the difference between *self-worship* and *self-worth*—self-worth gives you value because you're created in God's image).

Letting go allows God to transform you into a more effective servant for Him, being more in tune with pleasing Him. It develops more of a servant spirit in you. "How can I give more?" instead of "What do I get?" Remember that personal happiness is not about your visibility or receiving other's approval.

Letting go provides more patience with your family and friends, because you are no longer primarily focused on you and depressed or obsessed with receiving what you consider justice. This kind of thinking and behavior can result in a short temper with others. Letting go gives you more security with who you are in Christ. Consider the vineyard workers' principle in Matthew 20:1-16, this is God's ministry. *"He can do whatever He wants with me, when He wants. I am His!"*

Letting go elevates you to deeper level of worshiping God. It is a freedom to worship God as never before. God reveals more of Himself to you because you are now in a position to trust Him as you sit at His feet. You are now more open to learning whatever He wants to teach you, resulting in worshiping Him more for Who He Is, not for what He can do for you!

These verses will be helpful in letting go. Verses 10 and 11 of Second Corinthians 2 speak of the power in forgiveness. And Second Corinthians 10:5 says, *"Taking every thought captive to the obedience of Christ."*

You let go by an act of your will, not by emotion. Understandably, there can be great pain in letting go. But remember that Jesus promises to be your comforter and He will not leave your side as you walk this out. He, Himself, stands with you, comforting you. He only has the best for you, so hold on to that!

Applying 2 Corinthians 2:10-11 is easier if you ask God to help you focus on your present situation and help you not dwell on the break up. Negative thoughts can eventually hold you as an emotional prisoner. For example, instead of wishing your ex would call; consider this prayer:

God, I know wishing (name of person) would call is counterproductive, so help me control such thoughts and help me to mentally understand that I shouldn't desire someone who clearly isn't interested in me.

Instead, let me enjoy the freedom of not being in a relationship. And will You please meet my emotional need? Thank You for making me in Your image and letting me know I'm important to You.

If a negative thought enters your mind after your break up (for example, *Nobody loves me; I'm a reject!*), you simply pray saying, *God, this thought doesn't glorify You and I don't want to dwell on it. Please remove it from my mind.* Replace it with the truth either from scripture or with *He has His best for me no matter what.* This is taking every thought captive through the power of God. And remember, you can do all things through Christ who strengthens you—Philippians 4:13.

I certainly don't know how anyone else feels, but like many of you, I've experienced rejection throughout my life. You've read about my romantic failures, but I've also been rejected because of my physical appearance. Add to this my insecurity issues, regrettably, due to my poor choices. I'm a former pornography addict, so you can see I have issues.

But what motivated me to bring closure to issues and previous relationships? It is quite simple. I just got tired of how I viewed myself, living a defeated life, and repeating the cycle, particularly with the pornography. I also wanted to experience the best that life has to offer. And not bringing closure kept me living in the pain of my past, punishing my present, paralyzing my future, and perverting my purpose. Not achieving closure prevented me from experiencing God's destiny for me. I began seeing myself the way God sees me—as a person of value. I began telling myself, "I'm okay, not the best, but certainly not the worst." I had to stop equating my worth with whether or not I was in a relationship. I stopped telling myself I was inadequate or unworthy. I quit demanding that God *owed* me a spouse. And somehow, I had to come to terms with the fact that God is God and He is in charge. As God, He has the right to do whatever He pleases with me (Romans 9:20-21).

Yet, this all-powerful and all-knowing God loves me and His best for me is always right now—not yesterday and not tomorrow, but right now.

When I'm constantly focusing on yesterday or tomorrow, I'm missing out on what God is doing for me today. Lamentations 3:22-23 says, ". . . *His compassions never fail. They are new every morning.*"

Practicing these principles revolutionized the way I viewed each day. Automatically, I began focusing on the here and now, which helped me stop wasting away so much of my present time on the future or past. I told myself that I probably wouldn't get married and I'd be okay with that. I didn't do well living with expectation. It took tremendous pressure off of me. I relaxed.

So in some situations I forgave myself and asked God for His forgiveness. I believed Him and accepted His grace. I didn't base His forgiveness or acceptance of His grace on emotions, but faith that God is who He says He is! In some situations, I forgave others just as I had asked for forgiveness. Slowly and continually, I learned to like myself for who I am and for who God made me. And I learned to love myself, but not at the expense of others. I'm also continuing to learn to serve others. I'm admitting my faults, but refusing to be enslaved by them. I'm choosing to learn from my faults in order to be a better person. Learning not to take myself so seriously has been extremely helpful. I've become less concerned with "my rights," self-entitlement, and what I think others owe me. And my biggest motivating factor for closure is loving people with God's love.

Sometimes, a single continues holding on to a previous relationship because it's a way to stay connected to that person, even if it's unhealthy. To help you process what I just shared about my journey, you may want to count the costs of holding on to a previous relationship and compare it with the benefits of letting go.

How Do I Forgive?

A major step in freeing yourself from emotional slavery is forgiving the person who wounded you. This doesn't require or suggest that you be best friends. What we seldom realize is that unforgiveness impacts us subconsciously in every relationship we have.

As we approach this topic of forgiveness, keep in mind that forgiveness and emotional healing for followers of Christ are two critical, yet different issues. Unresolved hurts can grow into anger or rage. Anger is usually a secondary emotion resulting from an unhealed hurt. *Unger's Bible Dictionary* defines anger as:

> *"The emotion of instant displeasure, indignation, arising from the feeling of injury done or unintended. Anger is not evil per se. Anger*

is sinful when it arises too soon, without reflection; when the injury which awakens it is only apparent; when it is disproportionate to the offense; when it is transferred from the guilty to the innocent; when it is too long protracted and becomes revengeful." (Matthew 5:22; Ephesians 4:26; Colossians 3:8)

Often without knowing it, we let unresolved hurt become bitterness. Bitterness can become long-term resentment. How are we to apply the biblical principle in Ephesians 4:26-27? *"In your anger do not sin. Do not let the sun go down while you are still angry and do not give the devil a foothold."* This verse seems impractical to live out! I believe the context here isn't about major emotional issues. And I believe God gives us some grace here. Yet, this verse does imply that individually, we have an ability and responsibility to control our emotions and not allow them to run wild, even when someone else has hurt us. This doesn't eliminate accountability or responsibility of the person who wronged us. Nor do these verses ask us to deny our emotions.

At first glance, this command from God seems impossible and possibly, for some of us, unfair. But we need to back up for a moment and refresh our memory of who the God we say we love is. Remember as we saw in a previous chapter, that God loves us. So if God loves us, what is He trying to do *to* us and *through* us?

For those who are followers of Christ, we must remember that our God is supernatural. And from time to time our supernatural God may request or command supernatural things from us. We also need to understand Philippians 4:13, "that I can do all things through Christ who strengthens me." This means that God isn't asking us to do the impossible with our limited human powers. But God empowers us to do what He asks us to do. We need to realize that God has made us more powerful than we realize. This is the reason God confused the languages of people who previously spoke the same language at the Tower of Babel in Genesis 11:6. He said if He didn't, there was nothing they could not do as one people. These people were acting as God's enemies. Our problem may be that we don't utilize the power we have in Christ.

Also we need to understand that God gives us His grace when we need it, especially in crisis situations. But God commands us not to let the sun go down on our anger for at least two reasons. First, our anger, though not a sin, can take our focus off God and place it on revenge, which belongs to God (Romans 12), and second, our anger can lead us to commit a sin. God knows that revenge is a destructive emotional force that takes a toll on us. Therefore, we have to let God take care of injustices in relationships. The only way I, and probably you too, can do this is by the power of the indwelling Holy Spirit and by trusting God to bring justice in His own way and His own time. We must realize that revenge is God's business and not ours; so we may never see Him enforce it on those who mistreat us. But again, this isn't our concern.

God also knows that Satan gains a foothold on us when we aren't focusing on Him. Satan's goal is to destroy us, those that love us, and those who are watching our lives to determine if they want to become followers of Christ.

I believe that God knows that we tend to be controlled by our anger, which often results in our being out of control. When we do not have self-control, we aren't happy about our situation, sometimes with God Himself, and sometimes with ourselves. So His command is really to bring us to peace with ourselves, to get our lives back to normal as soon as possible. It may be a huge spiritual cop-out to try to justify our anger by believing it is too hard or unreasonable to control our angry emotions. Think about it. Would you like to end your emotional pain more quickly? Then Ephesians 4:26-27 could just be what you are looking for! Ask God to help you do what He is asking.

When we begin projecting this negative attitude to others (consciously or subconsciously), we begin attracting more of the same type of wrong people. Next, it becomes a blame game when we don't stop and ask the Lord to search our hearts. That's why forgiveness is undeniably necessary.

But how do we forgive? Maybe you have heard or even said, "I'll forgive when I feel better. It is going to take me some time." From a biblical definition of forgiveness, this statement isn't an option. As we mentioned previously, there is a difference between biblical forgiveness and emotional healing. We'll discuss emotional healing later.

First, let's get an understanding of biblical forgiveness. Several Bible dictionaries define biblical forgiveness as "removing guilt resulting from wrongdoing; pardon because of gracious attitude toward an individual." Psalm 103:12 says, *as far as the east is from the west, so far has he removed our transgressions (wrongdoings) from us* (NIV). Isaiah 43:25 says, *I (God), even I, am he who blots out your transgressions, for my own sake, and remembers your sins no more* (NIV). This Isaiah verse clearly states that God blots out our sins and transgressions. To sin is to actually be as good as you can, but still fall short of God's standard. To transgress is to know what is right and intentionally do wrong. It is similar to your parents telling you not to do something as a child, but you disobey anyway.

So if God forgives us, then we should forgive ourselves. I know that some of you struggle with forgiving yourself for your role in the break-up.

Recently, I've discovered that according to Luke 17:4, for a follower of Christ, forgiveness isn't an option and doesn't seem to be based on emotion. Luke 17:4 reads, *"If he sins against you seven times in a day, and seven times comes back to you and says, 'I repent,' forgive him."* I don't know about you, but I can get extremely frustrated if I'm mistreated once during a day. I can't imagine the same person offending me seven times in the same day and asking me for forgiveness and my granting it! But if I'm going to obey God, then I must set aside my emotions and forgive. Biblical forgiveness doesn't eliminate accountability, responsibility, or making restitution if necessary. And it doesn't require swallowing your anger. Yet, it is imperative that you process your anger as part of your emotional healing.

Biblical forgiveness does require treating the person cordially and graciously and it's the Holy Spirit that empowers us to do what we would normally not do on our own. It isn't promoting anyone's dysfunctionality, lack of accountability, weakness, or responsibility either. For example, if someone owes you money, you forgive him and treat him as if he doesn't owe you any money. But you don't continue giving that person money. So forgiveness is not an emotion, but more of an action, resulting from an act of the will. It is similar to God telling us in Matthew 5:44, *"But I tell you: Love your enemies and pray for those who persecute you."* Think of it as going to work on Monday, when you would rather stay home. But when Friday comes, you are so glad you went to work because you got a full paycheck. In that situation, you overrode your emotions and acted by your will.

Forgiving is critical for us because according to Matthew 6:14, if we don't forgive, God won't forgive us. And it isn't that God doesn't want to forgive us when we ask, but it is we who won't accept God's forgiveness. Say *what*? When we don't forgive, our heart becomes like a closed fist, not letting anything in or out. So when we haven't forgiven someone, but ask God to forgive us, when God tries to forgive us, we can't accept it because of our closed fist. Thus, we are rejecting God's forgiveness. Only when we forgive and open our fist, can we receive God's forgiveness.

Changing Bad Patterns: Breaking the Vow

Have you ever been so hurt after a break up that you either consciously or subconsciously swore, *I'll never let anyone hurt me like that* again! Or I *am never going to hurt like this ever!* You may have said it to protect yourself from getting hurt, but it becomes the DNA for all of your future relationships. Constantly, singles ask me, "Why can't I meet somebody nice?" The answer may be that many singles have created an invisible fortress as a result of their vow of self-protection.

In order to change your pattern, you must honestly answer some questions. Do you tend to attract the same kind of person that you really don't want to attract? Why do you think this is? Is it someone with a temper or someone who is emotionally detached? They may look and smell different from your previous relationship, but they may make you feel the same way. . . rejected, afraid, needy, angry, unloved, or used.

To change your pattern, you need self-awareness. If you have what you consider bad dating or relationship patterns, you need to ask yourself what they are and, more critically, why you have them. Then, ask yourself what is the end result of such an approach? These bad patterns sabotage healthy, long-lasting relationships.

Honesty with yourself is your first step toward eliminating detrimental relationship patterns and moving toward a healthy *you*, then possibly a healthy *relationship*. If your previously bad relationship patterns have changed, are you now ready for a healthy relationship? Have you identified the source of your former bad patterns and are you honest with yourself? If you feel you are unworthy and undeserving of a healthy and mutually beneficial relationship, then you may not be emotionally ready.

Answer the following questions:

- How do you know you have changed?

- What is going to keep you from reverting back to your old habits?

- Can you control yourself?

- Have you or are you usually sexually active in your relationships? Do you want to stop? Why or why not? Will you commit to stopping this pattern in your relationship?

- Who are you accountable to help you honestly evaluate your change?

If you remember making a vow about never getting hurt again, or other decisions that may be hindering your future relationships, you have the power to break it in the name of Jesus. A simple prayer that breaks the vow you made is:

In the name of Jesus, I repent for any vows I've made either consciously or unconsciously (name vows: i.e. I will never let anyone get close enough to me to hurt me again). *I break and renounce all agreements I've made with that vow and its effects in my relationships. I bind my mind, spirit, soul and emotions to God's abundant blessings and to His perfect will.*

Going to the Root of Your Pain

If you are experiencing pain right now, first of all, I'm sorry you're going through this. Hopefully, the following suggestions will help you.

When you break up with someone or someone breaks up with you, it's natural to go through pain. In fact, I recommend that you emotionally, physically, and spiritually process or take time to grieve. Part of mending a broken heart requires you to emotionally throw up, to get all the poison out of your system, like food poisoning.

I write to help me process or work through the pain of my emotions. Writing helps emotionally grey areas to become more black and white, bringing more clarity. Writing exactly how I feel is extremely therapeutic. Once I can realize what my emotions are and how I feel about them, then I can begin my first step toward healing. Some find it helpful to write a letter to their ex (without mailing it) expressing their emotions. Others may punch a boxing bag, jog as fast as they can, or talk it out with someone with whom they feel safe. Try several things to see what works best for you, but the emotions have to come out.

When I feel that people, whether followers of Christ or not, have needlessly hurt me, God has given me a phrase that has been priceless for me and often immediately alleviates my frustration: *There is no logic for sin.* Basically, it doesn't make sense, so you can't figure it out. And it is a waste of time trying to do so.

Sometimes the emotions are magnified because we have deeper root issues like damaged childhood memories, trauma, old hurtful relationships, or other painful experiences that are entangled together. And we can turn the break up into something bigger than what it actually is. In cases like this, you may want to seek biblical counseling (in which the Bible is used) or secular professional counseling. It is your call.

Suppose you don't need counseling, but your ex seriously wounded you. What do you do if you trusted someone, giving them your all, including your body, expecting the same in return only to discover that this special person lied, did things to hurt you, and maybe even cheated on you? As painful as this may be, consider yourself blessed that this person was exposed before doing more damage to you. Be grateful that you are no longer in such a relationship.

Unfortunately, many people—primarily women but some men, too—stay in such relationships longer than they should, hoping they can change the other person. Women's tendencies to remain in such relationships are usually attributed to their nesting instinct, which is essential in a healthy relationship, but destructive in an unhealthy one.

In reality, we can't change other people because if we could, we would have certainly already changed them, eliminating our problem with them. We would control their brains, causing those we think are a perfect match for us to like, love, and marry us. This is fantasy. God can change us and He can change other people, but we can only change ourselves.

Emotions are healthy, legitimate, natural, and appropriate. We shouldn't deny our emotions and feelings. Yet, it isn't healthy to allow our emotions to control us or our subsequent actions.

Frequently I tell married couples who have wounded each other through conflict to allow each other to work out their own emotional healing. Yet, I urge them to try to work through their conflict within a maximum of two days. Of course, a major breach of the relationship requires more than this limited time. But, for most cases, my reasoning for the time limit is to keep our emotions in check and not just let them run amok. Sometimes when we've been hurt, we actually enjoy rehearsing the hurt. At some point, once we've asked all the whys—answering some of them but realizing some will never be answered—we need to move on. We don't want to miss out on God's destiny for us by living unproductively in our past.

Some of you may think this is impossible, but I've spoken to tens of thousands of people about relationships over the years. And I've seen men and women process their emotions in a few hours, and some in two and a half days of an intensive biblical conference on communication and relationships, even with such issues as adultery.

Emotionally processing involves first expressing, venting, or emotionally throwing up all your anger, frustrations and hurts from the break up. Then, for followers of Christ, processing includes inviting Him into your broken heart to minister His healing balm, asking Him to help you see your situation from His perspective. For this, you may need the help of someone who can speak God's truth and perspective into your situation. And for some, help is needed with prayer and appropriation of God's power to do what is humanly impossible by actually practicing biblical principles that require actions overriding emotions. I often see all of these aspects as a relationship counselor for couples who are divorcing or trying to overcome betrayal or a violated trust.

Unlike biblical forgiveness, emotional healing is more of an individual issue. There seems to be no timetable or one technique for emotional healing, so it's important to pray about how the Lord would like to minister to you. It's a process that takes time and occasionally comes in waves or layers. Just when you thought you were over your previous relationship, the person pops up in your life, challenging some of your emotional issues.

For others, healing comes almost as instantaneously as it did when Jesus healed people on earth. Certainly I'm not saying either way is wrong. I'm just challenging the old premise that healing can only come one way. We have to be careful not to put people and God in *our* box because we are comfortable in our own box. Sometimes our comfort zones don't allow room for our faith in God to work.

As I mentioned earlier, having a support group, family, and close friends who love you enough to tell you the truth, even though you may not like it, is part of your healing journey. Trusted friends, pastoral counselors, or married couples can give you an objective, yet loving, perspective on your relationship. Consider that you may have experienced a painful loss, but explore with others the gifts or lessons that came with the relationship, new opportunities to grow, and how this will help you in the future. Having someone who loves you and holds you accountable may save you from unnecessary heartbreak.

Breaking up leaves an empty space for a while. Instead of filling it up with food or other unhealthy ways, take advantage of this time to ask the Lord to fill the void with His love. Dedicate the time you would have spent with your ex to the Lord and He'll fill your loneliness.

On the practical side, this is also your opportunity to learn new hobbies, explore new interests, and discover a new side of you!

Loving My Enemies—*Really?*

How can we love our enemies? In Mark 14:32-36, Jesus, before His crucifixion, asks His Father to change His mind and provide salvation by other means. It is implied that God the Father says, *"no"* to God the Son. Jesus responds, *"Yet, not what I will [desire], but what You will."* So Jesus' death on the cross for us had nothing to do with emotions and everything to do with action. Hence, biblical love is about action, which is why God can command us to love our enemies. His love is about how we treat people. So if your significant other has broken up with you or vice versa, that person shouldn't be your enemy, if at all possible. It doesn't require you to be best friends or friends at all, but when and if your paths cross, you can be cordial. Your ex does not need to dominate your thought life. Plotting revenge is so time consuming and self-destructive. And, as we've already mentioned, revenge is God's business.

And how can we do this? As followers of Christ, we have the Holy Spirit dwelling in us to empower us. Philippians 4:13 states, *"I can do all things through Him who strengthens me."* God Himself empowers us to do all He asks us to do. But He leaves the choice of obedience with us. Your ex should be better prepared for another relationship or marriage because of having dated you.

If You Are a Widow or Widower

If you are a widow or widower, your loss may have occurred suddenly or gradually from a long-term illness. In either situation, you may be wrestling with abandonment. Or you may be questioning or feeling upset at God for allowing this to happen to you. If this is how you feel, I hope the previous chapter was helpful.

Your healing may come in knowing that your spouse probably wouldn't want you to live the rest of your life alone. Of course, you may have no desire to date or remarry. My mother told me, "After your father died, I just couldn't imagine finding a man better than him." But if this isn't how you feel and you do have desires to date and remarry, don't feel guilty. Share your feelings with a trusted close friend. If you are a Christ-follower, pray about it and read chapters 8-10. Be careful not to lower your standards if you re-enter the dating world.

If You Are Divorced

If you are divorced, whether or not you had biblical grounds, or your spouse just walked out on you, or you were in sin, there is a natural tendency to feel like a failure because you aren't living happily ever after in your previous marriage. I've got good news for you. *God still loves you*, it isn't the end of the world, and there are some successful remarriages. But first, make sure you are healing emotionally and spiritually.

Here are a few suggestions. Forgive your ex, which doesn't require being in a relationship with him. Don't say negative things about him. If you have children, don't say negative things about their biological parent. They can and will see the truth! Don't let your divorce make you bitter. If you have children, please be extremely careful about bringing your dates home. Children get attached easily.

Evaluating Your Readiness for a New Relationship

How do you know you're ready to move on? I can't make any promises, but honestly answering the following statements to your support group will help.

A good sign you are ready for a healthy relationship is just wanting someone of the opposite sex to talk to and have a "safe place" to be able to talk about anything. But there's no desperation.

A few more good signs you are possibly ready for a healthy relationship:

- Having no ill will toward your ex

- Not necessarily looking for a new love

- Being content with yourself and your circumstances so that you're not looking for someone to meet your need.

Such a mindset gives you a perspective that you are complete, not needy, and thus not looking for a relationship from a sense of urgency. It also helps you avoid codependent relationships.

Though there aren't any guarantees, hopefully the suggestions above will prove helpful. The desired goal is to be set free, maybe like never before! Maybe it is learning more about yourself, as well as developing your relationship with Christ. And, as you see yourself as God sees you, you will learn to appreciate who you are, whether you are in a relationship or not. When you feel free, you send out signals, making you very attractive!

If you are a follower of Christ, pray to experience the fruit of the Spirit, which is love, joy, peace, patience, kindness, goodness, faithfulness, gentleness, and self-control (Galatians 5:22-23). Remember, biblical love is an action. So acting rightly— for example, forgiving someone who has hurt you—helps you become free and begin to feel more powerful, no longer trapped by the pain of your past or that particular person. Or you could pray to ask God to bless that person—I know it sounds weird, but doing so can take away your bitterness. What I'm suggesting is supernatural and God actually empowers you to do it. And as we act appropriately, according to God's will, our emotions will fall in line. The idea is not being perfect, nor is it totally eliminating our baggage, which I'm not sure that is even possible. But our desired goal is, when our baggage surfaces, we deal with it in a healthy manner, not letting it control us, or if we're in a relationship, cause division.

Next Steps

Believe it or not, we've actually finished this chapter. It was a long one, wasn't it! Recently, I memorized the book of Colossians. A verse difficult to forget and simultaneously challenging me is in chapter 3, verse 4. It says, *When Christ who is my life . . . . "* If my life is focused on Christ, then I trust Him for the very best. My trust in Him empowers me to wait, not demand, as well as to look for the best in all situations.

Let me urge you to work through the Action Points found in the following pages. Being honest with yourself as you work through the questions will help restore your emotional and spiritual health. A bonus of being healthy is that it will prepare you for future relationships or that special relationship. But let your desire to get emotionally healthy be *only* to get emotionally healthy and not to get a guarantee for a future relationship. If you are emotionally healthy, you will be more attractive to others, but more importantly—to you.

> *"He* (God the Father) *has sent Me* (Jesus Christ, God the Son) *to bind up the brokenhearted, to proclaim freedom for the captives and release from darkness for the prisoners. "* Isaiah 61:1 (part D)

SUMMARY POINTS

1. Your previous relationship experiences don't have to determine your future relationship experiences.

2. You can know if you have healed from a previous relationship and are ready for a new one.

3. There are warning signs that you have not experienced closure from a previous relationship.

4. You need to evaluate if you have bad relationship patterns and, if you do, you need to break them.

5. Having a person to whom you are accountable or support group is essential in evaluating your emotional and spiritual health, and in breaking or changing any bad relationship patterns.

6. If you are going to move forward from a previous relationship, you have to forgive and let go.

7. Our motivation for moving forward usually comes from being tired of living a life of defeat from our past.

8. Overcoming betrayal, the break up, and the break up after sex was involved, will take some time. It is essential that you ask and honestly answer how you got there and what can you to do prevent it from happening again. Having a loving support group can be invaluable for your recovery.

9. Learning and practicing biblical love are key steps in closure and gaining your emotional and spiritual health.

10. If you are divorced, it isn't the end of your world. You still can experience God's destiny in your life.

ACTION POINTS

1. In general, what has been your experience in your previous relationships? Why do you think this is so?

2. Have you experienced closure from your previous relationship? How do you know if you have or haven't? If you haven't, what needs to happen in order for you to experience closure?

3. What are the warning signs for you that you haven't experienced closure?

4. If you have bad patterns in your relationships, what are they and how will you break them?

5. If you don't have an accountability partner or support group, get one before getting into a new relationship.

6. How are you with forgiveness and letting go? Why? How can forgiving benefit you?

7. If you're having trouble letting go, what is it that you need in order to let go?

8. How does God's view of love differ from yours, or does it?

9. Has this chapter helped you? If so how?

Chapter Five

"I Been Lonely Too Long!"

*"Just as I have been with Moses, so I will be with you; I will not fail
you or forsake you."* Joshua 1:5

*"Be strong and courageous! Do not tremble or be dismayed, for the
Lord your God will be with you wherever you go."* Joshua 1:9b,
New American Standard Bible

Who are you? What is your purpose or destiny? If you know what your
purpose or destiny is, how are you doing in regards to fulfilling it? What are
your spiritual gifts and how are you using them? In biblical days, the way of
discovering your spiritual gifts was when another believer told you what
your gifts were because you ministered to that person with those gifts.
Christ followers didn't take surveys back in the day when the Bible was
being written to determine what their spiritual gifts were.

Why am I asking you so many questions about you? First of all, you are
important and have inordinate value. And what you do does matter. I could
be wrong, but I believe many people, even Christ followers, often react to
life instead of attacking life or being proactive. But it may prove foolish and
unproductive to attack life if you don't know who you are. Your spiritual
identity is critical, as it stipulates your direction regarding where and how
you are going in life, your life goals, and fulfilling your destiny. Why am I
being so nosy? What you do impacts your time and, for some of you, your
battle with loneliness. I believe time alone can be an incredible opportunity
or a tremendous deterrent depending on how you as an individual view your
time alone. Some people are victorious with their time alone while others
are defeated by it.

Now that I specifically know what God has called me to do, I regret all
the time I wasted. Some of it was wasted trying to impress people I really
didn't know and who couldn't care less about what I did. Some of it was
wasted attempting to be something I wasn't, in order to earn cool points
with people. I wasted so much time procrastinating about doing my
homework and other school-related obligations. Honestly, I think much of
my wasting time was simply part of my maturing process, and much of it
was wasted fighting the battle of loneliness.

Next Time You're Lonely, Don't Have a Pity Party

When you are alone, but you don't want to be alone, don't have a pity party. Pity parties just make things worse. Our natural tendency is to feel sorry for ourselves and then begin thinking of all the people who let us down, often including God. Once Satan sees an opening because of our negative spirit, he will say something like, *"Jesus doesn't care about you. Look how He has abandoned you . . . ."* Don't let loneliness cause you to deceive yourself by forgetting the fact that Jesus Christ does love you and has died and been resurrected to prove it.

When you are alone with no possibility of being with others, read Psalm 139:13-16

"For You formed my inward parts; You wove me in my mother's womb.

I will give thanks to You, for I am fearfully and wonderfully made;

Wonderful are Your works, And my soul knows it very well.

My frame was not hidden from You, When I was made in secret. And skillfully wrought in the depths of the earth;

Your eyes have seen my unformed substance;

And in Your book were all written the days that were ordained for me, When as yet there was not one of them" (NASB).

And remember, when you feel like having that pity party, look for someone you can help like Joseph of the Bible did.

Developing a Spiritual Mental Toughness

There is a spiritual battle between God and Satan for your mind. God has won this war with Jesus Christ's resurrection. But often, we experience unnecessary defeats.

Spiritual Mental Exercise

Memorizing scripture is an excellent method of developing spiritual mental toughness. Philippians 4:13, *"I can do all things through Him* (Christ) *who strengthens me."* We must also appropriate the power God has given us. Second Corinthians 10:5b states, *". . . and we are taking every thought captive to the obedience of Christ."* We do this by asking God to help us not to dwell on this thought or picture that has popped into our head. I believe Satan has access to our brain and can interject thoughts and pictures, but he can't control what we do with those thoughts or pictures. First John 5:14-15 reads,

> *"This is the confidence which we have before Him, that, if we ask anything according to His will, He hears us.*
>
> *And we know that if He hears us in whatever we ask, we know that we have the requests which we have asked from Him"* (NASB).

So God promises to answer "Yes" to our prayer requests which are according to His will.

Another step involved in this spiritual mental exercise requires refocusing on what is beneficial. Reflect on the many other times when He has blessed you. Focus on what He has done in your life and be grateful because Proverbs 23:7a states, *"For as a man thinks within himself, so he is."* Philippians 4:8 says,

> *"Finally, brethren, whatever is true, whatever is honorable, whatever is right, whatever is pure, whatever is lovely, whatever is of good repute, if there is any excellence and if anything is worthy of praise, dwell on these things."* (NASB)

Be prepared for those lonely episodes that come with Christmas, New Year's Eve, Valentine's Day, or wedding invitations. Set up reminders of the good things in your life. Use photographs, songs, or gifts that take you back to those times are good memories of God's goodness. For those particular commercial events that are often triggers for your loneliness, ignore them. Consider creating your own interpretation. Celebrate in a way that will feed your spirit *and* your emotions. For example, Valentine's Day is showcased as a romantic day. What if you, instead, consider it as a day to celebrate all friendships? Singer Taylor Swift, whom you think would be on dates nightly, said on a popular TV show that she and her single girlfriends got together for Valentines. "(We) just ate whatever we wanted and danced. We made these little profile cards about why we're single," said Swift, who has previously dated Joe Jonas and other celebs.

Don't be jealous of others and believe the lie Satan told Eve, which is basically that God was holding out on her. God isn't withholding His best from you. *"Do not let your heart envy a sinner, but always be zealous for the fear of the Lord"* (Proverbs 23:17).

Myrna says that during three years of an isolating chronic illness, loneliness was a constant companion in the beginning. She found that going on Facebook and seeing all the happy faces and activities made her feel miserable. "Why are they all having fun while I lay here feeling so sick," she thought to herself. Later, she discovered that many of these seemingly perfect lives where plagued with house foreclosures, unemployment, and relationship problems. Others, too, are trying to create a false image and be what they aren't, so don't focus on what others seem to have. It can be deceiving. Jesus was probably tested with loneliness, too. Hebrews 4:15 says,

> *"For we do not have a high priest who is unable to sympathize with our weaknesses, but we have one who has been tempted in every way, just as we are —yet without sin"* (NASB).

A Few Suggestions for Maximizing Your Alone Time

Joseph, Not Imprisoned by His Injustice

When Joseph was unjustly put in prison, he had at least two options. First, he could have had a pity party and blamed God for his circumstances. Joseph was innocent of the crime for which he was imprisoned. But God was doing a greater work of ridding Joseph of his pride while simultaneously preparing him for leadership.

Joseph's second option was what he chose to do while in prison. Instead of hosting his own pity party, Joseph used his gifts to help the chief cupbearer and chief baker, who were also in prison, with their issues. It was a time to grow his gifts even in a hidden place. Often other people are in worse situations than we are. By helping others, Joseph also helped himself: 1) he momentarily wasn't worrying about his own situation; 2) time tends to pass by more quickly when we are occupied with other things to do; 3) he wasn't lonely for a while because he was invested in others; and 4) typically, when we invest in others, others will sooner or later invest in us, just as the chief cupbearer later remembered Joseph and recommended him to the Pharaoh.

One Victory Over Loneliness

While on a business trip in Chicago, one of my daughters—who was a freshman in college away from home—called me because her friends disappointed her by not showing up. I shared some Bible verses with her as to who she is in Christ. To my pleasant surprise, she took the verses to heart—resulting in her leading a girl to a personal relationship with Jesus Christ!

Maybe some of you, like my daughter, may have acquaintances and not friends. Acquaintances will be with you only when it is convenient for them. Friends are with you no matter the circumstances.

That has been the case with Myrna during these past few years. She has discovered not only who her acquaintances are—the ones who disappeared when she became ill—but who her brothers and sisters are. They are those who accept her vulnerability and visit her without any expectations.

Paul—Not Just Doing Time for His Crime

Another person who was also unjustly imprisoned was Paul who did two things. While in prison, he, like Joseph, could have blamed God; but instead, he shared how he came to personally know Jesus Christ with the Praetorian Guard (Roman Imperial).

> *"So that my imprisonment in the cause of Christ has become well known throughout the whole praetorian guard and to everyone else, and that most of the brethren (*Christ followers*), trusting in the Lord because of my imprisonment, have far more courage to speak the word of God without fear"* (Philippians 1:13-14, NASB).

Paul also wrote a letter to local bodies of Christ followers. These particular letters are often referred to as the *Prison Epistles*. Paul and Joseph were both unjustly put in prison, but they understood that *their freedom wasn't based on where they were; but in whose and who they were!*

Interestingly enough, while Myrna is contributing to this book, she, too, is "imprisoned" by her body's weakness. Yet, God not only called her to help me in this book, but has given her the grace and strength that have increased her dependence on Him. Remember, all things work together for the good of those who love Him. Pray for the Lord to open your eyes to the opportunities He is giving you, even in the state you consider an intolerable loneliness.

Give Away Your Time

Next time you have some alone time, prayerfully consider visiting senior citizens from your church or at a retirement home. Many senior citizens' bodies have slowed down, but their minds are just fine and full of wisdom. When I spend time with men and women in their eighties and nineties, I get so much more than I give. It is an excellent trade-off. They receive the attention many of them crave, especially at their age. In turn, you can receive tremendous wisdom, which you may not have even known existed. These senior citizens may become mentors for you.

You can also visit the sick, including children in hospitals who will remind you of courage and your blessings. "I remember even praying for Jehovah's Witnesses to knock on my door because I just couldn't stand the isolation from being sick," says Myrna. "They came and I got the opportunity to share the Good News with them." Others who came were blessed by all the revelations the Lord was giving Myrna during her season of being alone—with Him.

The holidays, especially between Thanksgiving and Christmas, can be extremely difficult for singles, so be prepared with some strategies. Giving your time is one of the best medicines for the holiday blues because it takes the focus off of you and allows you to experience the true meaning of the season. God will show up wherever people are in need—homeless shelters, soup kitchens, college campuses with international students who can't go home, prisons, pregnancy care centers, crack babies who are wards of the state—the needs are endless.

You don't have to go far to give your time and create a special community. Myrna prayed about what to do regarding her isolation. She sensed the Lord say she should offer to care for her neighbor's newborn baby. It didn't make sense to Myrna, because of her chronic fatigue, but she responded in obedience. Myrna now takes care of the baby periodically, but only when the baby is about to go to sleep. Now, Myrna feels connected to her neighbors. They share their faith with one another and, most importantly, the baby brings much healing joy for Myrna! If Myrna, in spite of her illness can reach out to serve to create "community," then you can too!

Call: Reconnect

I was a single in my thirties living in Tulsa when I sent a *thank-you note* that resulted in my having dinner with the late Matthew and late Viola Daniels every day until I got married. At the time, I was a minister on staff at the same church Mrs. Daniels attended. She invited the pastor and me for dinner. I wrote a thank-you note because Mom taught me to do so. Mrs. Daniels called me to thank me for the note and invited me to eat every day with her family. Single and struggling financially, I readily accepted. The fact that her husband was an outstanding cook didn't hurt either!

Also while in Tulsa, another lady, Elreno O'Neal, heard me teaching the Bible at a different church and she also invited me to her home for dinner. Elreno and her late husband, Willard, had me come to their home every day for dinner.

I made so little money that I couldn't afford groceries. So every day, I ate twice a day at 4:00 p.m. and then at 6:00 p.m. I fixed my plate at the Daniels home and Elreno always put the food on my plate. It literally took me an hour to eat the plate she prepared. She thought I was too skinny. Since I wasn't dating, I spent every Friday evening with the O'Neals watching television until 10 p.m. Butch and Rushella Latimer also gave me refrigerator privileges. These two older couples and the Latimers became my friends and befriended my mother when she visited me.

You can also call family members you haven't seen or spoken with in a long time. Reconnect with your family. There is nothing like family. Who knows, you may discover family members who may actually live close to you. And with older family members, you can learn your history.

Prior to her work injury, Myrna was very busy travelling the world, so she didn't have much time to spend time with her family. Now, she and her mom are spending more time talking with one another and Myrna is learning about her family history, her mom's scrumptious recipes, and feeling much more connected. Myrna now knows she belongs to a family community.

Ask God

Pray—Ask the Holy Spirit to bring people to your mind for whom you can pray. This can be wild because the Holy Spirit is in complete control. He may bring all kinds of people to your mind. It can also be an amazing time of fellowship with God.

> *"Jesus answered and said to him, "If anyone loves Me, he will keep My word; and My Father will love him, and We will come to him and make Our abode with him"* (John 14:23).

> *"Call to Me and I will answer you, and I will tell you great and mighty things, which you do not know"* (Jeremiah 33:3).

> *"For I know the plans I have for you," declares the Lord, "plans for welfare and not for calamity to give you a future and a hope."* (Jeremiah 29:11)

One night, Myrna had a major breakthrough with the Lord after crying out for help with her isolation. That night, a woman called to pray for her and offered her a kitten. At first, Myrna was reluctant, not only because of the unexpected responsibilities, but because her apartment complex didn't allow pets. Well, they changed their rules for her since the Lord sent her a furry companion. Now, Myrna wakes up each morning, smiling at her playful unsuspecting answer to prayer. "Every time I look at my kitty, I am reminded of God's faithfulness," she says.

Myrna's answers to her prayer regarding her isolation didn't stop there. Since then, she has met many new people, even at her door, some from as far away as Italy. So, even though Myrna couldn't go out much to find fellowship, God has sent her people because He heard her cries. He is faithful and with you!

Practical Application

Next time you begin feeling lonely. Consider going outside and seeing if there is someone on the street you can help with such chores as yard work. Look for someone who may possibly need your assistance. I would ask God to guide you to a divine appointment. So the next time you are experiencing time alone, consider possible options.

Who's Yo Daddy?

In our battle with loneliness, it is critical that we don't forget who we are and that our identity is in Christ. Philippians 2:12-14 says:

> *"So then, my beloved, just as you have always obeyed, not as in my presence only, but now much more in my absence, work out your salvation with fear and trembling; For it is God who is at work in you, both to will and work His good pleasure. Do all things without grumbling and disputing"* (NASB)

From reading this passage, it is clear that we won't enjoy every moment of life; but we are commanded to do *all* things without grumbling and complaining. I have a tendency to blame others or circumstances and whine when things aren't going the way I want them to.

I also have to realize that God gives me all of my needs and not all my wants. Yet, He says in Psalms 37:4 that if we, *"Delight* [ourselves] *yourself in the Lord and He will give* [us] *you the desires of your heart."*

If God is our Father, shouldn't we act more like him? He tells us in Philippians 4:6-7:

> *"Be anxious for nothing, but in everything by prayer and supplication with thanksgiving, let your requests be made known to God. And the peace of God, which surpasses all comprehension, will guard your hearts and your minds in Christ Jesus."* (NASB)

What we should learn from these verses is that nothing is too small or too big for God our Father. I believe everything means *everything*, including managing our time alone. Then God promises to give us peace and guard our hearts. First Kings 8:56 says,

> *"Praise be to the Lord, who has given rest to his people Israel just*

as he promised. Not one word has failed of all the good promises he gave through His servant Moses." (NIV)

"In the hope of eternal life, which God, who cannot lie, promised long ago." (Titus 1:2, NASB)

If you aren't experiencing God's peace, could it possibly be because you aren't trusting Him? It seems as though Jesus daily sought time to be with His Father. Mark 1:35reads:

"Very early in the morning, while it was still dark, Jesus got up, left the house and went off to a solitary place, where He prayed." (NIV)

Could it be that Jesus, who came as a full man and God, sought to spend time with His Father for fellowship, direction, encouragement, and purpose for each day? I wonder if His doing this daily affected His loneliness battle. Maybe there were fewer daily questions such as: *What am I going to do today? Who has free time to hang with me today?*

I believe that as Jesus met with His Father daily, their fellowship and God the Father's direction helped Jesus fulfill His purpose, decreasing His daily possible battle with loneliness.

Jesus Created His Own Community

Jesus was proactive on earth, literally calling men to become fishers of men and thus, His disciples. His ministry, which changed lives for the better, also created a following, which included women.

Jesus was also a risk taker and a radical, which creates excitement— giving time alone, a black eye. In His encounter with the Samaritan woman in John 4, Jesus breaks a traditional law by traveling into the country of Samaria. Then, He goes to where the woman lives—the Great Commission in action. Next, Jesus meets this rejected woman on her own turf (the well), knowing she would be more comfortable in familiar surroundings. Jesus works around her schedule. Then, He speaks to a Samaritan woman, who is always ceremonially unclean to a Jewish man. Jesus makes Himself vulnerable to her by asking her for water. His vulnerability empowers her, which is a sign of equality, as well as dignity. By asking for water, Jesus is *meeting her where she is*. Her concerns and needs became His. And maybe most important is the fact that Jesus has *staying power*. When the Samaritan woman initially rejects Him, He doesn't leave.

Think about creating your own community if you don't have one. Jesus' encounter with the Samaritan woman was an all-day *thang!* He didn't get bored that day!

While single and living in Tulsa, Rudy was my best friend.

We talked about everything, including theology and women.

Since Rudy was a former tennis player for the University of Southern California and a teaching pro in town, women were constantly throwing themselves at him. Rudy was a model for me in how he handled himself. Once, a beautiful female employee at the club invited him to her apartment. He declined her offer. I asked him why. He said, "She doesn't have the best reputation, and I didn't want to put myself in a situation I couldn't handle, because I know me." I couldn't help but wonder how many guys would have accepted her offer.

I wonder if Jesus and his good friend Lazarus had such conversations?

Spending Time With our Heavenly Father

In Mark 1:35, Jesus scheduled *alone* time with God, His Father. If Jesus spent time with God, our Father, I can't help but think how much more I need to spend time with Him. So I do.

The following is what works for me, but you can create your own:

- I *schedule* to meet with God first thing in the morning when I get up (if you're *not a* morning person—do it when you are awake but not distracted—give *God* your undivided attention. Be intentional and write it on your calendar *as apriority* so that everything else is built around that centerpiece.

- I have an inexpensive notebook in which I record the day's date, where I am if I'm on the road (because I travel a lot), and the purpose of my trip.

- Under the day's date, I write, *Praise List*. Under this list, I try to write 7-10 things God did in my life the day before. This helps me see Him in my life each day. Psalms 68:19 says, *"Praise be to the Lord, to God our Savior, who daily bears our burdens."* This also helps me to be less selfish in my prayer requests later. This activity encourages me because I daily see God actively moving in my life.

- Next, I read a passage of Scripture. I just begin in Genesis to read through the Bible. I read to where there are breaks or subtitles in each chapter. I may read anywhere from 1-10 verses.

- I try to find one truth I can put into practice that day, which becomes my practical application for that day.

- I close by praying and thanking God for the truth He revealed to me and for an opportunity to apply this truth today. Then I pray for my family, ministry, work, people I may encounter during the day, and for the project I want to complete this day. You get the idea.

All of this takes approximately 20 minutes. You can make it shorter or longer. Can you schedule Jesus Christ into your day for 20 minutes? Daily meeting with Him can change your life forever!

Do You Hate Being Alone? Why?

If you hate being alone, ask yourself why? How do you feel about yourself when you are alone? Why do you feel that way?

I think some people hate being alone because they fear being by themselves with themselves. I believe some people sell themselves short—thinking they aren't enough on their own. I don't think they see themselves the way God sees them. If this is you, reread chapter 3.

Such people often feel left out. Their so-called friends don't call them. If this is you, realize those people who don't want to hang out with you are missing out on you. But don't fear being alone, because this puts you in another type of emotional slavery. Next time you are alone for whatever reason, ask God what He is trying to teach you. Then ask God to meet you in your loneliness. See what happens.

Can't Guarantee You'll Never Be Lonely

I wish I could guarantee that you'll never be lonely, but I can't. However, how you respond to your time alone is truly your choice. Honestly, I love having time to myself. So does Brenda. Not long ago, I was out of town. Two of my daughters are away in graduate and law schools. And my other daughter was out of town on a retreat. During my usual nightly call to Brenda when I'm on a business trip, I asked her, "How are you enjoying your time alone?" She responds, "I'm loving it!" We love each other, our children, and our careers. But our relationship with each other, our children, and our careers keep us incredibly busy. Consequently, we love having alone time to catch up with ourselves.

Being alone doesn't have to mean being lonely. As a matter of fact, it can propel you into becoming friends with yourself and with God. When people and your comfort activities are removed, it's actually a time to discover your true self. Myrna has always worked in *cerebral* strategic and communications roles, but now that she spends a lot of time alone, she's discovered new things about herself. Without the ability to go out and get distracted with other things, Myrna has been forced to explore new things in an unfamiliar context within her health limitations. Through YouTube videos, Myrna has learned how to paint, draw, do arts and crafts, and has learned a lot about nutrition and herbs for healing.

Even her time with the Lord has changed. She's digging deeper into the Word and has developed a strong interest for the Hebrew roots of the Bible. Why? In her alone time, she has chosen to learn about and become friends with new parts of herself and God.

So, next time you are faced with alone time, do you have choices you can make? Sometimes, in order to get what we want; we may have to give it to someone else first. Below is a song that may help you the next time you battle loneliness. Christina, my oldest daughter, wrote it for me when I was battling loneliness and feeling like a failure. I hope it helps you as much as it helped me.

You Will Never Leave Me

Lyrics by Christina Shuler Copyrighted© 2010 by Christina Shuler

I'm traveling down a road and I don't know where it will take me.

I could be soaring over mountain tops, or stumbling through a valley. I could be just walking on the road, or making my way through a turn. No matter where I go, no matter what comes my way, I'll be alright.

Chorus

Because you're my Rock You hold me in your hands Everlasting is your love

You will never leave me King of Kings

Perfect are you plans

On your promise I will stand You will never leave me, Lord

I'm traveling down a road and people join the journey.

One friend walks now by my side while another chooses a different way. As we journey on, I'll be forever changed.

No matter where I go, no matter who I meet, I'll be alright.

Repeat Chorus Bridge

I look forward to the day when all will be redeemed and the pain will be no more

I look forward to the day when all will bow and confess that Jesus is Lord

I look forward to the day when I can see Jesus face to face and worship at his feet

I will sing. . . .

SUMMARY POINTS

1. All of us at some point in time must face our personal battle with loneliness. Some of us learn to be victorious and some of us are still losing our battle with loneliness.

2. You have a purpose, a destiny, and, if you are a Christ follower, you have at least one spiritual gift.

3. When you feel lonely, don't have a pity party.

4. You don't need to fear having time alone.

5. Mental and spiritual toughness are required to win your battle over loneliness.

6. When lonely, you have options.

ACTION POINTS

1. Do you battle loneliness? Why or why not?

2. What do you do when you are experiencing loneliness?

3. What do you think your purpose is? Why?

4. What do you think your destiny is? Why?

5. How do you feel about you when you are alone? Why?

6. Do you fear being alone? If yes, why?

7. What is (are) your spiritual gift(s)? What makes you think this? Will you talk to God about your loneliness the next time you are lonely? Why or why not?

8. Do you think God keeps His word? Why or why not?

9. Will you try some of the suggestions in this chapter next time you are lonely? Why or why not?

10. Remember the next time you are lonely that *you do have options*. What will you do?

SECTION II:

CONFUSED ABOUT RELATIONSHIPS?

Chapter Six

Relationships With The Opposite Sex That Work: Friendships

"A man (person) *of too **many** friends **comes** to ruin, but there is a friend who is closer than a brother"* Proverbs 18:24, NASB

Developing friendships with the opposite sex usually provides excellent preparation for dating and, ultimately for most, marriage. Research seems to support that the best marriages are the result of a relationship that begins as friends, later blossoming into a marriage. One of the reasons why such marriages are so good is because the individuals in these couples learn to effectively communicate with each other about *every little thing* without worrying about impressing the other. These friendships with the opposite sex seldom have the added pressure of romance and emotion, allowing for more openness without the risk of losing the relationship. Simultaneously, these relationships alleviate loneliness, while reaffirming each person's gender identity. What do I mean by reaffirming each person's gender identity? Cross-gender relationships almost always have sexual tension. Sexual tension does imply or suggest the desire to have sex, as it does force individuals to recognize their gender differences. This recognition means we take into consideration that our friend is of the opposite sex, reminding us of our differences and our own gender. And this recognition will impact our conduct to some degree.

Such friends usually don't have hidden agendas. They simply enjoy hanging out with each other. Laughter, encouragement, community, trust, and surviving social problems are major aspects of these friendships. These friendships create a safe place, allowing you to be able to discuss anything, even your blind spots, without worrying about losing a friend.

Another bonus is having someone to *school* you regarding the opposite sex. Such friendships are priceless because these friends love you enough to tell you what you don't want to hear, but need to hear. Proverbs 27:6 states, *"Faithful are the wounds of a friend. . . ."* And these friends are loyal as described in Proverbs 17:17, which says, *"A friend loves at all times, and a brother* (sister) *is born for adversity."* There is nothing like a friend who will stick with you through thick and thin.

Meeting Friends of the Opposite Sex

For some of you, just meeting the opposite sex can be traumatic. You want to be in a relationship, but you aren't even comfortable trying to initiate a conversation with the opposite sex. You may be in middle school, out of college, divorced, or immersed in your job. I completely understand. You may be shy or have been rejected a lot in the past. But, remember, in this case, you're not after a dating relationship, but rather a friendship, so that should take off some of the pressure.

So what can you do? First, don't live in the past. If you do, your past will usually defeat you. Focus on the present and who you are now. Be confident.

Now, guys and girls tend to be different in their approach to establishing friendships. Due to ego, in most cases, guys still typically look for the visual first— even for friendships—instead of just having common interests. Girls, on the other hand, put more priority on having a trustworthy friend or common interests or activities. For some gals, after a certain age, a guy who expresses interest in them could be considered a potential husband. A friend laughingly told me that she and her friends over fifty years old joke around when they meet a guy and ask, "Does he have a pulse? That'll do."

If you find a potential friendship candidate, you'll have to figure out a way to approach them. I know texting is easy, but I prefer a face-to-face encounter for evaluating if a face lights up or is uncomfortable when you ask about being friends. Public places like coffee shops are great.

How do you find or make such a friend if you don't have any? Big cities, in particular, can be lonely hubs for singles. Everyone seems to be rushing to the next meeting or class, juggling different projects or activities, so the first step is to *make time* for friends. If you're always busy, how can anyone fit into your schedule?

Invite God into your desire to make friends with the opposite sex. Ask Him to send you friends who will be encouraging, authentic, or whatever other traits you are looking for in a friend of the opposite sex. Pray that He opens doors for you to meet friends and to give you discernment about whom you should allow into your life as a friend.

A principle I've discovered to be quite effective is giving to others first what you want from them. If I want to make a friend, I make myself friendly first. In other words, I initiate being friendly. I believe most people like being treated nicely and typically reciprocate when treated so. You may need to make the first step. Try it and see what happens.

Years ago, the music group, *The Main Ingredient* sang a song entitled *I Just Don't Want to Be Lonely*. Most of us feel the same way. Friends are often the easiest and best ways to eliminate loneliness.

But as you think about developing a friendship, let's explore this dynamic counter-cultural practice of *giving* before *getting*. I'm not suggesting money or gifts, but seeking to meet the needs of your new friend first before your own. Giving first is a biblical principle found in the following verses in the Bible. Amazingly, God never asks us to do anything that He doesn't do for us first. First John 4:19 reads, *"We love because he first loved us."* Matthew 20:28 says, *"Just as the Son of Man* (Jesus Christ) *did not come to be served, but to serve, and give His life as a ransom for many."* Another verse is in the Gospel of Mark 9:35 where Jesus says to His disciples, *"If anyone wants to be first, he must be the very last, and the servant of all."*

For example, ask how her day went first before sharing how your day went. Your giving is more of a consideration than anything else. It communicates to your friend, "I care about you and you are important to me." It is easy to unintentionally be selfish, and selfishness is a tremendous cancer to any healthy relationship.

As you are making new friends with the opposite sex, here are some questions you should ask yourself and answer: "What do I want to learn or receive from this friendship? What are some goals for having friendships with the opposite sex?"

Here are some suggestions:

- Learning to speak Man 101 or Woman 101. Males and females usually use the same words, but are often speaking a different language.

- Learning what particular traits attract you to the opposite sex.

- Learning more about yourself. When interacting with others, you learn more about yourself. Knowing yourself well is critical in establishing healthy and long-lasting friendships or more intimate relationships.

- Learning to relax more when you are with the opposite sex. Familiarity breeds comfort. When you are comfortable, you are relaxed and not nervous. This confidence—and losing the sweaty palms—makes you more attractive.

- Learning to some degree, how the opposite sex thinks (this could be enlightening and scary!).

You can create additional goals for friendships with the opposite sex.

Where to Meet Friends

- Consider participating in co-ed group activities at school or church. Don't be afraid to join outside groups with common interests such as hiking, bowling, tennis, etc. Volunteer at a local shelter for the homeless or get involved in a political campaign.

- Having friends who aren't followers of Christ is fine. Just make sure such relationships don't cause you to compromise your biblical principles.

- If you see someone you would like to meet—*bite the bullet* and ask her to join you for coffee, or something non- threatening in a public place during the day.

- Remember the worst that can happen if you ask someone for coffee is they may say no. If that person says no, it isn't the end of the world. Walk away confidently. And don't be ugly, but you might even say in a nice calm and manner non-vindictive, "I think we could have been good friends." No now, could be yes later.

- They might say yes. It is difficult for your prospective new friend to say yes if she isn't asked. Don't be shocked if she says yes. Most people want a trustworthy friend. If she does say, yes, don't be overly excited. It could freak her out and she might change his mind, thinking you want to be more than friends.

- Define what you mean by friendship. Be sure to discuss it. Explain the difference between a friendship and a dating relationship from your perspective. Then ask her to explain her definitions for friendship and dating.

One of the first girls I became friends with my freshman year in college said yes when I asked her to walk with me to the local church about seven city blocks from the school. For me, I just wanted some girls with whom I could talk. There was no romantic interest on my part, and I didn't sense any from them either. As a guy, I found girls to be sensitive, fun, and excellent listeners. But they also provided insightful and different perspectives on life.

Friendship Boundary Issues
(Emotional, Physical, and Sexual)

How do you know when someone is interested in you as just a friend? For me, and I'm sure this isn't true with everyone, friendships with those of the opposite sex always had some degree of sexual tension, which I came to monitor. Maybe this is just a guy thing or just my thing.

Honestly, I'm not sure you can always tell. Time and actions are usually good indicators. In such cases, your same-sex friends and family members can be invaluable. You may have blind spots, especially if you are hoping for more than just a friendship.

But if your interests are purely for a friendship, sometimes it can be confusing when you get mixed signals. For some, mixed signals may be frequent or daily calls (for example, more than your same-sex friends), going out a lot together, touching your knee or arms around the shoulder. In churches, there can be "spiritual dating" under the guise of a prayer partner of the opposite sex.

When you are becoming friends, it is essential to define your relationship. For example, the term "spiritual dating" is intriguing to me. Dating, to most guys, is dating. Now, you can't cover everything, and you have to understand that people come from various backgrounds—thus there will be some differences. A key in handling mixed signals is *immediately* talking about what just occurred that to you was a sign that your friendship is going to a new level, which you as friends haven't discussed. My rule of thumb *is to talk about everything and assume nothing* because most people are poor mind readers. So instead of guessing, stressing, and asking all of your same-sex friends to *interpret* what happened when you were with your new friend of the opposite sex, simply ask her about what just happened. Tell her how it made you feel and why. You need to understand that she is the expert on her motive for what just happened. Then, as two friends, make the necessary adjustment. This process eliminates a lot of unnecessary drama and sleepless nights.

Some men feel that too much information can be just as bad! They feel some things are better left unsaid. Some have expressed concern for discretion regarding when to say it and how to say it. As a counselor, if I am going to err in the context of relationship it would be on talking too much instead of not enough.

Otherwise you might find yourself in a "spiritual dating" situation like Leslie, who was heartbroken after having a "pseudo relationship" with a guy friend. In her innocence and willingness to help her male friend, Leslie would pray with him regularly, listen and minister to him, talk a lot on the phone, as well as go to church events and dinner together. Sometimes, while sitting together at church, Leslie's friend would tap her knee or put his arms around her chair. Being an older single woman who hadn't had much male attention, this aroused romantic feelings in her. Her hopes for a dating relationship ended when he told her he was dating and ended up marrying someone else. In Leslie's case, she could have told the man that, for her, his tapping her knee and putting his arms around her gave her mixed signals. Her response should have initiated a conversation about the exact state of their relationship as soon as possible. Leslie could have explained that such touching, from her perspective, was causing her to question herself. *Was their relationship changing into something deeper?* He may have said, "I do this with female friends, but it doesn't mean anything to me." Then she could have responded, "I'm sorry, but it does to me. Touch means a lot to me. So if we're not going to a deeper level, I'll need for you not to do that with me please." Everything is on the table. And his nonverbal (body language) response, as well as verbal, will inform her as to how he is really handling her concern. His verbal and body language can also reveal where their friendship is now as a result of their conversation.

The same is true for guys. For a lot of guys frequent calls and hanging out aren't issues. But the touching can be a problem for some. Ladies, when you are touching our legs or laying on us, those can be mixed signals. And we guys need to discuss these actions too. Years ago when I was single and in grad school, one of my guy friends introduced me to this girl who was his *nonromantic* friend. She was like a sister to him. She soon became my friend, too. One day, in front of her mother and my guy friend, she approached me as I walked into her house. She kissed me on the lips (no tongue action), without a hug or embrace. It blew me away! But I assumed it was no big deal because she did it with an audience. There was never talk about dating. And so, until I moved away whenever she met me, she kissed me. She was comfortable with it, but I never was, even though I never acted on it. I rather enjoyed the kiss and knew our relationship would never go beyond being friends.

Some of you don't want to hurt the other person and don't know how to set boundaries in a healthy way. Or you may be afraid to set boundaries because you fear losing your friend. In such situations, eventually someone is going to get hurt. It is less painful if you are honest about your feelings up front or as soon as something which makes you uncomfortable occurs. If you aren't honest initially, your friend may feel you deceived her.

Applying boundaries in friendships with the opposite sex also includes requiring respect. For example, Liza realized her relationship with guy friends was based on feisty kidding around. In her most recent situation, it resulted into badgering, which she hates. And this badgering created unnecessary stress for her.

She asked me about this relationship. I asked her why she was attracted to this kind of person. Liza traced it back to her good relationship with her dad. It was a special emotional bonding time for them. He taught her to debate with him when she was a child about the news, history, and politics. This became her pattern with guy friends, which was all right until it resulted in rude badgering. So for her, the initial debating or kidding is an attractive feature which is okay; but she can't let it evolve into destructive behavior, and the guy needs to offer more than finding her physically and intellectually attractive.

Liza couldn't stop the badgering because she tends to put other people's feelings above hers. In business, she is tough, firm, fair, and a leader; but in her relationships, or at least this one, that wasn't the case. Then she asked me, "Though I'm a strong independent woman, why do I have trouble transferring that to relationships?"

It was an excellent question. I've seen this problem before in successful businesswomen. Not sure I have an answer. But these successful businesswomen are able, like men, to compartmentalize themselves. Media tells women to be strong, feisty, independent, and better than men. So in the marketplace, women learn to successfully compete with men. However, church tells women to submit to men, usually without doing a good job of explaining biblical submission, resulting in confused instead of empowered women.

The confusion results because many women expect men to be strong, masculine leaders, in relationships but when men acquiesce to the strong woman who often has difficulty shifting to the nurturing role, women can become resentful.

What came first—the acquiescing male who triggered women leaders in the relationship or the dominating woman who castrated guys into complacent roles in relationships? These women are tough at work (don't let them see you cry) playing by the guys' rules, but in personal relationships, they are soft and wanting to give—not bad attributes. But when these women are giving in against what they really want, then I believe it is about insecurity and inadequacy. It could be that, after working in the office all day, they want to feel and be treated more like a woman. I believe these women can achieve this, but they can't violate their conscious. And this is true for men as well, because we are often captivated by a woman's physical beauty.

It is interesting that many successful businesswomen view nurturing—a core value for women—as a weakness. This may be a learned behavior, a result of today's culture. Whether male or female, we must not allow our meekness to be misinterpreted as weakness.

Constantly giving in to what we really don't believe in or want isn't healthy for our significant other, our relationship, or us as individuals. It is unintentionally dishonest. Eventually, it comes back to bite you on the butt. This is where having a loving support group is advantageous.

What About Friends With Benefits (Sex)?

A friend with benefits sounds so good in theory, but theory doesn't take into consideration our emotions. Friends with benefits tend to do just the opposite of what they are intended to do. We have a friendship, and our sexual intimacy is just a physical act for a guy's release and, for the girl, it provides closeness, with no strings attached. But in reality, such relationships don't have to include sex. We'll talk about friends with benefits, which include sex, in our chapter discussing sex.

In my ignorance, I once made an agreement with a girl to just be friends, but it included kissing. I had just come out of a serious relationship and had no interest in a new commitment so soon afterwards. But I did want to enjoy some fringe benefits. I asked this very nice young lady if she was "down" with this arrangement. She said she was fine. I took her at her word. So we spent a lot of time together until one evening, after heavy kissing, she expressed her feelings had gone beyond just being friends. Oops! Mine had not. I'll never forget her words, "Didn't you feel something while we were kissing?" Her parents had been giving me the "future son-in-law" comments and looks, which I had ignored because their daughter and I had an agreement.

I learned a vital and painful lesson that evening. My selfishness and insensitivity had just devastated a very nice girl. I learned that, for this girl, kissing meant commitment. Even though her mouth said no, her emotions said yes. She took it very hard when we broke up. I initiated it. She desired to get married. As great a girl as she was, I didn't want to marry her. She said yes to everything I wanted to do. I needed someone who would challenge me, or else I'd walk all over her. A mutual friend said she moved out of town, and that she was depressed for many years. I felt incredibly guilty that my selfishness for a little pleasure had hurt such a sweet young lady for a long time.

So I think no matter how clear either person may be about friendship with benefits, our emotions have difficulty with our mental and verbal commitments. If you have friends with benefits, they are no longer "friends." They are much more than that and it's best to clarify your relationship.

What If Your Single Guy Or Gal Friend Gets Married?

If your single guy or gal friend gets married, you should definitely expect a shift in your relationship. Often, singles prioritize friendships, if they aren't involved romantically with someone. But when one of the single friends begins dating someone else, the relationship noticeably changes. They spend less time with their single friends, and it dramatically decreases when they marry. In some cases, a new spouse can be threatened by a friendship with someone of the opposite sex and may even demand the termination of that friendship. This is a worst case scenario. It really depends on the married couple.

If, as a single, your friend of the opposite sex gets married, and if he struggles in his marriage, especially early on, be careful about allowing him to share with you negative and intimate details of their problems. Your friend needs to learn to work through difficulties in his marriage by effective listening and communicating with his spouse. You may become an unintentional crutch hindering this essential process for married couples, especially newlyweds during this time of adjustments, which may be difficult for some. Working through difficulties is what really bonds couples together to build a foundation for emotional, intellectual, spiritual, and physical intimacy so their marriage can last a lifetime!

What About Friends in the Workplace?

What if you work with this person and she gets married, but your job requires you to continue working together? What do you do when your job demands a lot of travelling together, then eating together, and working together all the time? Relationships, business as well as personal, can get foggy.

If your relationship has been appropriate before the marriage, there is no reason it can't be restored to one of respectability. It really depends on the individuals working together and their integrity.

If you're a single whose job requires traveling for business with married colleagues of the opposite sex, anything can happen if you don't watch your boundaries. Working long hours together on the road and spending all meals together can confuse your emotions for one another because you can genuinely like each other as people and co-workers. How can you tackle these situations? No one likes to eat alone, but as the single person, you could suggest one or two of the evenings of the business trip that your married colleague Skype her spouse and have a meal together that way. Such a gesture may lay the foundation for the spouse of your single friend to grow to trust and love you—okay maybe like you. You never know. Such an action may make it easier for the new spouse to feel more secure about all the business trips with someone of the opposite sex.

As the single friend, occasionally order room service or go out to one of the better restaurants in that city to which you haven't been before and have your own adventure. And you can call one of your same-sex friends so you won't be lonely. Skype with them, and you both can eat dinner and talk.

My friend Heidi had a male boss who was constantly text-messaging her even on weekends. The texting was about basketball games he was watching on TV or other non-work-related topics. Heidi wondered how his wife felt about it, but was uncomfortable saying anything because the Christian workplace environment was so friendly and she didn't know if this was part of that work culture.

One thing Heidi could have done is ask this question: "(*Name*), you know I appreciate you as my boss and sharing basketball stuff, but since you are married, how does your wife feel about you texting me so much?" If he says, "She doesn't care," this isn't a good response. It's a signal there is trouble in their marriage and Heidi shouldn't be the person to whom he is running. Heidi could have legitimately said, "I'm not comfortable with you texting me so much outside of work about non-work things because you are married, especially if your wife doesn't know about it." This response isn't a rejection of her boss, but a word of wisdom from a friend. If the relationship is one in which you can speak freely, then you can say, "Since you are married, I'm not comfortable with you texting me so much on weekends or weeknights about non-work stuff, but we can talk about the games at work." Certainly, we don't want anyone to lose their job, so these are just suggestions. You have to make the decision as to what works best in your work culture.

What If You Don't Have Friends Of The Opposite Sex?

What is this saying about you? Not having friends of the opposite sex isn't necessarily saying anything negative about you. I've been told that in some cities such as Los Angeles, New York, Washington, D.C., and Miami it is difficult to make friends. For some people, it is or was easy and fun to have tons of friends of the opposite sex in high school or college. Of course, this is or was not the case for many. But regardless of your situation, as you get older it's much more difficult. After college, the pool for friends seems to shrink. And people get married or are just not around.

You might ask yourself if there is something that you fear about having a friend of the opposite sex. Perhaps, you're afraid that it would become more than a friendship, and you wouldn't know how to set your boundaries without hurting the other person, so you're safer not even starting a friendship with the opposite sex. So what do you do? I suggest trying the tips for making friends mentioned earlier in this chapter. Or, you might be projecting your bad dating experiences with the opposite sex onto a friendship level, which could be done subconsciously. Some of us constantly compare our present to our past. If so, go back to the previous chapter to deal with issues of the heart.

Should Girls Initiate Friendships With Guys?

If you are simply initiating a friendship, I don't see a major problem with it, but some guys will apply the same perspective of you as they do of the women who initiate dating them.

Most men like mystery and most men like to pursue women, so these women typically will get first priority.

What Happens When One of You Begins Liking the Other More Than a Friend?

If your friend asks you for advice regarding someone he is thinking of dating, it can stir up your true feelings. Such a request lets you know where your heart is regarding your friendship with this person of the opposite sex. If you have no romantic interest in your friend, then such a request won't bother you in the least. But if there is a tug in your heart or you become jealous, then you have to honestly examine your feelings for your friend.

But what do you do if you are jealous? You have at least two options. One is to tell your friend your feelings and risk termination of friendship. The other is putting your friend's happiness ahead of your own and giving her the best possible advice so she can establish a good relationship with the person she is interested in. Both options work; it simply depends on your friend. Being protective of him in advising is one thing, but you must be careful not to base your advice on your romantic feelings for your friend.

When one of you in the friendship begins liking the other more than just a friend, I suggest praying about it initially by yourself, then maybe getting a close friend of the same sex to pray with you to hear what God may be saying to you. If your feelings persist, then consider telling your friend of the opposite sex. I'm not telling you to do this. You have to make your own decision.

If the feeling isn't mutual from your friend, then the friend who doesn't feel the way you do may end the friendship. Or that friend may allow the friendship to continue with the condition that the one who has a "thing" for the other can control his emotions and doesn't freak out.

If your friend likes you more than a friend, but you aren't feeling it, then consider a suggested response: *"Name, I really appreciate our friendship and I wish I felt about you like you do for me, but I don't have those same feelings as you do."* It is CRITICAL that you are completely honest with your friend and yourself. If you say you do like your friend as a potential boyfriend or girlfriend, when you really don't, you are leading your friend on indefinitely. This could get *oogly*, which is way past ugly! What if your feelings never change? You will eventually have to break off the relationship and may lose a friend unnecessarily. Yes, you may lose your friend temporarily or for good when you tell your friend initially about your feelings. But at least you can be at peace with yourself for being honest and not leading your friend on. You may have to deal with the emotional pain of losing a friend, but it won't be accompanied with feelings of guilt.

If the feeling is mutual, then let the dating begin!

Concluding Thought

Developing friendships with no benefits (you feel me?) with the opposite sex are vital and not just limited to intimate relationships. Friendships with no benefits will actually improve your relationship and intimacy when you do marry. It has been my experience, along with several of my single guy friends at the time, that friendships with the opposite sex can lower your sex drive—helping you see the opposite sex as more than sex objects. I haven't done research on this—just several single guys' experiences. As you may desire a friendship with the opposite sex to eliminate your loneliness, consider wanting such a friendship to help someone else eliminate his loneliness. I've often wondered if this was true of Jesus, who was single and often surrounded by women. Recall that Hebrews 4:15 says,

> *"For we do not have a high priest who is unable to sympathize with our weaknesses, but we have one **who has been tempted in every way**, just as we are—yet without sin."* (NIV)

So Jesus was tempted in this area too. Of course, my personal experience and the experiences of other male friends may not prove true for you, but consider testing it. See if spending time with the opposite sex as friends reduces your sex drive as you see your friends as people and not sex objects.

SUMMARY POINTS

1. Friendships with the opposite sex without romance can be beautiful and wonderful experiences.

2. Such friendships allow for completely honest relationships because the worry of trying to impress or the concern of losing a friend is minimal. These friendships create "safe places" in which these friends can talk about anything.

3. Laughter, encouragement, community, trust, and surviving social problems are major aspects of these friendships.

4. In trying to make new friends, consider initiating the process instead of waiting for someone else to make the first step.

5. Friendship boundary issues usually can be more easily resolved if dealt with immediately.

6. If your single friends begin dating and get married, expect your relationships with them to drastically change, as they should.

7. If you don't have guy or girlfriends, it doesn't mean that something is wrong with you.

8. When one of you in the friendship begins liking the other more than just a friend, you both have choices to make and possible risks to take.

9. Friendships with no benefits can lay an essential foundation for a long-lasting and mutually beneficial relationship or marriage down the road.

ACTION POINTS

1. If you want to make a new friend, when you see someone you think you would like to meet, just walk over to that person and offer to treat him or her to coffee or go dutch. Worst that can happen is that this person says no, but you might hear a yes. If this is too big of a first step for you, simply show yourself to be friendly. Don't just say "hello" first, but think of a nice compliment to give to the person you want to meet. For example, say something nice your potential friend about his or her hair or clothing, or smile.

2. If your friend of the opposite sex gives you what you consider a mixed signal, in which you are not sure if the relationship is changing, or something occurs which makes you uncomfortable, immediately but politely tell your friend exactly how you feel about the action and why.

This helps both of you to honestly evaluate your friendship and redefine it if necessary.

3. If your single friend of the opposite sex begins dating or gets married, give your new married friend space. Marriage will require your friend to focus on the new spouse. If you really want what is best for your friend, you will be patient and happy about the marriage.

4. If you begin liking your friend more than just a friend, I suggest praying about it first before speaking with your friend. Next, you have to make the decision to share your feelings or not, and weigh the possible consequences. (I would tell my friend, but this is me, and I'm a risk taker).

5. Developing friendships with the opposite, sex with no benefits, will greatly benefit you both when you enter into a serious romantic relationship.

Chapter Seven

God is Really Into Sex!

"There's more to sex than mere skin on skin. Sex is as much a
spiritual mystery as physical fact. As written in Scripture, 'The two
become one.'" 1 Corinthians 6:16, The Message

It's Natural

Ever since that first neighborhood party in my backyard during my first
slow dance with the girl on whom I had a crush, my introduction to my sex
drive occurred. As sixth and seventh graders, our party was chaperoned by
all the mothers in our neighborhood. Mom told me I always liked girls
because I was kissing them in kindergarten. But this was different. During
this slow dance, for the first extended period of time, this girl's breasts were
pressing against my chest. I wasn't a Christian then, but I was silently
singing, *Yes, Jesus loves me!* There was no space between this girl and me.
For a very brief moment, life was perfect! Then, all of a sudden, without
any warning, a part of my anatomy stood at attention! Even though I was
embarrassed, there was nothing I could do. Couldn't she feel it pressing
against her? How could she not? What was she thinking? No way was I
going to ask her! What was I supposed to do? No one prepared me for this
moment. The song wasn't close to being over. So, I pretended it was
normal, finished the dance, and thanked her for dancing with me. Evidently,
it wasn't a problem because she became my girlfriend the next week.

But as a young boy journeying to manhood, I loved this new experience
and wanted more, even though I didn't really understand it. I wished Dad
and I had been closer so I could have asked him about what happened.
Fortunately, I didn't know what was involved in sexual intercourse; I just
knew I loved being close to girls.

Does this sound similar to what I hope was an innocent introduction to
your sex drive? For the remainder of most of our lives, it becomes a force
with which to be reckoned. Sometimes it controls us, and at other times we
are able to control it. So, what do you do about sex as a single person? It
seems natural. Our sex drives are incredibly powerful! Can you ever
remember letting it take control? It could get us into some places we may
regret later. So what is the big deal about having sex whether you are
married or not? Why fight the feeling?

Why Does the Church Say No to Sex Before Marriage?

If sex is so natural, why are Christ followers told to avoid sex outside of marriage?

Did your parent(s) tell you not to have sex before marriage, yet no one explained why you shouldn't, not even your pastor? Girls have told me their mothers said not to have sex because it would always be painful. Yet the Bible considers it pleasure. The non-verbal and often even the verbal communication was that sex, even for Christians, was evil and sinful. And if you ever did have sex before marriage, it was the unforgiveable sin!

Did you find yourself behaving one way with your parent(s) and people at church and another way at parties—living the double life? Did you or do you often find yourself trying to obey your parent(s) and the Church while wrestling with your powerful sex drive and thinking all the time that God is against sex? As a teenager and new to following Jesus, I remember not wanting to die before getting married so I could have legalized sex. This is terrible, but true.

Let's see exactly what God's plans were for creating sex.

God is Really Into Sex!

Maybe the first fact we ought to consider in attempting to tackle this topic is that God created sex! So, God is not some prude desiring to keep the people He created from having sex. He is quite the opposite. God wants us to have sex on a frequent and regular basis...in marriage! Read what God says in passage in 1 Corinthians 7:1b-5, especially verse 2, which is written below:

> *"First, is it a good thing to have sexual relations?*
>
> **Certainly**—*but only within a certain context."*   The Message

I don't want to put any of you singles to sleep or for you to zone out on me, but in order to understand why God is so into sex, you will need to view sex from His perspective. One of my friends, Johnny Parker, says, *"Any two people can have sex, but it takes three people to make love, which includes God, your spouse, and you."*

The context referred to in verse 2 above is marriage. So as I speak about sex, it will be from God's perspective. Some of you singles may think, "How is this going to help me?" Understanding and applying God's principles regarding sex may very well save your future relationships and possibly give you a marriage that will last a lifetime! Most relationships and marriages break up because of a lack of knowledge and application of God's principles. I want you to get God's principle that sex is designed *only* for the context of marriage. When you finish reading this chapter, I want your brain to always connect: MARRIAGE+SEX.

What if you're single and your sex drive is killing you, but you are trying to stay out of bed? What if you're a follower of Christ, but you are losing the battle and are sexually active? First, know I'm not going to judge you. Second, if you keep reading, you may find some very practical help.

My goal is for you to see the *beauty of sex* in its Godly context—in a Godly relationship. Thus, I'll write about sex in the context of marriage, resulting in my using the terms husband and wife. To appreciate what you are about to read, you need to understand that God is all about relationships—first, His with you, and then yours with others.

If you are single and aren't in a relationship, then if God has a relationship for you down the road that gets serious, you'll already have your relationship map. So please don't quit reading as this old married man and counselor tries to help you avoid the problems that plague his relationship clients, both the singles and the marrieds.

Now, let's read the rest of the First Corinthians 7:2-5 passage:

It's good for a man to have a wife, and for a woman to have a husband. Sexual drives are strong, but marriage is strong enough to contain them and provide for a balanced and fulfilling sexual life in a world of sexual disorder. The marriage bed must be a place of mutuality—the husband seeking to satisfy his wife, the wife seeking to satisfy her husband. Marriage is not a place to 'standup for your rights. Marriage is a decision to serve the other, whether in bed or out. Abstaining from sex is permissible for a period of time if you both agree to it, and if it's for the purposes of prayer and fasting— but only for such times. Then come back together again. Satan has an ingenious way of tempting us when we least expect it. The Message

The first truth extracted from this passage is that God says it is a *good thing* to have sex! Amen! I certainly didn't hear this growing up in my church or I'd have definitely attended more often! God acknowledges that our sex drives are strong, so He provides the context of marriage for our sexual relationships. But the kicker is that sex is good only within the environment in which God created it, the marriage relationship. God wants our sex life to be fulfilling and satisfying. WOW!! Go God!!

YOU BECOME ONE

An essential purpose of biblical sex is found in 1 Corinthians 6:16-17, which says,

"Or do you not know that the one who joins himself to a harlot is one body with her? For He says, 'THE TWO WILL BECOME ONE FLESH.' But the one who joins himself to the Lord is one spirit with Him" (NASB).

The implication of these verses is that you bond your spirit to whomever you have sexual intercourse. In the context of marriage, this is ideal because this bonding of your spirit to your spouse's builds oneness. Bonding of spirits is like emotional and physical glue, helping a couple to be monogamous—lowering the possibility of adultery or divorce.

You want to be careful with whom you bond your spirit. Bonding your spirit to the wrong person or multiple people may be difficult to break, but we'll talk about this later in this chapter.

Ladies, pay close attention here. Not only do you bond spiritually with your sex partner, but physically as well. When you have sex, the male actually deposits his DNA in you. What is DNA, you ask? It's the substance that carries an organism's genetic information. This is the means by which hereditary characteristics pass from one generation to the next.

Forensic experts can actually take DNA from a rape victim up to three days after intercourse, but no one is actually certain how long the DNA of a man can remain in a woman after sex, whether voluntarily or not.

And that's not all the bonding that takes place during intercourse. During sex, the hormone oxytocin is released in the woman to increase her bonding with the man she is having sex with. Even if it's a one-night stand or a live-in arrangement that doesn't end up in marriage, you have physically become one with this guy. God wasn't kidding around when He said *the two shall become one*. That's why He set up sex to spiritually and physically bond a couple as part of a covenant marriage. So, if you're having difficulty getting your previous boyfriend(s) out of your mind after a break up, this might be a powerful factor.

Your Body is Extra Special!

"Or do you not know that your body is the temple of the Holy Spirit who is in you, whom you have from God, and you are not your own? For you were bought at a price: therefore glorify God in your body and spirit, which are God's." 1 Corinthians 6:19 (NKJV).

Your body was created to glorify God, the Creator, who made us in His image. When you have sex, you and your partner's body immediately go into Creation mode, a God-like trait. The reproductive system goes into full gear with the man launching countless sperm, acting like heat-seeking missiles looking for the woman's egg to become one and create life. Naturally, it doesn't always hit the target because of birth control or other reasons, but the creation process is indeed triggered during sex. The God who created the universe created us in His image with His unique trait of creating human life. Our bodies become sacred temples during sex as internal systems position themselves for the miracle of creating human life.

Outside of marriage, you become vulnerable to many consequences— like pregnancy or sexually transmitted diseases that can derail you from your purpose and destiny. Is the risk worth it? God intended sex to be safe in the context of marriage.

What About Sexual Compatibility?

People say that you should *test-drive* your partner for sexual compatibility before marriage. When most people voice concerns about being sexually compatible, they're not worried about the intangibles that make the physical possible. They're more concerned about biology, but the plumbing almost always works. Usually when it doesn't, it is an emotional or medical issue.

Do you know how you can determine sexual compatibility without having sex before marriage? I'll share some secrets with you. If you are single and dating, ask yourself these biblical principles, "How well do the person I'm dating and I...?" You'll see what I mean as I explain the biblical passage. There'll be questions for you as a single to process.

How do you communicate with each other?

Remember as you read, I want you to think *"Marriage+Sex"* whenever you think sex. As we write about sex, it is in the context of marriage. Therefore, even though you are single now, let's suppose you get married. You are going to want to satisfy your spouse sexually and be sexually satisfied in return. It will require effectively communicating to each other what the two of you like and dislike sexually. If couples are going to satisfy each other sexually, then it may also include intentionally and voluntarily seeking to bring pleasure to your spouse, even though you may not particularly care for a specific sex act. But this is voluntarily, given with love as the motivation, not demanded or forced. It is not about demanding that a spouse perform an uncomfortable sex act. Effective communication translates into being heard and understood as well as into hearing and understanding your potential future spouse about sex. It also seems to imply that if couples are to have mutually pleasurable sex, they have to be able to work through conflict and forgive each other before entering the bedroom.

Now that you've read about the importance of communicating about sex in a marriage covenant, if you are single and dating, you should ask yourself, "Do (*person you are dating*) and I communicate well?" "If not, what do we need to do to improve our communication?" "How effective are we at resolving conflict?" Answers to these questions will be invaluable to you, especially if you marry this person. Learn to communicate before you get serious or get married.

How Well Do You Serve Each Other?

The New American Standard Bible translation, probably the most literal Greek to English translation states in 1 Corinthians 7:4:

> *"The wife does not have authority over her own body, but the husband does; and likewise also the husband does not have the authority over his own body, but the wife does."*

This passage concludes with two crucial emphases. Whether in the bed or out of it, married partners should serve each other. So, if Brenda wants sex and I'm not really in the mood, watching the game, or whatever, I need to *serve* her in this area. The first emphasis is that I need to sacrifice *"my rights"* and have sex with Brenda. Naturally, if one spouse is sick, he shouldn't be forced to have sex. But aside from being sick, the Bible does say it is better to give than to receive. And I don't want Brenda to miss her *blessing.* But seriously, think about this, sex is about giving and serving, not just about self-gratification. In fact, when a couple desires to bring pleasure to each other sexually first, then this is when they both can experience what I call **maximum sex!!**

So, the second emphasis in finding out if you are sexually compatible is serving one another. Serving is the foundation of a healthy, mutually beneficial, and long-lasting marriage. If a married couple is having problems in the bedroom, it is because they are having problems outside the bedroom, which are not being resolved.

So ask yourself, "How good are we at serving each other?" "How about sacrificially serving each other without demanding something in return?"

God's Big Picture

Biblical sex is so much more than a physical act. For followers of Christ, it is an act of worship. If you process all that you have just read, you see that

God's design for sex is quite beautiful. Being sexually active within the marriage structure is an act of worship because worshiping God is about giving. In the sexual act, man and woman give themselves to each other in the most intimate physical and spiritual act. Since biblical sex is about giving, then it is also about worship. To experience sex the way God intended requires a covenant of an emotional, intellectual, and spiritual oneness relationship, which is culminated by a physical oneness— sexual intercourse.

Sexual intercourse is to be pleasurable. In Genesis 18:12b,

"After I have become old, shall I have pleasure, my lord being old also?" (NASB).

Most Bible scholars say that Sarah is referring to having a child, but it also includes the physical pleasure of sexual intercourse. Even in her old age, she looked forward to having sex with Abraham with anticipation. Yet, marriage isn't about sex on demand. This oneness isn't perfection. It demands a constant working at the relationship, such as forgiving each other.

Does the person you are dating demand sex of you? If so, that's not love. Having sex doesn't necessarily equal love. Biblical love is about giving! You may need to break up with this person.

Both the woman and the man are giving each other their all. Their love has created a safe place for both of them. Interdependency is foundational to this relationship. This level of intimacy and vulnerability is designed to be shared only with one person. Every time a married couple is sexually intimate, they are renewing their marriage covenant with God and themselves.

What you also need to know is that the longer you're married, the better the sex, is because all the emotional, intellectual, spiritual, and physical oneness can't happen in one night. It is perfected over years. I've heard husbands married to the same woman for more than twenty years say, "The sex we're having now can't compare to our early years of marriage!" And that is the way it is supposed to be as our love for our spouses increases and, we get to know them better as well. That is why it's so difficult for one-night stands to be better than sex in a healthy marriage!

But Sex Outside of Marriage Is Also Great—Really?

That's apparently what most Christian singles feel about sex before marriage. According to a *Relevant Magazine* 2012 article, 80 percent of Christian singles are having sex outside of marriage (http://graceforgrace/2011/10/13/80-of-christian-singles-admit-to-pre-marital-sex/). Listen to this. You may be thinking this is great, but as premarital sex has risen, the marriage rate has declined. So, if you'd like to eventually get married, you may want to reconsider the effects of premarital sex on your chances of getting married.

Sex outside of marriage can also affect the quality of your future marriage. Data from the *National Survey of Family Growth* found that "women who are sexually active prior to marriage faced considerably higher risk of marital disruption than women who were virgin brides." It could be that self-control during singlehood builds a strong character, a person much more willing to go to greater lengths to avoid divorce.

In a study looking at factors impacting increased marital stability, Brigham Young sociologist Tim Heaton concluded from his studies that divorce is more likely among the sexually active and cohabiters because they have established their life together on *"relatively unstable sexual relationships."* And, if you start having sex in your teen years, you double the risk of divorce later in life compared, to women who had sex in their unmarried adult years.

Some teenage girls say the sex hurts and the guys are in a rush. And many of these girls say there is no communication. As a matter of fact, some studies show that more and more teens are having sex without even dating!

Another issue I hear from teenage girls is that their first few times, their sexual experiences aren't what they expected. Their male counterparts often ejaculate in a few minutes and are done. Once the act is over, for some girls, that is the end of their relationships. For others who continue having sex with the same partner, the relationship is only about the sex. If the sex stops, so does the relationship.

In 2008, statistics revealed that 69 percent of all teens that had sex by age 14 said they have gone through one or more types of abuse in a relationship. The survey was commissioned by Liz Claiborne Inc. and aired originally on CBS News, where his excerpt appeared: "We were surprised at how many tweens or kids ages 11 and 12 are dealing with these issues," Liz Claiborne Inc. Vice President Jane Randel told CBS' Early Show national correspondent Tracy Smith. What's behind it all? Researchers believe early sexual activity tends to fuel dating violence among teens and tweens, Smith reported.

This is another reason teenagers need to wait before being sexually active. Yes, your bodies are obviously big enough to have sex. But emotionally, you aren't ready. It is like some twelve or fourteen year old trying to drive a car. In fact, some states are in the process of increasing the age for getting a driver's license from sixteen years old to eighteen or nineteen years of age due to the lack of maturity.

Amazingly to me, the Bible comments on sex before marriage. In 2 Samuel 13, Amnon, the half-brother of Absalom, becomes so lustful for Tamar, Absalom's sister, that he devises a plan to be alone with her. He rapes her. What a sad event. After Amnon rapes Tamar, he hates her with the same passion that he lusted after her before sex with her. The aftermath of this event is tragic. But when we allow our lust to take over, seldom do we think of the individual as a person, nor the consequences of our actions.

Action Point

Don't accept my opinion or even the Bible's principles regarding premarital sex. Take the time to evaluate a real-life scenario of premarital sex for yourself. Determine if it is the kind of sex you want or if you would prefer to wait for God's best.

If you are over eighteen, consider doing this action point now. If you are offended, then please let me apologize to you in advance, but I do want to speak about what sex outside of marriage has become for some singles.

Tucker Max, author and movie producer, is known mostly in college crowds for drinking to oblivion, and having sex with girls, and then describing it in graphic detail on his site. Log onto: http://www.lemondrop.com/2009/09/23/i-slept-with-tucker- max-the-internets-biggest

If you are a female, is this the kind of sex you want? If you read the comments posted on the site, what do you think it says about the value of a female? Why do you think Steph went along with this? Isn't it interesting that Steph likes being in relationships?

If you are a guy, why do you think Max doesn't ask Steph if she enjoyed the sex? Do you think he was afraid to know or didn't care? How do you think he would feel if he discovered that he's not satisfying all the women with whom he is sleeping? Would communication have improved the sex? But in order to have that communication, there would need to be some kind of relationship based on caring for the other person. Maybe God knows what He is doing by wanting sex to be protected and respected in marriage?

How does this sexual account compare to God's view of sex? Why do you think they are approaching sex this way? How would you feel about yourself if you were in this situation?

God's design for sex is countercultural to the world's outlook on sex, which is selfish. It is all about self-gratification. For many, there is usually little or no concern as to whether your sexual partner was satisfied. It is more about quantity of your conquests. As a matter of fact, the question "what's your number?" now also means "with how many people have you slept?"

Sleeping around may be part of the trend today, but consider the possible consequences:

- There is no 100 percent guarantee of preventing pregnancy from any contraceptives, except abstinence.

- The federal government recommends abstinence as the safest way to avoid HIV. Condoms can break or leak.

- Sex before marriage creates cycles of single fathers and mothers for the next three-four generations before such a cycle is broken. Think of the impact of children growing up without a father or mother. This is not a jab at single parents, but a realization that the best environment for raising emotionally healthy, stable, and productive children requires a father and a mother. This certainly isn't saying that single parents haven't raised outstanding children, but even these parents will usually tell you they wished they had received help from a female or male parent.

Steve Harvey's 2012 movie, *Act Like a Lady, Think Like a Man* seems to be Mr. Harvey's attempt to warn the secular community that **sex without a relationship equals emptiness and loneliness**. So Mr. Harvey doesn't appear to approve of one night stands. I think he would simply call sex without a relationship a *booty call*.

His 90-Day rule before having sex is to help individuals not jump in bed with someone where there is no chance of relationship or with someone that you will regret having sex with after the fact. Mr. Harvey's 90-Day rule encourages individuals whether they are following Christ or not, to at least slow down in the area of casual sex. And it may help with less sexually transmitted diseases, short-term broken hearts, lifetime emotional wounds, unwanted pregnancies, and abortions.

Is a coincidence that secular research is agreeing more and more with biblical truths? So if you are a teenager, college student, single in the workplace, or divorcee, *sex is worth waiting for!*

Guys, What You Need to Know About Women Regarding Sex

Gentlemen, is you care about women, you need to know what is required of most females to have sex.

"For the woman to have sex with her husband, she has to open herself to him. What he is doing is a physical intrusion to her. It is invasive. In order to have sex with her husband, she has to decide to become vulnerable to him. Thus, the physical union requires a depth of emotional involvement in order for her to fully enter into the act. She becomes both physically and emotionally open and moldable in order to receive him into her. This requires a great deal more trust for her than for him."

Abel Ortega and Melodie Fleming, authors of *The Dance of Restoration: Rebuilding Marriage After Infidelity.*

Guys, if you really care about girls, then, understanding the vulnerability of women in sex should for you eliminate one night stands. For most women, sex is all about relationships, not merely a physical activity. Sex is about connecting with a woman emotionally, intellectually, and spiritually. Sex is the expression and celebration of this connection. Marriage is the best context for this relationship.

Ten More Reasons to Wait for Sex

Dr. Tom Lickona, a development psychologist and Director of the Center for the 4th and 5th Rs, wrote an article entitled *10 Emotional Dangers of Premature Sexual Involvement*[1]. They are:

1. Worry about pregnancy and disease

   One high school girl told a counselor: *"I see some of my friends buying home pregnancy test. They are so worried and so distracted every month, afraid that they might be pregnant. It's a relief to be to me a virgin."*

2. Regret

   "Since that first night, my boyfriend expects sex on every date. When I don't feel like it, we end up in a big argument. I'd like to end this relationship and date others, but after being so intimate, it's awfully tough." Karen, age 16

3. Guilt

   "In the movies, when people have sex, it's always romantic. Physically, it felt good, but emotionally it felt really awkward. I was worried that

our relationship was now going to be a lot more serious than it was before. It was like, 'Now what is she going to expect from me?'"

Lucian Shulte

4. Loss of self-esteem and self-respect

   *"There are girls in our dorms who have had multiple pregnancies and multiple abortions. The ironic thing is that practically all the girls who talk to me say they **hate** the whole scene—the bars, the parties, the attitudes, and sexual expectations of guys. But because they have such low self-esteem, they will settle for any kind of attention from guys."*

   Young woman, residence hall director

5. The corruption of character

   "It was like a drug. The more sex I had, the more I wanted. I couldn't control myself, yet I wasn't satisfied at all."   *Young man*

6. Fear of commitment

   "I first had intercourse with my girlfriend when we were 15. I'd been going with her for almost a year, and I loved her very much. She was friendly, outgoing, and charismatic. We'd done everything but have intercourse, and then one night she asked if we could go all the way. A few days later, we broke up it was the most painful time of my life. I had opened up to her more than anybody, even my parents. I was depressed and nervous. I dropped out of sports and felt like a failure. In college, I've had mostly one-night stands. I'm afraid of falling in love."

   Brian, college senior

7. Depression and suicide

   "I want to spend more time with him, do stuff like go shopping or see a movie. That would make it a friendship for me. But he says, no, then we'd have a relationship, and that's more than he wants. It seems like I don't get the 'friend' part, but he still gets the 'benefits.' It's hard for me to be with him and then go home alone."   Heather

8. Damaged or ruined relationships

   "Sex became the center of our relationship. Like a cancer, it took over. New things entered—anger, impatience, jealousy, and selfishness. We just couldn't talk anymore. We grew very bored with each other."

   Jennifer, 24

9. Stunted personal development

   "A girl who enters into a serious relationship with a boy very early in

119

life may find out later that her individuality was thwarted. She became part of him and failed to develop her own interests, her sense of independent identity."   Dr. Samuel Kauffman

10. Negative effects on marriage

"Sometime during my wild college days, I picked up an infection that damaged the inside of my fallopian tubes and left me infertile. I am now married to a wonderful man who very much wants children, and the guilt is overwhelming."   A 33-year-old wife

Dr. Armand Nicholi, Jr., professor of psychiatry at Harvard Medical School, describes a study that sheds light on the emotional consequences of sexual behavior: *"When Harvard students adopted a strict sexual code, their relationships and academic performance improved."*

Dr. Thomas Lickona is a co-author with his wife Judith and William Boudreau, M.D., of *Sex, Love, and You:* **Making the Right Decision** (2003); www.amazon.com; and co-author, with Matthew Davidson, of *Smart and Good High Schools* (2005); www.cortland.edu/character

To read this *must-read* article in its entirety, go to
http://www2.cortland.edu/dotAsset/199337.pdf

What Singles Really Want

Why are the majority of Christian singles having sex outside of marriage? For many women, there is much more to sex than the act itself. They want *intimacy*. Intimacy can include sex, but it doesn't have to. Having asked thousands of women to define intimacy in one word, they define it as *closeness*. A woman can enjoy being with a man without having sex. Unfortunately, some women strive to keep a guy around by giving sex. They think that's the only way to have a relationship with a guy. But at the heart level, most women want an emotional, intellectual, and spiritual connection, which is culminated in a physical expression of oneness through a commitment of marriage. So, what single women are truly searching for is closeness, but they often confuse it with having sex, or, compromise—giving sex in return for intimacy. Some single women may feel physically intimate, but, without the commitment, they may simultaneously experience insecurity or emotional loneliness and emptiness.

When the woman gives her body, it is the ultimate gift a woman gives her man. It is an act of trust and vulnerability—the giving of herself, not just body, but emotions, intellect, spirit, and soul.

Men have a slightly different perspective on sex and intimacy. Whereas most women have to be in the *mood*, most men simply just need to be in the *room*! If we're breathing, we're ready to have sex. For men who know very little about women, sex can be all about the man.

Generally, males are stimulated by sight. Good looks are vital to women, but seldom their determining factor. How they are treated or the man's character has a greater impact than a guy's physical appearance.

Guys, not only is having sex crucial for us, but how well we perform affirms our manhood. That is why we want to know if we brought pleasure to our sexual partner. People have made a joke about it: "It was good for me; was it good for you?"

Men also have a sexual cycle, approximately every three days, in which a male needs a physical release. According to Dr. Juli Slattery's article, *Sex Is a Physical Need,* a man's sexuality has tremendous impact on his emotional, marital, and spiritual well-being.

The best way for a woman to understand this dynamic is to relate it to another physiological need. If you've had a baby, you may relate to the experience of milk building up in your breasts a few days after giving birth. The buildup of breast milk becomes annoying (and even painful) until the milk is expressed. You may have even had the embarrassing experience of leaking breast milk when it was not expressed. A male's semen buildup is sometimes released through nocturnal emissions if it is not otherwise relieved. Just as with breast milk, sperm production tends to "keep up with demand." The more often a man has sex, the more semen his body is likely to produce.

Source: http://www.focusonthefamily.com/marriage/sex_and_intimacy/understanding-your-husbands-sexual-needs/sex-is-a-physical-need.aspx

So, most men have physical pressure for sex. "Wet dreams" are often God's release for this pressure. Guys, you can pray for these wet dreams.

In our society today, where men are constantly being demeaned, sex plays a more critical role for a man emotionally, mentally, and physically than ever before!

The terms intimacy and sex for most guys are interchangeable. Guys typically don't talk about intimacy, at least not openly. But our need for companionship and attention can be seen early on.

Easily, 90 percent of the guys I speak with who are sexually active aren't satisfied with one-night stands, nor having sex with their girlfriends over a long period of time outside of marriage. Society portrays men as being void of emotion, but this isn't true. Men do care about relationships. Sex outside of marriage negatively impacts men too! Men typically just don't have a safe place to talk about it.

Saying *No* To Premarital Sex

Suppose you really don't want to have sex before marriage? What do you say to those wanting sex from you? For some people, a firm "no" is sufficient. Others might try: "I'm flattered that you're attracted to me, but I only want to have sex with one woman the rest of my life, with the person I'm emotionally, spiritually, and intellectually connected to." "I'm not ready to have sex with anyone." "I don't want to risk STDs or getting you pregnant, and nothing but abstinence is 100 percent safe!"

How Did Our Culture Develop Such a Low View of Sex?

We are talking about sex before dating because we want to protect you and your date. In the dating chapter, you'll discover that men used to court women by going to their homes where these women lived with their parents. Fathers were the natural protectors of their daughters. Then women left home to live on their own in cities. Courting gave way to dating. Dating had less or no parental influence.

Not only was there less parental involvement, but, the 1960's Sexual Revolution claimed to "liberate" men and women from traditional roles in relationships and sexuality. Public acceptance for sex outside of marriage grew with the advent of the pill, which for the first time separated sex from reproduction. With the help of TV shows, radio, film, and print media, sex outside of marriage is more of the norm today, and being a virgin is a target of jokes or considered odd.

For the first time, women in the 1960s could have sex without getting pregnant, and guys didn't have to worry about *having* to marry their girlfriends when they became pregnant. Women using the pill outside of marriage unintentionally lowered their value to the men sleeping with them. They were more liberated and less respected!

Our society went from seeing twin beds for Ricky and Lucy Ricardo's bedroom in *I Love Lucy* in the 1950s and Rob and Laura Petrie in *The Dick Van Dyke Show* in the 1960s, to 2011 films like *"What's Your Number"* that refers to the number of men the lead female character has slept with. Initially, I thought it was about asking a gal for her phone number!

Before this sexual revolution, studies show that 77 percent of white women were virgins when they married. Today, that number is 5 percent[1].

Countless numbers of women today are complaining about being single in their thirties, forties and fifties. What's going on? The separation of sex and reproduction led to a new phenomenon: couples living together without being married.

Before this, only one-fifth of one percent of all couples cohabitated, but today it's 19 percent. Once upon a time, 80 percent of all American households were comprised of married couples. Today that number is down to 51 percent, the lowest *marriage rate* than at any time in U.S. history.

Below is research by the Administration of Children & Families (2004) about why unmarried couples live together:

- Couples attempting to avoid divorce by living together.

- Convenience, market forces (i.e. sharing living costs), pragmatism are reasons they choose to live together.

- Fear of commitment or fragile bonds are also reasons.

- The average cohabitation for an unmarried couple is 2 years, then, they either marry or split. The majority of couples that do marry, divorce within the first five years of their marriage.

Behavior is different than married couples in spending, fidelity, leisure, and household duties because of the previously mentioned issues of fear of commitment and fragile bonds. Cohabitation tends to make it more difficult for couples living together to work through issues of money and household duties as easily as married couples. Also the fidelity during conflict and how to spend leisure time can become issues due to selfishness and less commitment.

What women thought would be liberating for them has actually been more liberating for men. Consider this. Why did men used to marry? To live with the woman they loved and have children. Why should men make a marriage commitment to get what they want when they can get it without getting married?

Ladies, don't buy into the lie that by sleeping with your guy, he'll marry you. Look at the stats again. It's not working. As a relationship counselor, when I ask couples why they are living together, 90 percent of the time, the girl says, "If I had known it would take this long for us to get married, I would have never moved in with him." Then, the girls are surprised to hear their men often say, "I wasn't committed until now." The look on the girls' faces is always priceless!

If I Can't Have Sex, Can I...?

It's not about what you cannot do. It's about what's best for you, your relationships with the opposite sex, and with Jesus. There are reasons why God gave us guidelines. It's because He cares for you and wants the best for you. It's not about denying you like Adam and Eve were made to believe in the Garden.

Here are some of the activities many singles ask about and explore instead of intercourse:

- **French Kissing**—It's not sex. Just be attentive that you don't get carried away, especially in an isolated environment.

  Dr. Helen Fisher, an anthropologist published a book, *Why Him? Why Her?*[2] According to Dr. Fisher who studied the effects of kissing on the brain the whole brain gets involved in kissing, triggering various hormones that affect your emotions. She says that the testosterone found in saliva increases lust. For men in long-term relationships, kissing increases their oxytocin hormone which helps intensify attachment. Meanwhile, dopamine hormones drive the emotions of romantic love.

  Dr. Fisher also says that first kisses can be critical to relationships! Over 50 percent of men and women who start liking somebody will stop liking them after their first kiss if they are a bad kisser. Does Dr. Fisher get your attention?

- **Masturbating**—Please, be careful. I've heard one well-known relationship expert say if a couple is married and the woman is pregnant and can't have sex, he has no problem with the husband's masturbating looking at pictures of his wife and not *Playboy*. But he said this should only be done for a short time until his wife can resume having sex.

  As a single, I masturbated initially after watching pornography. I loved the sensation and the physical release. Eventually, my body became addicted to it. I stopped simply because I didn't like being a slave to my body. As a single, I relied more on "wet dreams" or natural releases.

Possible Problems with Masturbation:

- What if you masturbate while single, then get married, only to discover you enjoy masturbating more than sexual intercourse with your wife? I'm actually counseling a married man with this problem.

- Intimacy is much better than masturbation could ever be.

- Sexual intimacy requires vulnerability; masturbation doesn't.

- Sexual intimacy is about trust and giving; masturbation requires no trust and is all about you.

- Sexual intimacy is about serving your spouse; masturbation is about serving yourself.

- Masturbation can cause premature ejaculations, which can be a major issue during sexual intercourse, especially because most women require more time to become sexually aroused.

- Masturbation is *incredibly addictive* and *much more difficult to stop* than most guys could have ever imagined!

- **Pornography**—This sets you up with neurological pathways to keep expecting the same "high" that you'll expect from your future wife or husband. With the increased use of the Internet, Christian women are also getting addicted to pornography. Today, 30 percent of Internet pornography consumers are women. Of those women exposed to pornography, 19 percent of Christian women are addicted, while 44 percent felt hopeless in overcoming it[3].

  - Pornography lies to you. It will please you, but only temporarily. It gives a false sense of sexuality and intimacy. Pornography never tells you it will enslave you, but it does.

  - Pornography is about selfishness and self- deception. It is about laziness, possibly damaging your appreciation to communicate during sex and putting you at a disadvantage once married.

  - Pornography addiction can be defeated, but it isn't easy.

  - The Witherspoon Institute reports that some studies show that pornography use undermines marital and other intimate relationships of its users. It can make men sexually incompetent with a real partner, and for some, can lead to growing attractions to images and behaviors of a "hard-core" nature. Women not only face new expectations of sexual behavior, they also are confronted with increased chances of divorce, infidelity, and less happy marriages.

- **Oral Sex**—Yeah, I know former President Clinton said it wasn't sex, so the rate of oral sex went up after that speech. It is an intimate sexual act.

- **Petting**—This is putting your hands outside or inside your date's clothing and may include touching sexual organs. Often leads to premarital sex and pregnancies.

- **Sexting**—Sending nude pictures or sexual messages is nothing but pornography and inappropriate flirting. Sexting should be a red flag that this person isn't ready to date yet because of a poor self-image possibly resulting from emotional or sexual abuse. Sexters have baggage that hasn't been resolved or healed. Bringing this unresolved baggage into a new relationship can be extremely destructive and dysfunctional. Usually this person is struggling to like him or herself and will have difficulty genuinely liking you. Another problem with sexting is when you break up, it has become common practice for your "private nude" pictures to be posted on Facebook. Once you hit that send button, you lose control over your pictures forever! Criminal charges can be pressed against you for pornography and being a predator even if you're a minor.

Staying Sexually Pure Until Marriage—*Seriously?*

There are singles who are successful in maintaining their virginity or second virginity. Here are some people who are successfully living an abstinent lifestyle, such as Olympian Lolo Jones, who is often criticized for being a 30-something-year old virgin. But she is proud of this fact.

Another who won his fight in keeping his virginity until marriage is former Los Angeles Laker star, A.C. Green. Many years ago, A.C. Green took pride in being a Christ follower, remaining a virgin until he married at the age of thirty-eight in 2002. He is still married. Hopefully, he will remain so. But even if he doesn't, his ten years of marriage at the writing of this book are longer than the average marriage today. Sixty-five percent of marriages today are ending in divorce in their first five years.

Below are some of A.C. Green's quotes and others' quotes about him:

- **On marriage and sex:** "Being married . . . and all that comes with it… is wonderful. It was worth the wait."

- ***Miami Heat teammate Anthony Mason (who doesn't profess following Christ) on A.C. Green:*** *"You would think of [A.C.] as a goody-two-shoes from the outside looking in. It was something to make fun of when you weren't there, but to see it up close, to see how his life has benefitted, you realize that's the way you're supposed to live."*

- **On his teammates trying to break his resolve:** Initially his teammates in the NBA didn't believe that he was waiting till marriage. Of this, A.C. says *"But as time went on, when the guys saw some consistency to the way I was handling my life, they gradually came to accept it, to the point where some asked me to talk to their sons and daughters."*

- **On the meaning of abstinence:** *"[Abstinence] doesn't really have anything to do with a person's religious background. It's about self-control...identifying your core values as a person."*

- **On his wife, Veronique:** *"She's exceptionally beautiful, and she has a great sense of character. She's an accountant, she teaches dance, and she's a singer."* They were friends for four years before they started dating. *"We were able to have fun together, to laugh together, struggle and cry together. We were able to develop a friendship before it became physical, before it was a sex interaction. Now, we're committed—for life."*

Lolo Jones is as famous as A.C. Green used to be, but what does the average person do to stay sexually pure? I asked males and females from various cultures from the ages of twenty to fifty years old, some virgins, some second-virginity people, and divorcees exactly what they do to stay sexually pure until marriage. Below are some of their comments:

"My stance on this topic went through stages. My first stage went a little like God gave me these feelings, I want to act on them so I did, and it was the only time (since I have been a Christian) that I was intimate with a woman that I was not married to. Afterwards I felt so guilty, dirty, and condemned that I just vowed that I could not do that again. It has been three years since I have been with a woman and let me tell you it has been the toughest thing that I have ever had to do in my life but here is the thing. People say that they love God with their mouth but I believe that God judges your actions when it comes to you truly loving him. If He says do not commit fornication, do not commit adultery, that is clear to me with no negotiation. I believe that God looks at you loving Him if you follow His commandments. It could be that He is preparing your spouse and he or she is not ready or it could be that He is still preparing you as a person so that you will be ready and so that you will not repeat earlier mistakes. All I know is I do not want to prolong my blessing or disappoint my heavenly Father by disobeying something that He clearly outlines in His word, so the sex before marriage issue is settled for me." Forty-something male

"I try not to think about it! And when I sense those thoughts coming, I try to focus on something else! I work to guard my eyes and ears from sexually-charged movies, TV shows, music, etc. I'm also wary of overtly sensual guys." Twenty-something female

Are you mad at God about it? Why or why not?

"No, I'm not mad at God about it, because He has allowed me to see

what a tremendous treasure my virginity is. The more I mature, the more thankful to God I become. And after reading those statistics [on premarital sex's impact on marriage]... I'm actually even more grateful to Him for it!   Leah, 23 years old

"I had my days where I was upset with the Lord and I was mad at my situation and countless days of sexual frustration, and the questions of why can I not have a mate, but this is the bottom line: if God created you then I believe He knows what is best for you."

Walter, 40- something

What Can *You Do*?

Christians used to marry at younger ages, decreasing the length of time they had to cope with sexual temptations. Now, more are remaining single even into their thirties, forties, fifties, and older, naturally grow tired of waiting. If you're one of these singles and have remained pure, you're my hero!

Some Christian singles, after waiting until their late twenties or thirties have been faithful and want to throw in the towel. "I've waited and been faithful, but I'm still not married, so I might as well have sex." It's not about doing to get, but honoring God because of your love relationship with him.

Singles should not feel guilty for wanting sex. God has made us sexual creatures. Having sex has to do with whether we have a license to drive.

If you've had sex before marriage, but you plan on embracing a second virginity until marriage, or if you have always been a virgin, how do you plan on making it happen for you?

It begins with a decision to remain sexually inactive until marriage. If you have previously been active, we'll help with that later in this chapter. Regardless of your sexual history, trying to remain sexually pure until your marriage is no easy task. It is hard work! But it *can* be done! Once you've made your decision, then you must create a game plan. Waiting to have sex until marriage is possible.

I speak from experience, being a technical virgin into my thirties. I use the term, *technical* due to my pornography addiction, which led to my masturbating, but I didn't have sex with a girl until marriage. I was never attracted to guys.

I know there are many pressures out there to have sex, so I'm not going to leave you hanging all alone out there. Here are some practical tips to help keep you pure.

Plan ahead and make a firm decision about how far you can go with kissing and touching without risking falling into a slippery slope and end up having sex. If things get out of hand, be firm and don't give mixed signals.

- *Stay away from tempting situations.* When planning your time together, consider that your environment may put you in compromising situations. If you know that having a candlelit dinner with wine and romantic music in her home will put you in the mood for sex as dessert, then don't do it.

  Ladies, be extremely careful about compromising dating environments, especially right before your menstrual cycle. Women's sex drive increases before their menstrual cycle because of hormonal shifts.

  During this time, be attentive to avoiding situations that put you at risk like being alone in a secluded or seductive place with your date.

- *Look for public or group activities.* They take tremendous pressure off the one-on-one date. Some countries like Brazil encourage group dates until a couple gets serious about each other. More and more online dating services such as Match.com and Meetup.com are promoting group socials. And as we mentioned earlier in our chapter on friends, cultivating friendships with the opposite sex often lowers your sex drive, while also lowering the times of being alone.

  As far as public activities, did you know that an Austrian study found that sunbathing increases a man's sex drive because Vitamin D boosts testosterone levels? Have you noticed that you feel especially "hot" after long hours in the sun? If you're one of these sensitive people, then avoid dates where you're sunbathing or after you've been out a long time under the sun. This may sound like silly advice, but like they say, the devil is in the details.

- *Guard your eyes, which are the keys to your mind. Ladies, help your brothers out by the way you dress. Avoid showing cleavage, wearing short tight skirts, and skin-tight clothing. We guys are responsible for controlling our eyes, but you can help us.*

- To Young Women, From a Young Man:

  "Ladies, do you want to attract a man that will love you for who you ARE and not what you offer? Then cover up! Stop with the booty shorts and low v-necks. You can't trap and capture the true committed man you want by using those methods. Because men of character try to AVOID women showing skin. And honestly the men that give you attention because of your cleavage will most likely

leave you unsatisfied and down in out in a relationship. Also covering up increases a sense of femininity and innocence which men are attracted to MORE in the long run. Promiscuity just brings one-night stands. So there you go, a man's perspective (it takes one to know one). Girls, deep down you know what you're doing and it's a cheap way to get looks. I'm not suiting to "diss." I'm saying this in a constructive manner, to help you get the man you want. Because in order to get the loving man you need, you have to be the respectable woman HE needs. Love you, gals! Live with God."
  -18 yr. old from Colorado, Abstinence Clearinghouse, 9/24/2013

I agree with this young man. While watching a rerun of *Matlock*, a TV series in the 80s and 90s, I noticed that the women dressed in loose-fitting clothes, long dresses, and jackets. I'm not saying you should dress like the 80s, but guys do like mystery. And when women wear stylish clothing that covers more skin, it causes guys to look at their faces and eyes more than their breasts. Which would you prefer?

Cory Schortzman, author of *Out of the Darkness* and a licensed professional counselor in Colorado Springs says, *"The more skin a woman shows, the more wounded she is."*

- **Be aware of your body.** If you have an unexplainable sex drive where you have to have *it* no matter what, consider having your hormones medically tested. An imbalance in hormones for both men and women can cause unexplainable sex drives. Like the great theologian, Dirty Harry, says, *"A man's* [woman's] *gots to know his* [her] *limitations."*

Exercise is a tremendous release and alternative for your sex drive. But be careful about the gyms and times you workout because they can be pick-up places too!

- **Being alone too much or never being exposed** *to the opposite sex can set you on fire more easily.* Imagine some dry brush. It will ignite more quickly the drier it is. As I previously shared, my sexual drive as a single guy decreased the more friendships I made with girls. It helped me see them as people instead of objects for self- gratification.

- **Be accountable.** Find some Godly friends or couples who will hold you accountable for your actions in dating relationships. Not only will you keep them in mind as you make decisions regarding your choices, but they will support and celebrate your courageous stand, even if the secular world ridicules it. You can't do it alone.

- **Have communion before your date.** I find that it strengthens me and increases my intimacy with the Lord. It may help remind individuals during their dates to include the Lord.

- ***Consecrate your singlehood and celibacy to the Lord*** for full-service and deep love and intimacy with him. It's more common in the Catholic Church with priests and nuns, but some in Protestant circles are also subscribing to this lifestyle.

> *"And I will betroth you to Me forever; Yes, I will betroth you to Me in righteousness and in justice, In loving- kindness and in compassion, And I will betroth you to Me in faithfulness. Then you will know the LORD.* Hosea 2:19-20 (NASB)

Misty Edwards, worshiper at the International House of Prayer in Kansas City, is a beautiful thirty-something-year-old who has chosen to neither have sex nor marry. She has set herself apart specifically to minister to the Lord because she loves Jesus with an incredible passion. Like a dove, which has no peripheral vision, her eyes are fully focused on her love for Jesus. Periodically, she revisits this lifestyle with the Lord to see if she's on track, and who knows, maybe someday she may marry. For this to work, I think you have to have a community of like-minded believers that understands and supports this way of life.

Biblical Examples of Abstaining From Sex

Joseph is a single in his late twenties. He is a God-follower. He is being sexually harassed on his new job. Let's see how he handles it. Read the Genesis chapter 39:10ff account below:

> *"And it came about as she spoke to Joseph day after day, that he did not listen to her to lie beside her, or be with her. Now it happened one day that he went into the house to do his work, and none of the men of the household were there inside. And she caught him by his garment, saying, 'Lie with me!' And he left his garment in her hand and fled, and went outside. When she saw that he had left his garment in her hand, and had fled outside, she called to the men of her household and said to them, 'See, he* (Potiphar, her husband) *has brought in a Hebrew to us to make sport of us* (is she a former slave?)*; he came in to me to lie with me, and I screamed. 'And it came about when he heard that I raised my voice and screamed, that he left his garment beside me and fled, and went outside.' So she left his garment beside her until his master came home. Then she spoke to him with these words, 'The Hebrew slave, whom you brought to us, came in to me to make sport of me; and it happened as I raised my voice and screamed, that he left his garment beside me and fled outside.' Now it came about when his master heard the words of his wife, which she spoke to him, saying, 'This is what your slave did to*

me,' that his anger burned (against his wife). *So Joseph's master took him and put him into the jail, the place where the king's prisoners were confined..."* (NASB)

Joseph has a choice to make. He can sleep with his master's wife or he can literally *run* to keep his commitment to God. I imagine his sex drive was up and running. Timothy, in the New Testament, also, a virgin, single, and about thirty years old, is told by Paul, his spiritual mentor, to flee from the temptation of sexual immorality. Reflecting on being in my thirties and a virgin when I was married, I strongly believe that if Joseph hadn't run from Potiphar's wife, he would have succumbed to her temptation. As Christ followers, I don't think we can play with sin, or be *cool* with it either, by telling ourselves that we are mature followers of Christ. I believe Joseph ran because he knew he could fall. Sometimes, we need to run from sin if we're going to win over temptation.

The apostle Paul gives this advice to Timothy, in 2 Timothy 2:22, *"Now flee youthful lusts, and pursue righteousness, faith. . . .."* (NASB). Timothy is told to avoid even the occasion to commit this particular sin. Flee means to literally run or move hastily.

> *"There is a sense in which sexual sins are different from all others. In sexual sin we violate the sacredness of our own bodies, these bodies that were made for God-given and God-modeled love, for 'becoming one' with another. Or didn't you realize that your body is a sacred place, the place of the Holy Spirit?"* 1 Corinthians 6:18-19, The Message

> *He* (Moses) *chose to be mistreated along with the people of God rather than to enjoy the pleasures of sin for a short time.* (Hebrews 11:25)

Not only do you need to understand God's Big Picture regarding sex, you'd *better know* Satan's Big Picture as well. Satan will gladly give us pleasure for a short time in order to *hook* us. He intentionally fails to inform us of the long-term consequences of our actions, such as guilt, shame, feelings of unworthiness, or even a surprise pregnancy, abortion, or socially transmitted disease that could affect your life forever!

If you refuse to accept being sexually harassed on the job, you may lose your job. So life may get tougher for you, but God will be with you in the midst of your injustice. And life may get worse before it gets better. But if you wait on God, when He brings you out on the other side, your past pain won't be able to compare with God's blessings in your new position! Read the rest of Genesis 39 and see how God in His time promotes Joseph and deals with his singleness!

This isn't a guarantee to end your singleness, as much as it is a view of how God often works through injustice and suffering for standing for your values. And that injustice and suffering are often experiences God uses for our spiritual promotions. It helps us see who or what is really first in our lives and it helps us see if we are free or being encumbered by someone or something.

Keeping It Real

I realize some of you did not make the same choice Joseph did. And I'm not condemning anyone. You already know I've messed up.

Even though unmarried couples that are sexually active become physically intimate, it is no guarantee that they are emotionally, intellectually, and spiritually intimate. And it is common for these couples to feel guilt or shame. As I previously mentioned, when counseling these couples, I often watch the majority of girls' mouths drop open when they hear, for the first time, their boyfriends say that, even though they are living together, he isn't totally committed to their relationship. Most of the girls regretfully say, "I thought we'd be married by now." Research reveals that premarital sex is almost the kiss of death to most couples desiring a long-lasting relationship.

When couples have been sexually intimate, the sex tends to cloud their decision-making ability. Some partners will avoid communicating problem issues in order to have sex, even though this couple really needs to learn how to work through conflict. If a couple doesn't learn to work through conflict before marriage, it can be much more devastating in the marriage. Couples that are sexually active have much more intense attachment issues, making it more difficult to break up, even though the couple knows they should.

When you are used to having sex on a regular basis, but you have broken up with your partner, dating can become stressful. A friend I knew in graduate school said he had been sexually active before becoming a Christian. He was dating a virgin. He said there were times she would want to kiss all night, but he had to stop after about ten minutes because as he put it, "Henry was at attention." He said he had an internal fight over not beginning foreplay with this girl, whom he liked very much. He never married this girl, not because of anything she did wrong. He said they simply weren't God's best for each other. He also said he is glad he treated the way her did because he could look in her eyes without regret.

Some of my other Christian friends, who have unintentionally slept with Christian girls, have regretted it. One said to me, "Once I started kissing her, I couldn't stop! It was like a blur! He was sorry he had hurt her and himself as well. Now, he said, "I don't love her, but I feel attached to her. And it is awkward seeing her at church now." The girl had been sexually active before as well. She was a single mom. But she was a Christ follower too and wanted sex as much as he did. She said, "I certainly didn't want or plan for us to have sex. But I am lonely. But this can't happen again!'"

Being a faithful follower of Christ who is not being sexually active is hard work! And all Christ followers who are singles have to make a decision, every day and all daylong: either God is enough or He isn't.

A twenty-five-year-old Christ follower shared a personal situation about his fiancée. She was a college student and Christ follower. She told him, "I want to know what it feels like before marriage." He accommodated her. Both actually demonstrated a lack of faith and trust in God. After they had sex, they both prayed like crazy that she wasn't pregnant when her period was late. They asked me to join them in this prayer. Many Christian singles, like this couple, sadly end up pregnant and have abortions that leave them with deep scars for years, and sometimes for a lifetime. Is premarital sex worth all of this?

Sexual purity reveals your integrity and commitment to God. Will you keep your word, no matter what? Are you trustworthy? If God can't trust you with yourself, why should He trust you with His gift of a spouse?

What If You're Single and Already Had Sex?

God has "good news" for you. God is a God of forgiveness and more chances. So read the following verses from The Message Bible.

> ". . . if we admit our sins—make a clean breast of them— he won't let us down; he'll be true to himself. He'll forgive our sins and purge us of all wrongdoing." (1 John 1:9)

> "As far as sunrise is from sunset, he has separated us from our sins." (Psalm 103:12)

> "No matter how many times you trip them up, God-loyal people don't stay down long; Soon they're up on their feet." (Proverbs 24:16)

> "Forget about what's happened don't keep going over old history. I'm (GOD) about to do something brand- new." (Isaiah 43:18-19)

> "But I (GOD), yes I, am the one who takes care of your sins—that's what I do. I don't keep a list of your sins." (Isaiah 43:25)

So based on the verses above, God is the God of second, third, fourth, fifth, and countless chances. Therefore, if you have given away your virginity, God will give you another opportunity for virginity. So it is not too late for you. You can heal from and receive closure from previous sexual encounters.

Second Virginity is a term for those who have been sexually active in the past, but have asked God for forgiveness and have committed to remain, from this point on, sexually pure until their marriage.

Why am I talking to you about sexually purity?: (1) emotional and spiritual devastation accompany sexual intercourse before marriage; (2) sex before marriage lowers your ability to commit to a lifelong marriage; (3) sex before marriage increases your chances of divorce; and (4) sadly, in our society today, many once-divorced people aren't just remarrying once and that is it. They are often now marrying and divorcing three to four times because the ability to stay committed diminishes more and after each divorce and being sexually active before marriage.

Breaking Up After Sex

Telling many singles, even those professing to be followers of Christ, not to have sex before marriage, doesn't make me popular with them. Often they ask, why, which is a fair question. I tell them that if they like or love the one they are sleeping with and marry that person, research reveals that such couples actually have much less sex after marriage due to trust issues. And that according to government research and my own thirty-plus years of relationship counseling, most of these couples break up before marriage; and of the couples that do marry, most of them divorce or struggle staying married, which often includes affairs.

I share all of this before even addressing the additional problems, such as guilt and unworthiness that those followers of Christ have because they are sexually active.

Breaking up after sex can have all of the issues mentioned above but with much more complicated circumstances due to the emotional, physical, and spiritual bonding, to which some refer to as *soul ties*[4]. These ties make it more difficult to make objective relationship decisions. As mentioned earlier, this is one reason some women will stay in an abusive relationship. They have bonded and now have a soul tie to that person, even if he isn't the right person for her. What is a soul tie? The Bible often speaks of relationships in which our hearts are bonded or "knit together." We see this in Colossians 2:2, *"that their hearts may be encouraged, having been knit together in love"* (NASB). We use the term "bond." There can be soul ties with sexual partners regardless of their marital status. Soul ties in the context of marriage are to help a couple be monogamous by bonding their spirits together. Genesis 2:24 supports this when it says, *"For this reason a man will leave his father and mother to be united* (knitted, bonded) *to his wife, and they will become one flesh* (sexual intimacy)."

Woman wasn't created from the dust of the earth, but from Adam's rib, because she was formed for an inseparable unity of fellowship and life with the man, according to the Commentary of the Old Testament. Sexual intercourse is actually to be a physical expression of this inward commitment—the knitting together of emotions, intellects, and spirits.

Because of this bonding of spirits, it appears to be more difficult to bring closure and healing to a break-up after the couple has experienced physical intimacy than it is for those couples who haven't been sexually intimate.

Relationships naturally bring some wounding and hurting, but much of it usually unintentional. With the increase in casual sex before marriage, it is tougher to overcome these wounds and move forward. Once you have sex with someone, even though it's casual, you're connected forever both spiritually (soul ties) and physically (cellular memory).

Do you have soul ties from your past and want to destroy these ties? Some of you are thinking, *Jesus has forgiven me of all my sins,* and this is true. But we still have to deal with the consequences of our sins. For example, a boy gets a girl pregnant. Suppose they both become followers of Christ and ask for forgiveness. Jesus forgives them, but the girl is still pregnant and the boy is still the father of that unborn child. And Jesus loves them, but this couple still has to make a life-changing decision.

If you would like to break your soul ties, then please pray the following prayer:

Dear Heavenly Father,

Thank You for your unconditional love and mercy and for your Son Jesus Christ who died and rose from the dead so that I might have abundant life. I am sorry for having offended you by having sex before marriage with (name of partner). *Please forgive me and have mercy on me. I renounce and sever all ties, physically, spiritually and emotionally with* (name of partner) *in the name of Jesus. By the power of the blood of Jesus, I cancel all evil assignments against me because of my sin. In Jesus' name, I shut every opening to* (name of partner) *and to the enemy, and I appropriate the blood of Jesus over my body, emotions, mind, and spirit that were touched by this act. I speak blessings over my relationships and I commend them into your heart. Help me to live in your perfect and pure love. In Jesus' Name. Amen.*

Praying this prayer can change your life and eliminate much of your baggage that you would have taken into your next relationship. Thus, you are much healthier for a new relationship or in a better place if you remain single.

For those of you who prayed this prayer to break your soul ties, there is a *Purity Covenant* for you on my website: www.clarenceshuler.com. It's a free download; just click on the bookstore tab.

What You Need to Know About Marriage and Sex

Some of you singles erroneously think, *"If I could just get married."* Some of you think, *"If I could just have sex before I die."* Just getting married or having sex won't solve any of your problems. In fact, if you get this order wrong, it creates many problems.

But let me let you in on an amazing issue for married couples. Increasingly, more and more married couples aren't having sex! Approximately ten years ago, while speaking at a predominantly white men's retreat, for the first time, I encountered a husband who hadn't had sex for nearly a year! Totally freaked me out! I couldn't imagine it. And naively, I thought this was a cultural issue applicable primarily to white couples. But now, I counsel black guys whose wives haven't slept with them in a year! WOW!!

In fact, one of my friends said that if you want to stop singles from having sex outside of marriage—give them blood transfusions from married couples because married couples ain't having sex. So while singles are trying to have sex, married couples are having less sex—why? They're not friends and have disconnected emotionally, intellectually, and spiritually, which makes connecting physically extremely difficult. It is almost impossible for these couples to have mutually satisfying sex because it is a celebration of oneness—being connected. *So you can have sex with anybody, but it does take three people to make love—God, your spouse, and you.* This quote of Dr. Johnny Parker is making more and more sense. God is into relationships. Sex in the framework of marriage helps solidify them.

And no, God isn't blessing unmarried Christian couples having sex because God can't bless sin. On the contrary, He will discipline those who are having sex before marriage because He loves them.

And as long as we carry all this invisible baggage inside, it's difficult to let anyone else in. We're so full of our past. Maybe that's what's causing the epidemic of people living alone and not getting married?

Conclusion

I can't believe I'm saying this, but I'm tired of talking about sex. Hopefully, you see why God is so into sex. And hopefully, it should be an experience you look forward to having with the right person in the context of marriage. But it should not dominate your life, making you feel less-than or not loved by God. You've got to understand and embrace the fact that God's Best for you is always ***RIGHT NOW!*** If God knows the number of hairs on your head, and if He knows all of your days, then He knows what's best for you, because He LOVES YOU!

SUMMARY POINTS

1. Having sexual desires is natural.

2. Since having sexual desires is natural, we should not feel guilty for wanting to have sex.

3. Sexual intercourse is only for the context of marriage.

4. God loves sex and created it for our pleasure.

5. God wants married couples to have sex on a regular basis.

6. Sex before marriage can destroy your relationships.

7. God does forgive premarital sex and can give you a Second Virginity.

8. You can be healed of sexual wounds.

9. Struggling to keep your virginity or second virginity is hard work, but doable.

10. Other professing Christ followers might think you are crazy for being sexually inactive.

11. There are examples of people in today's culture and in the Bible who defeated sexual temptations.

ACTION POINTS

1. Do you remember your first introduction to your sex drive? Hopefully, it wasn't abusive. How did it make you feel?

2. If you are a Christ follower, if your parents told you that you couldn't have sex, how did it make you feel? Why do you think you felt the way you did?

3. Why do you think the church offers so little help for singles, whether teenagers, college students, married couples, or divorcees with singles' sex issues?

4. How do you feel about the fact that God created and encourages sex? Does this change your perspective of God? If so, why?

5. Why do you choose to be celibate or sexually active?

6. How do you feel about God's design for sex? Do you see this act the way it is designed as beautiful between a man and a woman? Why or why not?

7. Does God's design for sex make it worth waiting for you? Why or why not?

8. If you had sex before or outside of marriage, did your expectations match the reality of your sexual encounter? How did you feel about your experience after it was over?

9. Consider committing to and signing the Purity Covenant that you can download from my website: www.clarenceshuler.com

Chapter Eight

Taking Some of the BluR Out of Dating

"Do not be anxious for anything, but in everything, by prayer and petition, with thanksgiving, present your requests to God. And the peace of God, which transcends all understanding, will guard your hearts and minds in Christ Jesus." Philippians 4:6-7 (NIV)

Dating over the years has seemingly become more confusing, leaving many singles with lots of questions: *What's the right way to date? Should I date if I'm a Christian? What's the use of dating anyway?*

Some singles feel that dating is such a mess that they've given up on dating. Trying to have romantic relationships with the opposite sex can be an emotional roller coaster even at an early age.

Why all the anxiety about dating? Let's begin with some of the fears associated with it.

For Guys: *Fear of Rejection and Ridicule*

Do you remember your junior high days? If you are a guy, do you recall that girls seemed to run in herds, like cattle or horses, making it difficult for a guy to start a conversation with a girl who was in a group?

Guys, ever reminisce about the middle school, high school, or college parties, when you had to make that dreaded walk across the room from the safety of *you boys* to ask a girl for a dance? She was hanging with her girls. Inevitably, one of her girlfriends spotted you coming. Then, they all turned inward toward each other, giggling as you approached. By then, it was *too* late to turn back because everyone in the room was watching! You saw the girl with whom you wanted to dance. You tried not looking at her, but you couldn't help but stare at her more, the closer you got. All the girls knew exactly who you were going to ask. Again they turned into a circle, laughing as they asked her, "Are you going to dance with him?" The tone of their question informed the girl of their approval, rejection, or if she had options. Thus, her personal preference may be overridden by peer pressure. Her group often determined if you'd get the dance.

Finally, you arrived. Walking across the room seemed like it took two hours, but it was only seconds. You had to ask this girl for a dance in front of all of her friends and everybody else. If her answer was "yes," you earned *cool points.* If her answer was "no," you lost *cool points,* and risked not dancing the rest of that night, as everyone took their cues from this group's response to you. Even more difficult than asking this girl for a dance in front of her girls was the long walk back to your homeboys if she turned you down.

For Ladies: *Horror Stories and Broken Hearts*

Myrna tells me that lots of women complain that guys these days don't know how to behave on a date. "I've sat among many women with incredibly laughable stories about what guys did on a date," she said.

"One guy, after dinner, took me to see the site where the killing of O.J. Simpson's wife took place, then offered to take me to the cemetery where celebrities are buried," Myrna said laughingly. "Another one scheduled our second date at the same place (Starbucks), at the same time. When my blood sugar started dropping because it was dinnertime, I told him I needed to eat something because I felt faint. He then walked me to my car and I rushed to the nearest restaurant and ate by myself!" she added. Either this guy had *no* money or was very tight with it!

If you're a gal, you'll also recognize this line after what seemed like a great date, or even a relationship: "I'll call you." Then, you never heard from him again. That's what happened to Irma, who had been going out with a guy for a few months. He wanted to introduce her to his family on Father's Day, so she baked a pie as a gift for the family, but he never showed up or called her back.

How Did Dating Get So Confusing?

Research done by the Healthy Marriage Initiative in 2004 provides a brief overview of *courting* and mate selection. We will focus only on courting.

In the sixteenth century, courting was defined as "to pay amorous attention to; to woo (Jeffrey Osborne—*You Should Be Mine-The Woo Woo Song*), with a view to marriage." There were also various expected rituals and manners. Withholding sex, whether you were religious or not, was anticipated. Couples' energy was directed toward admiration, longing, and devotion, which are foundational for a long-lasting relationship or marriage. *In the 1920s*, a man came "calling" to a woman's home.

Back then it was common for single women to live at home until married. One of the reasons was to protect her reputation and physical body, a role of her father, who would approve and screen potential suitors.

"These home-centered activities required men to have conversational skills and manners, but not necessarily lots of money." Beth Bailey, *From Porch to Back Seat*

As our society changed or *progressed*, so did the way men and women approached each other in their premarital interactions.

Courting was replaced with *calling.* In the early 1900s there was the rise of urban centers. Women became more independent of parents, fathers in particular, and men in general. These independent women were described as *"She had her hat on,* indicating she was a single woman who had moved out of her parents' house to town to her own place and space.

Men's money then became the basis of the dating system. Lower classes had no place to court and no money to *take a girl out.* Going to a girl's home didn't require money. Often the guy got a free dinner, usually cooked by the girl, demonstrating one of her potential wifely skills. By then, the upper classes had the freedom from the restrictions of courting—less need to worry about manners or being approved of, especially by the girl's father. Some women lost the protection of their fathers, and some probably escaped abusive ones.

The Healthy Marriage Initiative's research terms the change from *courting* to *calling* as *transforming power dynamics.* These dynamics resulted in loss of father's protection, possibly fewer men of character, but wealthier men for dating, and lower requirements for men entering premarital interactions. This also created greater freedom for youth because there was less parental involvement and control. With *calling,* men only had to "win" the woman's favor, not her father's or mother's. In *calling,* the man would still go to the woman's apartment or house.

Calling changed to *dating.* With dating, men were expected to initiate the date. In the age of courting, a father or mother could initiate this process. The Healthy Marriage Initiative states, "The emphasis turned to the man's economic success over wit, intelligence, and character because the poor couldn't afford to date, resulting in the *commercialization of mate selection.*"

According to the article, *Limitations of Modern Dating,* adapted from J. Harris, 1997, *I Kissed Dating Goodbye,* there are now radical changes and consequences from yesterday's courting to today's dating:

- Process largely excludes parental wisdom.

- Sex no longer a "benefit" of marriage (lessening the ability to commit, bond and be monogamous—simultaneously increasing promiscuity).

- Leads to intimacy, not necessarily commitment.

- Places romance over friendship (reversing a foundational relationship order).

- Dating as recreation rather than mate selection.

With the advent of the feminist movement in the 1960s, traditional relationship roles between men and women began to evolve, leaving many singles confused. Because of the social climate and the absence of fathers, some men became more passive. Meanwhile, women assumed more leadership roles in the workplace and at home as single moms, and thus became more dominant in some relationships.

Confusion in men's and women's roles has spilled over into relationships. Men today struggle more with how to treat a woman. This often results in unintentionally being more passive or appearing to show less respect for women, who want to be treated as equals to men in the workplace, yet still be treated like women outside of it. It's very confusing for guys.

Likewise, women are also confused about their roles in a seemingly decrease of "strong men" willing to take the lead in initiating relationships or taking responsibility for fathering. As of 2011, 11.7 million families in the United States were headed by a single parent, 85.2 percent of which were headed by a female[1]. To make matters worse, studies show that testosterone, the hormone responsible for masculine behaviors, has been on the decline in men for decades[2].

Our God is not about confusion. He wants you to know your true identity and that only flows out of your intimacy with Jesus.

Are There Any Biblical Guidelines For Dating? If Yes, What Are They?

The Bible doesn't specifically address dating. During the days the Bible was being written, parents arranged marriages that seemed to work out well for their children, and dating was non-existent. There was no such thing as dating or falling in love in the Bible. Falling in love before marriage wasn't a major consideration, as most biblical marriages were arranged. Love occurred after the wedding. Genesis 24:67 says, *"Isaac brought her into the tent of his mother Sarah, and married Rebekah. So she became his wife, and he loved her . . . ."*

This concept appears to continue to work in some cultures. Believe it or not, according to the latest research, over 90 percent of marriages in

India are still arranged, with only a 5 percent divorce rate. Research reveals that arranged marriages are on the rise in America because of immigrant populations. (Source: http://www.statisticbrain.com/arranged-marriage-statistics/)

Americans by and large believe in finding soul mates. So, most Americans would object to marriage arranged by their parents. In our Western culture, falling in love is more of an emotional state of closeness that can be triggered by sight or a kiss.

While the Bible doesn't specifically speak about dating, it does contain biblical principles that are critical to establishing relationships that glorify God. The following verses reveal foundational relationship truths. In the New Testament, 2 Corinthians 6:14 reads, *"Don't become partners with those who reject God...Is light best friends with dark"* (The Message)? The truth of this verse is not that followers of Christ are better than non-followers, but that for the sake of unity in the relationship, Christ followers should not be joined together with spiritual opposites, with partners who are spiritually incompatible (non-believers), because it could result in spiritual disaster, loneliness, and conflict in such issues as raising children. This principle begins with whom we date.

What If You're Not Dating?

For some, the question is: To date or not to date? I don't think it is wrong to date or not to date. Years ago when the popular book *I Kissed Dating Good-bye,* was written, I heard many singles— including young adults in their twenties—say they wouldn't date until it's the "one." How will they know it's the *one*? *It is because they have been friends*, they said. *Why expose yourself to those who aren't meant to be your spouse* they added.

Years ago, when I was working with teenagers in a local mega church, one girl who was a follower of Christ said she wasn't going to date until she met the man she was going to marry. As captain of the cheerleading squad at a high school of over 2,000 students, she could have dated any guy, but she chose not to. She did meet a guy at our church camp, and he is the only person she ever dated. And they've been married over thirty-five years and have adult children!

I, on the other hand, dated a lot before marriage. I've been married to the same woman for nearly thirty years and have three wonderful adult daughters. So there doesn't appear to be one particular formula, except seeking the will of God.

Remember, if you are a follower of Christ, you *are complete* and don't have to be in a relationship. Also remember, if you aren't content being single, you probably won't be content in a dating relationship or marriage. We should not *need* a date or a spouse, but desiring one is quite normal.

Dating isn't the only avenue in which to meet or get to know someone for a potential romantic relationship. Sometimes, a romantic relationship can grow from friendships in shared activities at church, work, or other common-interest groups. Eventually though, you will have to be intentional about your goals in those relationships.

If you're confused about whether you should date, seek God on this. He may want you to fast from dating for a season, especially after a break up, so you can heal; or the Lord might want you to immerse yourself in something else until He brings you someone without dating. Only He knows, so ask Him.

Being Intentional

People frequently share their dating frustrations with me. Typically I ask them, "What was your game plan?" Stunned, they often give me this "Dating isn't a game" look. And dating certainly isn't a game. But did you have a goal for dating? If not, why not? "I never thought about it," is the usual response. "Why," I inquire. "Weren't you specific about whom you wanted to date?

When the date would be? Didn't you have a place or event planned?" Usually, the response is yes. "So if you were this specific, why not have a goal for your dating?" I ask this to make them think.

If you are not intentional, it may create confusion about whether it's a date. High school and college students "hang" together with blurred lines in their status. When you don't know if you're on a date, the awkwardness sets in especially, when the issue of who pays for the meal comes up.

Myrna shared her blurry "Is-it-a-date?" experience. "I met a parole officer at a Christian event and shared that I was working on a crime-related topic for a TV show. The next day he called and said I could go with him to a youth boot camp to shoot some footage for my show. Naturally, I thought it was business related. However, as he drove me to the camp, I suddenly began to feel that he was interested in me. When we got there, he pulled out a lunch he had prepared for us. He later started calling and asking me out."

For many guys, being one-on-one with a girl is a date. My rule of thumb is, assume nothing, ask questions about everything. Remember, communication is to relationships what location is to real estate! It takes the guesswork out of the equation and eliminates a lot of drama. When one or both individuals are too shy, afraid, or insecure to ask, it can cause confusion. In my racial culture, most girls will tell you up front whether having dinner or attending an event together is a date.

So, if the Lord is calling you to date, consider answering the following questions before your next date. It will be helpful to you and your prospective date:

What Is Your Purpose for Dating?

Initially, this may seem like a silly question. But before dismissing it, be honest with yourself. Why do you want to date? Is it because you feel everyone else is dating and you don't want to be considered odd or strange? Or do you want to date because you are lonely? None of these are good reasons for dating and may lead you into an unsatisfying dysfunctional relationship. But if you think spending time with a particular person could be fun, go for it! Dating probably has different purposes for different people. For teenagers, a date may be to get to know someone that you like a lot, with no immediate thoughts of engagement, marriage, or even a long-term dating relationship.

For me, a date was a one-on-one event to confirm a girl liked me and that we could get along and have some fun. It could be for doing certain activities with certain girls. For example, there were girls I dated in college who needed no advance notice to go on a date and weren't concerned with what we were going to do—see a movie or go to a concert. They were the adventurous types who trusted me. Naturally, there were those who wanted to be asked out a week in advance.

Basically, for me if it was a girl and she was breathing, she was a candidate for a date.

Dating for me in high school and college was an opportunity to get to know the opposite sex—learn about girls. It was about becoming more comfortable being around them—less nervous, so I could actually talk to the ones to whom I was really attracted. Dating in school was just about having fun, some exploration—kissing, hugging, and being able to carry on a conversation. There were those few couples that actually met the love of their life in high school and got married.

College was more of the same, but the stakes seemed to be higher because everyone was older, thus closer to marriage. The older you get, the more dating becomes an opportunity to learn what you like and don't like about the opposite sex and begin identifying a life partner. I'm not sure if I have a problem with dating as recreation or fun, that doesn't require a serious commitment. Certainly, I'm not implying that individuals have fun at their dates' expense. And maybe this is one problem with today's dating because it is defined differently by males and females, and also based on our various backgrounds. Possibly, our differing dating definitions could result in unintentionally or sadly perhaps intentionally, one individual wounding another on a date.

Dating is one of the occasions where mutual respect should reign, but many end up brokenhearted. While society elevates dating, few singles are equipped to have healthy relationships. Many haven't healed from either childhood or relational wounds and end up hurting others while dating.

Dating can be a tremendous source of joy and excitement, but for some, it can sometimes be devastating.

Regardless of your reasons for wanting to date, be intentional about it. Do you want to explore a romantic relationship but are not ready to marry? Be clear with yourself first, before you date. Then, be clear with your date.

Do you want your dates to like you? They probably already do to some extent (or else they wouldn't go out with you), unless it is a blind date. Do you want to establish a long-term relationship? Do you want your date to be a better person and potential long-term relationship partner for having dated you? Dating you should benefit whoever dates you, whether you marry them or not because of your character, integrity, sensitivity, and your faith in Christ if you follow Him. Is dating just a game, to see whom you can get to go out with you? Do you just want sex and no long-term relationship? If these last two reasons are your motivation for dating —don't do it—you may cause irreparable emotional damage to yourself and your date.

In the old days, fathers used to ask the guys courting their daughters, "What are your intentions?" So, be clear and open about your intentions, and it will save you lots of confusion and heartache.

Men's and Women's Dating Perspectives

Women's Perspective:

It may seem obvious, but maybe dating is different for men than for women at different ages. For many women out of college, the determining factor for going on a date could depend on whether a guy is marriage material. If she's not interested in marriage, dating can be for fun *(sharing similar interests or activities)*, wanting to be in a relationship, or getting to know how to relate to the opposite sex.

Men's Perspective:

Certainly, I can't speak for all men, but most men I know, especially when we were in high school or college, asked out girls we thought were pretty. If they said yes, it was a date.

What kept me interested in the girl was her personality and character. Her good looks didn't hurt. But I did go out with some very attractive girls whose ugly character was so bad that it overshadowed her physical beauty! Be clear about this: guys want to be in relationships! Girls may not know this, due to the stereotyping of guys.

Do You Consult God About Your Dating?

Or do you just go for the cutest-looking one? Do you pray about whom you ask or accept for a date? Do you think God cares about you, whom you date, and if you date? Are you considering God's will in your dating? Genesis 24:1-4 reads:

> *"Abraham was now an old man. God had blessed Abraham in every way. Abraham spoke to the senior servant in his household, the one in charge of everything he had. 'Put your hand under my high and swear by God— God of Heaven, God of Earth—that you will not get a wife for my son from among the young women of the Canaanites (non-followers of God) here, but will go to the land of my birth and get a wife for my son Isaac"* (The Message).

It seems the principle here is that Abraham, the father, is praying for his son's future wife. The biblical application here is that we should pray for our future dates. We should also get our family and friends to pray for our future dating as well. Pray for what? How about praying for wisdom, character, emotional health, or other qualities you like. You could pray that, no matter how attracted you are to your date, God will help you discern His best for you.

What Attracts You to the Opposite Sex?

Certainly this varies with people. Guys tend to be more visual *(face, smile, anatomy, the way she walks, etc.)*, which doesn't insinuate girls are blind. Both genders are usually physically attracted to each other. But be careful about how you talk about the opposite sex. It shouldn't be like you are ordering fast food at McDonald's or Chick-Fil-A: "Gimme a breast, thigh, and butt."

Women tend to be more holistic, being more concerned with a guy's character, mannerisms, and other qualities. Typically for women, visual stimuli does not get the same priority that guys give it, but good grooming and looks are a plus. For us guys, the visual gets our attention, but the girl's character—her inner beauty—is what usually keeps us in the relationship. Some women tell me that they are attracted to intelligent or athletic guys, while others say that a guy who is rooted in the Lord is attractive. For both men and women, someone who exudes confidence is certainly attractive.

What attracts *you* may not necessarily be what you are attracting. If you are a strong, independent woman, chances are you'll attract a guy who is not as strong as you. Remember, there are some "mama's boys" who are looking for a mom, and a dominating woman is a great attraction for these guys. If you're needy and dreaming of Mr. or Mrs. Right, you might draw in an abusive person instead.

In order to attract your "ideal" partner, you need to become a person who will attract that person. Confidence in your masculinity or femininity will more likely bring someone into your life that is more compatible.

Guys who are successful, especially financially, often find themselves targeted by women. So they must have wisdom to make sure a woman wants them for who they are and not what they have.

How to be Dateable

As previously mentioned several times, an essential indication you are healthy and ready to date or are dateable is that you need to like yourself. You embrace self-worth, not self-worship. You understand that you are complete in Christ—not lacking as an individual. Often, I say, *Don't seek to find God's Best, **concentrate on being God's Best** because God is not going to send **His Best** to **mess**!*

If you've had emotional struggles from your childhood or previous relationships, I hope that you've sought counsel and are working out your issues. If you have been in dysfunctional relationships, do you know what role you played and why? How did it end, or are you still in it emotionally? If you haven't stopped to assess what role you played and learned and changed from it, and don't know how to prevent it, then you are probably not ready to date. If you do, you'll continue attracting the same kind of dysfunctional people or hurting others along the way.

If you have a fear of dating, it can be a signal of deeply buried wounds that God wants to heal.

Another dateable characteristic is that you aren't desperate. Yes, you desire to be in a relationship, but your world doesn't rise or fall based on whether you are in a relationship.

Become interesting! Will you freeze if your potential date asks you what you like to do for fun? If you go from work to home every day and to church on Sundays, what do you have to offer for fun to your potential date? Yes, fun is important, so find a hobby or get involved in sports or some activity. What are you passionate about—in addition to God? This is part of knowing who you are.

Desiring to date is a fundamental dateable characteristic. Potential dates can sense your energy. A time-tested method of informing potential dates of your availability is *flirting*. Flirting can be appropriate as well as inappropriate. I think respectful flirting is quite natural. Making eye contact, winking, smiling, and saying appropriate words to the opposite sex can be fun, letting both of you know if you like each other.

Since many Christian singles are careful of the "sex" issue, some might shut down their "signals" toward the opposite sex, not flirting or thinking about being dateable. Unfortunately, some religious and Christian leaders may tell you flirting is a sin. I disagree. Have you ever seen a ten-year-old boy doing cartwheels to impress a girl? He was flirting. Most girls are excellent flirts, especially with their eyes. As a follower of Christ, the Holy Spirit will let you know if you are crossing the line. That is one of His jobs.

The other extreme is the message that pop culture tells women: expose EVERYTHING physically to attract men. It implies that this is what guys want. Is that really what guys want? Ladies, if you expose your body, most guys are going to look. But don't confuse staring and lusting for affection. Exposing a lot of cleavage or nudity (sexting, for example) sends a message that you are easy for possibly a one-night stand, but not a long-term relationship. It also communicates that you don't respect yourself, so why should the guy? Maybe the most damaging thought it communicates is that you will do anything for this guy. Is this what you really want?

Being yourself is an attractive and necessary dateable feature you need to display. Such behavior helps you and your potential date in decision-making about dating and a potential relationship. Trying to be someone else to impress another person is difficult, uncomfortable, and dishonest. What do you do when the *real you* accidently slips out or you just get tired of playing a role? What will your date do, especially if you have established a relationship?

In order to date, you have to intentionally set up time in your schedule, because relationships take a lot of time and work. When someone sighs, "I'm so busy!" then complains about loneliness or not dating, it's time to re-evaluate their priorities. In her 30's, Ana was intentional about marrying so she quit her job as a vice president in a public relations agency and became a freelancer to open up her time for Mr. Right. She is now married with three lovely daughters. Typically, guys aren't going to leave their jobs to focus on finding their mate, but some women are willing to do this.

What Do You Usually Want To Happen When You Date?

What qualifies as a good date is a subjective question, depending on the couple. If two individuals find each other attractive, enjoy each other's company, sense of humor, have similar values, goals, and the like, that sounds like a good date. And if their differences also create an attraction to the extent they want to see each other again, then I would say this qualifies as a good date, too.

Asking For a Date

Guys, if you want to avoid the experience mentioned in the first paragraphs of this chapter, then devise a plan to cut the one you want out of the herd. You may have to catch her doing something by herself, like going for refreshments, or returning from the restroom. If you have a girl who is a good friend, she may be able to help you with this. Or you might want to approach her later, away from the party in the hallway at school, or at the library, or walking to her car. I'm not suggesting stalking—don't be everywhere she is. And don't be desperate.

Outside of this scenario, you can either call her or go to where you know she hangs out and ask her, "Do you think you'd like to go out sometime?" Or, if you know she has an interest in certain foods or activities, invite her to that. Her interest will peak, and you'll simultaneously show her that you care about and share her interests.

How to Act On a Date

Guys on my dorm floor, in college, particularly the athletes, would have their girlfriends come watch them play "pick-up" basketball games. I watched these girls who were bored out of their minds. I always thought that it was incredibly selfish to have your girl come watch you for a meaningless game! To me, it was the height of arrogance. I was arrogant, too. I was just in denial, but I never did that.

One guy, who considered himself to be a lady's man, approached me the next day after one of my dates. He said, "She said you were the best date she has ever had! What did you do?" I thought to myself, "What I always do. I asked her questions about herself without it making like an interview—such as: "Tell me what brought you to Moody Bible Institute? What is your major and why? How and why did you become a Christian? Tell me about your family?" I made sure the conversation was all about her, not me or basketball. I made sure she laughed and had fun. Naturally, I reciprocated if and when she questioned me. Then, when I was taking her back to the dorm, I always stopped, not to get a kiss, but to pray for and with her. I didn't pray on every date with the same girl, but I usually did on a first date. I thanked her for the date and then went to my dorm.

How should you act on a date? Treat your date with respect, be attentive to the other person's needs and be genuinely interested in learning more about them by asking questions. This applies to dates where you discover that you don't have romantic feelings for this individual.

A Word to Guys

Guys, as you date, focus on treating your dates well. This will usually inspire them to respect you, which is critical for you as you initiate the relationship. I believe your date should be better for having dated you, even if she isn't *the one*. Understand that biblical leadership is about serving. Serving is a choice. I'm not suggesting you be a doormat. One way of serving is spending most of the date time listening to her, not talking about you. Let her do most of the talking. This allows you to get to know her priorities, dreams, values, and lets you know if you want another date with her. Look for women of character who want to be with you but who don't need you for their survival. Her character will be reflected in how she dresses. Even though most guys would love to see as much cleavage as possible because they are turned on by sight, the less cleavage your date shows, the better for her and you.

Her relationship with her dad will help you see her commitment, loyalty, and respect for a man. If you are a Christ follower, then you need to initiate (not preach) the spiritual aspects of the date. Pray for the food and thank God in her presence for your time together. This will also help prepare guys who are followers of Christ to become spiritual leaders, which most female Christians want in their guy. Being the spiritual leader in a relationship isn't equivalent to being a dictator. Leadership is always about serving and sacrificing.

Guys, a woman's impression of you starts with how you dress. Even if you ask her out to lunch, please don't show up in shorts! A woman will even notice the fine details you've gone through for her, like taking a shower, wearing a nice shirt, how you smell, and washing your car for the date. Open doors as a sign you are serving her. If she responds with a feminist line, tell her you were just showing her how much you respect her. Ask what kind of food she likes so you can pick a restaurant accordingly and make reservations. If you already know you like her, consider bringing her a rose. Make her feel special when she is with you. Myrna tells me that a guy once won her heart because he wrote her poems. Women like to be romanced, pursued, and made to feel special.

As a Southern boy, I always made sure that my date got home safely. In these changing times, guys often meet their dates at a certain location, which is a safety ploy many single women are wisely using. Often on a first date, a single woman may not want you to know where she lives, due to stalking or safety precautions. A simple, "Call me when you get back home with your doors locked," will go a long way with a woman as you indicate your concern for her safety.

Guys, during the date, don't feel you have to force things. Try to let things happen naturally. Usually, good dates flow. They have rhythm. If the date doesn't flow, but you like her, try for a second date. If the second date is awkward, I'd just ask her how she feels. She may feel the same way. If you're not sure if you'd like to see her again, do not tell her you will call her. She will actually expect and wait for you to call and may get hurt. It's best not to say anything if you're not sure.

A Word to the Ladies

Ladies, this is probably a double standard, but most guys don't want you to call to see if he made it home safely. If you call him immediately after the date that night, he will think you really like him or are needy.

Ladies, guys love it when you treat them with respect and don't verbally compare them with your other dates. Ask him questions, smile, and be grateful for him treating you to dinner or whatever else you do.

Men are visual, so exposing a lot of skin in tight spandex may lead your date to misinterpret it as a sexual invitation. There are many feminine, stylish clothes that not only increase your attractiveness, but also enhance your mystery, which is attractive to guys because they love the "hunt."

If you're a businesswoman dating on a weekday, wearing your corporate suit and talking all about your work may put up a wall between you and your date. In the book, *Captivating*, John and Stasi Eldredge refer to three types of women: dominating, desolate, and alluring. "The dominating woman," they write, "refuses to be vulnerable...kills her heart's longing for intimacy so that she will be safe and in control." It's tough to switch from a businesswoman in charge to a dating situation where you share your true feminine self.

The desolate woman, on the other hand, is needy and desperate for love but hides behind busyness, spirituality, or even baggy clothes. If this is you, try role-playing before your date with friends to build up your confidence, but more importantly, seek counsel to help you identify your root issues for this false identity.

According to the book, the alluring woman is a woman at rest, not striving, and comfortable in her feminine beauty. So on a date, be pleasant, confident in your femininity, a good listener, and enjoy the moment. Adventure is good for the soul! Remember, not every guy is perfect for YOU, but he may be the best for someone else, so treat him with respect.

As you date, are the men in your life protecting you from negative elements such as people who say unflattering things about you, which may even include you? Does he provide for you? I'm not just talking about taking you to nice places to eat. For example, does he create a "safe place" for you, so you can talk about anything with him? And you shouldn't want him to spend a lot of money on you before marriage. But does he provide emotional security for you so you can bloom and blossom? Is he the kind of guy with servant-leadership (not dictatorship) you would be willing to follow? Leadership doesn't translate into not having any input from you.

Reading some of the horror dating stories, I see many women have been bruised by men. There is no place for verbal or physical abuse in relationships. I realize that because of the feminist movement, which shifted male and female roles, guys may not treat you as well as you would like because they are trying to keep from discriminating against you as a female. So he may not open doors for you, or help you out of the car (if he drives), and he may expect you to pay for your dinner. If this isn't how you like to be treated, set your standards with him.

If he has unresolved wounds, he just may not be as sensitive to you and your needs. That may be your alarm bell to run through the exit door!

Debriefing

What is the gift from this date? What did you learn about yourself? Did you learn anything new that improves your life? What didn't you like about how you or he acted? What did you like? Did the date dig up old wounds of fear of rejection or abandonment, or did it resemble your negative dating pattern? If so, maybe the date was a catalyst for you to seek healing. Remember, no matter how the date went, you want to protect your date's reputation. Evaluate how you felt about the date and why. Will you see that person again? Why or why not?

Ladies, After Your Date:

Please don't live for the phone call. If a guy doesn't call you in a few days after your date, let him go. If he doesn't realize what a great lady you are, then, he is missing out. But don't waste so much time regretting or feeling rejected because he didn't call you back.

For some guys, saying, "I'll call you," is simply a nicer way of saying goodnight; but it doesn't mean anything to the guy and definitely not a commitment of any kind! Saying, "I'll call you," to some guys is like the greeting, "How are you doing?" Most of us, male and female, when we say this, it is merely a surface greeting. Few of us, really want to know in detail how the other person is doing. Ladies, in the future, it may be wise to receive "I'll call you," in the same manner.

Please don't think like some girls who believe that all this prospective boyfriend or spouse needs is a direct or indirect push from you. If you do, you may be pushing him for the life of the relationship or marriage. What is an indirect push? It is getting one of your date's guy friends to push your date your direction. Don't become a slave to this situation. Remember your self-worth.

Guys, After Your Date:

Please don't end your date promising to call her. The way most women, certainly not all, are wired is that they seem to live and die waiting for that "promised" phone call. Even if you are trying to be nice, you actually unintentionally cause more pain. If you do promise to call—then call! It isn't a commitment, but it seriously reflects on your character.

Guys if you have no interest to pursue a relationship with your date, be polite, sensitive, yet do not lead her on in any way. Be as sensitive to your date as you would want someone to be with your sister if you have one or your female relatives. This is an act of kindness.

Alicia Keys epitomizes the agony many girls experience when guys who promise to call them don't in her song, *How Come You Don't Call Me.*

Do You Share Your Faith Story (Testimony About Christ) on Your First Date?

Should the two of you share your faith story on the first date? I strongly suggest you do if you want to practice being equally yoked (2 Corinthians 6:14) in a potential serious dating or marriage relationship. Doing this allows you to make the decision whether to date this person again. If you have convictions about not dating someone who isn't a follower of Christ, this may save you from investing your emotions and then trying to break off a relationship that never should have become one.

Please hear me! I'm not saying that followers of Christ are better than those who aren't following Him. Nor am I saying that followers of Christ can't date those who aren't. I'm just asking you to think about your decisions and possible consequences.

What should hearing your date's faith story (testimony) confirm for you? I think hearing your date's personal faith story about how he came to have a personal relationship with Jesus Christ is a requisite for continuing dating this person—if you two want to build a spiritual foundation so that you are on the same spiritual page.

What four elements should you hear in a faith story? If your date shares his faith story, you want to hear four things. You want to hear: (1) about their life before becoming a Christ follower; (2) what sparked their interest in becoming a follower of Christ; (3) when and how they actually asked Jesus Christ to forgive their sins and to come into their life; and (4) what life has been like since becoming a follower of Jesus Christ.

Does this testimony guarantee your date is a follower of Christ? No it doesn't. People can lie. But it usually is an excellent indication that your date is a Christ follower. Another principle I believe is that the indwelling Holy Spirit can confirm in your spirit that what your date said about his relationship with Christ is true, just as we can sometimes sense if another is a follower of Christ. Romans 8:16 says, *"God's Spirit touches our spirits and confirms who we really are. We know who he is, and we know who we are: Father and children"* (The Message).

As you get to know each other, some of the factors that would help confirm his faith walk are if he prays over your meal. Is your date involved in Bible study or other efforts such as evangelizing, serving the poor, or discipleship? Does your date financially support a church or ministry? Has he or she received pastoral or biblical counseling when facing challenges or is your date accountable to an elder or church leader?

Often, I hear some followers of Christ say that dating gives them the opportunity to share their faith. You can share your faith in Christ as friends before becoming romantically involved. Once our emotions are turned on—objectivity can frequently be lost.

Do You Pray On Your Dates?

Is there any possible danger in praying with the person you're dating? My answer may shock those of you who are followers of Christ, but when I dated, naturally, I would pray over a meal if we had dinner, pizza, whatever, as mentioned earlier. I would especially on the first date. I would pray at the first date's conclusion—thanking God for my date and the time we had together, especially if it was good. But I didn't pray on every date with the same person because, just like you can bond your spirits sexually, I believe you can also bond your spirits spiritually. So, I would pray at the conclusion of the date, maybe every third or fourth date with the same person.

Do You Have Physical Boundaries You Refuse To Cross?

"If you stand for nothing, you'll fall for anything" (*quote source possibly originated by Alexander Hamilton, Peter Marshall, Ginger Rogers, or Malcolm X*). You need to have your standards and stick to them. When you lower your standards and get into a poor relationship, your guilt can be overwhelming.

If you like being physical with your dates kissing or petting, are you aware this petting is foreplay and often leads to unexpected sex? And unexpected sex often leads to unprotected sex. I'm not condoning sex before marriage. Know that the physical power of sex is nothing to play with. I do believe there is a "point of no return" in regards to being physical in your dating.

What Role Does the Physical Play in Your Dating Relationship?

Too often in dating, the physical aspect of the relationship becomes its primary emphasis. When the physical is the priority in dating before marriage, it usually will destroy the relationship. Often, when couples are involved in heavy petting or are sexually active before marriage, it is common for one or both partners to avoid, issues, which may create conflict, in order to have sex. The problem with avoiding conflict is that this avoidance hinders the couple's growth in the area of communication. In fact, it can become a handicap. When couples don't learn how to effectively work through conflict, often their problem issues are never resolved. So they learn to coexist with frustration, which constantly builds. Typically, one will "go off" on the other at unexpected times. If a person continues stuffing issues, eventually, somebody's top is going to blow! If a couple with this preexisting situation marries, divorce is often around the corner within the first five years of their marriage.

Will You Kiss on Your First or Second Date or Not Kiss Until Your Wedding Day?

You probably need a game plan for kissing or not kissing on your dates. I'm not suggesting there is a right or wrong here. It is your call. Better yet, ask God and get Him involved.

Suppose you don't want to kiss your date, but your date wants to kiss you? What do you do when she is leaning in and puckered up? If you kiss her because you don't want to hurt her feelings, you are likely to go home frustrated. And she goes home happy and full of anticipation. What do you do when she calls for a second date, but you knew during the first date she didn't meet your standard, or ring your romantic bell? Your kiss communicates to her that you like her and are interested in a relationship. Few people ever want to hurt anyone's feelings, but briefly hurting your date's feelings at this awkward moment will be much better than leading someone on in which more commitment and emotion has been invested—devastating your date later.

Initiating the kiss is no longer true of just guys. Young ladies and guys both tell me often the girls are just if not even more so the initiators of kissing.

Also consider that when you kiss someone, you are giving a part of yourself away to someone else. You may want to re- evaluate the value of your kiss and what it means to you. Leah Holder, daughter of two of my best friends, Olus & Nikita, is a beautiful young lady, a former outstanding high school basketball player, and an excellent college student who was recently accepted into a prestigious law school. Recently, she and I spoke about single relationships. She said, "I broke up with a guy and I'm so glad I didn't kiss him. I can't begin to imagine how difficult it would have been if I had more emotional involvement by kissing him." Leah speaks about sexual purity in her new book, *No Trespassing: I'm God's Property*. She is a much sought after speaker. Visit her website: www.goinghigherministries.com

Recently, I counseled a twenty-year-old young man who had been sexually active before becoming a Christ follower. He told me that he doesn't plan to kiss again until his wedding day. Again, Myrna and I aren't telling you what to do, but you should have a plan.

Where are the Dates?

Have you ever wanted to date to the point of desperation (which is part of the problem), but there wasn't any eligible person around? There are many singles who haven't been on a date in years—some by choice and others because they seem to have no eligible choices. By far, the most natural place to meet a potential date is where you hang out such as an activity or event that represents your mutual interests (political campaign, church, sports, dancing). If you haven't met anyone in your routine environment or through friends, then ask the Lord about how or where to meet a potential date.

Consider being a risk taker to some extent when it comes to dating. If you see someone to whom you are attracted at the transit system or Starbucks, go over and start a conversation. For example, if they are reading a book, ask them if it's a good book because you're looking for something to read. Or, go up to them and say, "I noticed you when I came in and I wanted to introduce myself. Can I buy you a cappuccino or something else?" The worst he can do is be unresponsive, but he could say yes. Guys tend to do this more than girls. Here are some other options to pray about:

Blind dates:

Just because a friend knows a single and you're single doesn't make a dating match. However, sometimes this connection can at least help you start your dating engines, especially if you have been out of the dating world for a long time. Cross-cultural blind dates require caution because some cultures don't know what is attractive in another culture. In some cases, blind dates eventually end in marriage.

Online Dating Services

I'm not for or against online dating. It seems that the rate is 20 percent of relationships today begin online. Continue to be wise no matter how you meet whom you date. More and more Christian couples that Myrna knows are getting married after meeting their mate online. Be cautious of online scams or relationships that later request money. Many women have lovingly given away their life savings to someone who ended up being a scam artist.

Fast Facts[3] regarding *Mindful Matchmaking:*

- Online dating, a billion-dollar industry, offers singles an unparalleled opportunity to meet and arrange dates with people outside their own social circles.

- Often these services encourage the user to rely on decision-making styles that are not well suited to the development of successful relationships.

- Awareness of the obstacles in this psychological terrain can help online daters make the most of these services.

- A large body of research shows that people are better at choosing from small sets than larger ones, whether at a supermarket or on an online-dating site.

- Deprived of the social cues that modulate dating behavior in face-to-face interactions, online daters tend to contact the most objectively desirable people at much higher rates than other individuals.

Meetup Groups

While these aren't dating services, they offer an opportunity to meet others with shared interests without the pressure of a pick-up. The group activities include hiking, book clubs, foodie outings, sports, and many other activities. The website meetup.com is free and there is no obligation to attend any of their events.

Does Age Difference Matter?

Again, answering this question depends on individuals and their maturity or lack of it. There are no hard, fast rules.

In high school, there seems to be a huge emotional and sometimes physical growth gap between a fifteen-year-old and an eighteen-year-old. For example, the middle school experience, according to a majority of educators, is a failure because of the age differences. Exposing six graders to eighth graders is not a good situation in most cases. School districts, that can afford it, have returned to the more traditional 1-6 grades and 7-9 grades and then high school. So age difference does matter more in certain circumstances.

Freshmen entering college tend to drastically and rapidly change in their thinking and experience between this time and their senior year. I think there is a big gap between twenty-one to twenty-five years of age in how much you learn, change, and develop during this time. It seems that the older one gets, the wider the age range. And yes, there are exceptions.

Today, men and women are dating people twenty years younger. It would be weird for me because I would feel like I'm dating one of my daughters. But this may work for some couples. If they are Christ followers, I would suggest they seek God's guidance, as all Christ followers should.

What About Older Women Dating Younger Guys?

In ninth grade, Glen, a classmate, was constantly pursued, not only by high school girls, but also by college girls! To all of us guys, he was our hero! All the girls in our junior high were crazy about him too, but they had no chance. They couldn't compete with these older beauties, their cars, and their money.

Dating an older woman appeals to most guys' egos because it appears to validate manhood, making you irresistible to girls your age because they figure you must have something going on—even if they can't see it. Other guys become envious. During the summer of my sixteenth year, I attended a national denominational camp where I was shocked that a gorgeous, twenty-year-old from New York was interested in me. Of course, I was really cute back then. I loved being with her, but really didn't know what to do with her. I didn't have to try to be cool, even though at times I did. Just being with her was magic, even though we didn't have to touch or anything.

At that same camp, another older New York girl educated me on the fine art of French kissing. We didn't talk much. She just took me to a solitary area and started class. It was similar to my college freshman year in Chicago. I told my basketball teammate that I liked his girlfriend's friend. He told his girlfriend's friend that I liked her. She called me up to meet with her. This junior girl who was not only older, but taller, let me know she was interested in me too. And, the dating began. These were a few of my experiences dating older gals. You never know what God has in mind, even if it seems far-fetched. Take Derek Prince, a famous international preacher, who married a woman twenty-five years his senior. She ran an orphanage and had eight adopted girls, six of whom were Jewish. They were together until her death. God brought them together for His purpose.

Characteristically, older women don't play all the head games, so there is usually less drama in the relationship. Typically, they are very direct because they seem to know exactly what or who, they want and go after it or him. So, they can be aggressive. They know how to make you feel like a man (and I'm not talking sexually). They understand how crucial it is for guys to be respected. Most are able to provide this respect because they tend to be comfortable with themselves. And they usually know more than the younger guy they are dating, and have no problem sharing this knowledge. They have often been wounded by men their age. So sometimes, dating a younger guy initially appears to be less risky. From their perspective, younger guys are moldable.

Should Girls Ask Guys out on Dates?

Certainly, my ego was seriously stroked when an attractive girl asked me out. I don't ever remember saying no. Please remember, we are dealing with generalities. But before you say this doesn't apply to you, bounce what is being said off the people who know you and love you.

Typically, when a girl asks a guy out, he doesn't have to work at the relationship. He always knows this girl is his *back-up*. This allows him to pursue other girls with whom he has to work at the relationship. Guys like mystery, challenges, and pursuing. When a girl asks a guy out, she is no longer a challenge. As a guy, our egos love it, but it isn't good in most cases for building a long-lasting relationship.

When this guy runs into a girl for whom he has to work to get a relationship, he will value her more. If her parent(s), demand(s) he comes by her home before she goes out with him— he is working. This builds respect in the guy for the girl. When a girl asks a guy out, he doesn't have to respect her, nor does he have to work for this relationship. Working for a relationship also builds commitment. Respect and commitment increase desire and reveal his investment, laying an excellent foundation for a long-lasting relationship.

Ladies, most men like to pursue you. So, if he doesn't have to pursue you—his ego loves it; but it actually lowers your value with most men. Guys feel they don't have to work for you and you'll accept any kind of treatment they give you because you want them so badly. You lose most—if not all—of your leverage in this relationship. If you're a girl who wants to date or get married, you don't want to be in a relationship with a guy who feels he doesn't have to work at the relationship because you chased and caught him.

Who Holds You Accountable Regarding Your Dates?

You might want to have some older people or a married couple who love you, help you evaluate your dates by providing their insight. You make your own decisions, but relationships of the heart can always use an outside perspective.

As I was channel surfing on one of my flights (free TV—the only way to fly!), my surfing stopped when I discovered a program revealing the tricks of illusionists. Their primary method of tricking us is termed *unintentional blindness*. Their goal is to distract us by what is obvious, so that we don't see what else they are doing. These illusionists also shared the fact that our vision can't effectively multi-task; it is extremely compartmentalized. Sometimes in relationships, our emotions create an unintentional blindness, and we may need the help of those who love us to help us *see all* that is going on.

At the time of the writing of this book, all three of my girls are in their twenties, one in law, one in graduate school, and one lives with us. All have been out with guys before. But none of the previous guys did what one young man did. This twenty-seven-year-old man called my wife and me, requesting permission to date one of my girls. I was pleasantly surprised. My wife and I appreciated the respect he showed us as well as our daughter. He asked if we had any questions about him and then we asked him if he had any for us. Our daughter and he have been Skyping for months, after being introduced by a friend of ours. He wanted to fly to town to see our daughter, but wanted our permission first. He said, "I do not want to just date your daughter, Sir. I'm dating with the intention that it will lead to something." I asked what was the something. He replied, "marriage." I'm trying not to like this dude, but I have to respect him. Actually, I do like him. This is weird!

I never asked any father-in-law if I could date Brenda. I wasn't that mature. In fact, a bad experience with a father when I wanted to date his fourteen-year-old daughter when I was fifteen gave me a fear of dads. I missed out on dating some girls I really liked because their fathers insisted that I come by the house to spend time with their daughters before I could take them out on a one-on-one date. These men knew my parents well and I knew these fathers, but I refused to go.

I greatly respect these fathers now, because they were requiring me to court their daughters. And they were protecting their daughters, which I can appreciate now.

I'm certainly not demanding that guys do this, but it does make an incredible statement about your character to the parent of the girl with whom you want to spend time.

Single Parents Who Date

As previously mentioned in Chapter Four, but worth repeating here, your children's routine as well as their emotional health need to be protected; especially from attaching themselves to someone, only to have to needlessly deal you're your child's perspective of abandonment or rejection later. If this person isn't marriage material, then don't expose your date to your children. And unfortunately in this day and age, you need to do a background check on this individual.

More information about single parent (both genders) dating can be found in the book, *What All Dads Should Know* in the introduction, pages 22-24, by Dr. Jeffrey Shears.

Divorced Men and Women

One of the most common mistakes divorced people tell me they make is assuming that since they have been married before, they don't need to invest as much time in their next potential spouse.

Counseling those who were formerly divorced in their latest marriage reveals this is a terrible mindset! They often rush into marriage because they hate being alone, but then they have to rush out of that marriage. Often before their next marriage, they are sexually active thus lowering their chances at a long-lasting and loving marriage.

> *"I praise you because I am fearfully and wonderfully made; your works are wonderful, I know that full well. My frame was not hidden from you when I was in the secret place. When I was woven together in the depth of the earth, your eyes saw my unformed body. All the days ordained for me were written in your book before one of them came to be"* (Psalm 139:14-16).

> *"But seek first His kingdom and his righteousness, and all these things will be given to you as well" (Matthew 6:33).*

> *"Don't seek to find God's Best, **concentrate on being God's Best**. God's not going to send his Best to mess!"* Dr. Clarence Shuler

Is Physical Appearance a Major Factor for Your Dating?

Attending several Christian educational institutions, I've learned not to make decisions purely on physical appearance. First Samuel 16:7 says,

> *"Looks aren't everything. Don't be impressed with his* (her) *looks and stature. I've already eliminated him. God judges persons differently than humans do. Men and women look at the face; God looks into the heart."* The Message

So when I was single and dating, I tried to learn to *look into the heart*. I was pleasantly surprised that a lot of my best dates weren't always the drop-dead, gorgeous girls, but the girls whose internal qualities made our time together special. Now there are plenty of drop-dead, gorgeous girls who also possess these internal qualities. I'm just encouraging you not to allow only external appearances to be your only criterion for your dating decisions.

Saying *No* to a Date

If you are asked for a date by someone you have no desire to date, may I suggest you be polite and sensitive. Realize that you are receiving a compliment when someone thinks enough of you to ask you for a date. Also understand that he or in some cases, she, may be extremely nervous in just asking you for a date.

So if you don't want to go on a date with the person, say something like, "Thank you so much for thinking enough of me to ask me for a date. As much as I'm honored to be asked by you, I don't feel that way about you. But thank you again for asking." This is just a suggestion. I'm sure you can say this much better than what I've written here. Please don't unnecessarily wound anyone by being insensitive or uncaring.

Another option is to consider a group date, which is usually fairly safe and much less romantic. Being asked by an individual to join him for a group event isn't a bad thing. While you may say no to that same person for a solo date, you could say yes on such a group venture.

What Determines if You Continue or End a Relationship?

What is a deal breaker for you—lying, being religious, non- religious, weight, height, complexion, education, unemployed, money management, premarital sex, cheating on you, verbally or physically abusive? Whatever it is, be extremely careful about overriding your conscience and lowering your standard. Equally as vital is your understanding of what is necessary for you to stay in a relationship. What makes you want to continue in a relationship? Consider discussing it with those who love you.

Neither should we be in relationships with people who only *need* us; they should want us. Needy people often feel they're incomplete, thus needing someone or something outside of themselves to complete them— for happiness, peace, or confidence and so on. Such a mindset puts their girlfriend on a performance track to please them, leaving the needy person vulnerable to external or superficial circumstances for his emotional needs. Needy people unintentionally create dysfunctional relationships, which usually self-destruct due to a selfish motivation, of which they may or may not be aware.

If you decide to end a relationship, please do not do it through a text or e-mail no matter how great of a writer you are. Your relationship was 3D, in living color, and so should be your break up regardless of the high-tech world we live in.

If You Decide You Are Going to Date, Then....

Define your relationship as soon as possible. Being in a relationship with no title usually results in unnecessary wounded hearts.

Relationships that have no title, such we're dating or boyfriend and girlfriend, can become detrimental. Such relationships often become ones of using each other or worse case, booty calls.

This untitled or defined relationships may feel good initially, but typically, one or both of you will get hurt because an undefined relationship allows for both in the couple to see or date others due to the lack of commitment to one another.

Be Careful of....

Ladies be careful of being financially vulnerable to guys. For example, it seems to have become a common practice for some women to buy their male friends phones. Gentlemen be careful of accepting a phone as a gift because often women who give phones, do so in order to track you!

Ladies be careful of initiating going to visit your male friends, especially if they live out of state, at your expense. If a guy really wants you to come visit him, usually he will pay for your trip because he values you. Most men have the core value of providing for the female in whom they are interested. So if he isn't providing most of the expense for your relationship, you may need to try to discover how he feels about you.

Guys be careful of a woman who showers you with money. I know it feels good for our egos, but we still usually rather pursue a woman than be pursued. Of course, there are exceptions to the rule; but be very careful. Such a girl or woman may view your acceptance of her money as commitment to the relationship, when you are not committed at all.

SUMMARY QUESTIONS

1. Most people have experienced fear and rejection in dating.

2. Dating in America seemed to become confusing when our culture transitioned from primarily rural to city. We went from courting, to calling, to dating.

3. Guys and girls have different perspectives and purposes for dating.

4. Being dateable is debatable. And it may require some work.

5. Asking a girl for a date can still be nerve-racking for some guys, but it is better to ask, because a girl can't say yes if you don't ask her.

6. Consider having a goal in mind when you date that is mutually beneficial.

7. It isn't a sin or wrong for a girl to ask a guy out, but it may not be a girl's best option.

8. If you are a Christ follower, sharing how you came to have a personal relationship with Jesus Christ will bring clarity to you about whom you date or continue dating.

9. Having dating guidelines may keep you out of trouble and help you learn how to discover what you enjoy about the opposite gender and which personal attributes you find attractive.

10. If you are dating much older or much younger people, be sure to check your motives. Make sure you are doing what is best for them and what God has called you to do.

11. If possible, have some accountability people (family or close friends) for your dating.

12. As a single parent, be sure to protect your child in your dating situations.

13. As a divorcee, try to make sure you are healed from your divorce before re-entering the dating culture.

14. You need to be emotionally and mentally clear as to what constitutes continuing a relationship and ending one. Be sure not to violate your conscience.

15. There is no place in relationships for verbal or physical abuse. The abuser was most likely abused as a child and needs professional help. Encourage this person to get counseling. Usually a person abusing you isn't your fault. Don't enable someone in their dysfunctionality.

ACTION POINTS

1. Should your date be a better person and potential long-term relationship partner for someone else because they dated you? How or why?

2. What do you think a girl needs from a guy on a date?

3. What do you think a guy needs from a girl on a date?

4. Why do you think that when the physical (particularly sex before marriage) is the priority in a dating relationship, it usually will destroy the relationship? What has been your experience?

5. Are you confident enough to date? Name five things you like about yourself that would be attractive to a potential date.

6. What attracts you to the opposite sex?

7. What is your purpose for dating?

8. Do you consult God about whom you date? Why or why not?

9. How do you think you can glorify God on a date?

10. Do you feel comfortable sharing how you came to have a personal relationship with Jesus Christ on your first date? Why or why not?

11. Do you kiss on your first or second date or will you wait until your wedding day? Why or why not?

12. Do you pray on your dates? Why or why not?

13. How much does a person's physical appearance factor into your dating that person?

14. Single parents, prayerfully consider doing a background check on your dates.

15. What are deal breakers for you in relationships? Why?

16. What determines if you are going to stay in a relationship? Why?

17. If abused, seriously consider calling the police, so the abuser gets the message and is held accountable.

18. What's the best way you can think of to end a relationship that you think would be the least hurtful for the person you are dating?

SECTION III:

BEFORE YOU SAY "I DO"

Chapter Nine

Finding Mr. or Mrs. Right

"Find a good spouse, you find a good life —even more: the favor of GOD! Proverbs 18:22, The Message

As previously discussed, if you are in Christ, you are complete and don't have to be in a relationship. But if you do want to be in a relationship that leads to marriage, this chapter has suggestions that may be beneficial.

Many singles believe that finding Mr. or Mrs. Right is all about romance and warm, fuzzy feelings that will last a lifetime. Myrna calls this the *Fairytale Syndrome.* It is a belief that basically after marriage, you'll live happily ever after. As a marriage counselor, I have, unfortunately, worked with many married couples that have struggles in their marriages over various issues, including loneliness, disillusionment, and unmet expectations. Marriage can be an amazing, exciting, and fulfilling experience, but you need realistic expectations and preparation for Mr. or Mrs. Right.

In seeking Mr. or Mrs. Right, the word *commitment* surfaces. *"The issue isn't compatibility; it is commitment. And the more committed you are, the more compatible you'll be as a couple."* For those of you who love dating, but want to get married, you need to begin focusing on one person. You can still love the opposite sex; but from here on, one person will represent the opposite sex. For example, I loved dating because I love women. Now that I'm married, that love is expressed to only one woman, Brenda, my wife.

Another relationship principle previously mentioned, but worth repeating, is that you will need to develop a counter- culture mentality that switches from receiving to giving. Instead of looking for someone who will serve you and meet all your needs, you look for someone *to serve* the rest of your life.

If I may take the liberty of paraphrasing the verse listed under the chapter title above, I would say:

"Find a godly [boyfriend/girlfriend] *or spouse, and you find a good life—even more: the favor of GOD!"*

I paraphrased this verse to include those of you who may be in high school or college who have just begun dating. There are some young people who get married at this age, but most don't. And for those who aren't

170

married, I don't want you to feel the pressure of *having to* get married. I'm not trying to discourage marriage at this age. I just want you to marry for the right reason and when you are ready.

Another reason for my paraphrase is that finding a godly boyfriend or girlfriend can significantly prepare you for marriage down the road. Learning how to be friends in a romantic situation is invaluable. Hopefully, experiencing a godly person of the opposite sex can help to improve your understanding of them, especially in areas such as speaking *Man 101* or *Woman 101*, or learning how to and why you should work conflict through to a healthy closure in the relationship.

Proverbs 18:22 states that relationships are a good thing. This is true because relationships expose many of our shortcomings, such as selfishness, insecurity, and poor communication skills. Therefore, you learn that if you are going to have a successful relationship, you must become less selfish usually more than any other character issues. Be secure in God regardless of your relationship status, and communicate effectively. As a single person, you may not notice behaviors that are potentially detrimental, but in a relationship, they can pop up when you least expect them. If you are in a relationship with someone who cares for you, he will lovingly let you know about these behaviors. His motivation isn't to embarrass, or hurt you, but to help you be a better person. This is exactly what God does for us in the Person of the Holy Spirit when we are listening to Him.

When seeking Mr. or Mrs. Right, whether dating or pursuing marriage, look and pray for a person who will care for you enough to tell you things you may not want to hear but need to hear for your benefit as an individual and for your benefit as a couple.

Just make sure that your significant other's ability to confront your problem areas is emotionally healthy. Conflict resolution requires respect, strong listening skills, and patience. Some people can't deal with confrontation, so they bury their emotions, which can unexpectedly surface at the wrong times. How will you resolve problems that are bound to come up in marriage?

If you've read this book this far, hopefully you've gotten some insight about how to find the right person, such as knowing your true identity in Christ, being content and confident as a single, and allowing the Lord to heal your broken or hardened heart. It is really about *your* focusing on being the right person.

Dr. Gary Chapman has discovered nine biblical principles for finding Mr. or Mrs. Right from Genesis 24. They can be found in his book, *The*

Marriage You Always Wanted, which isn't just for married couples. It is also for engaged couples. These are time- tested principles that I believe are critical for establishing healthy, mutually beneficial, and long-lasting relationships. Here they are:

1) Principle of Parental Vision for Child (Children)—*vv.* 1b-3

Abraham had the vision as a parent to plan and secure the best possible spouse for his child's future and family legacy. What a tremendous example for parents. Brenda and I prayed for our girls' birth, for each girl to develop a personal relationship with Jesus Christ at an early age, for a good education, for their dating years, and for their future husbands.

My prayer for my girls' future husbands is this: *"Lord, I pray that the men my daughters marry will love You first and them second. If possible, these men will come from families that faithfully follow Christ, and their parents will have modeled a godly marriage to their sons. I pray that these men will be morally and financially faithful, outstanding fathers, and will be helpful around the house; that they will never emotionally, nor physically abuse my daughters; and that they will be spiritual leaders for my daughters and their families."*

My daughters have also given me their specific prayer requests related to marriage. The only two that I can share with you are: (1) that their husbands will be followers of Christ, and (2) that their husbands will love Christ first and them second.

They expect me to be praying for their future spouses and they should since I'm their father.

2) Principle of Commonality—*vv.* 3-4

The principle of commonality is about having priority issues or beliefs in common. Abraham tells his trusted servant to go get a wife for his son from his extended family because they are people who have the same beliefs he has about God. Abraham forbids his servant from getting a wife for his son from the Canaanites or others who didn't believe in God.

The practical application is that, as followers of Christ, we should date and marry those who also follow Christ. Having different spiritual beliefs can cause major division for a couple instead of increasing their oneness.

There are other critical values that can make or break your marriage, so it's important to discuss them BEFORE you choose to marry. Here are major values to consider:

- **Finances:** Money issues are one of the leading factors for divorce. If one brings serious debt issues into the marriage, it affects the other as well. What are your values about money? If you disagree on how to handle money, consider taking financial management classes such as Dave Ramsey's *Financial Freedom University.*

- **Parenting:** Do both of you want children? If so, how many? If you are from different Christian denominations, how will you raise your children? For many couples, this can be a deal-breaker after they marry. My friend Carmen wanted desperately to have children, but her boyfriend already had grown sons, so they broke up. Her boyfriend later agreed to have a child if they should marry. After they married, he changed his mind, and she divorced him.

- **Goals:** If you're dating someone with aspirations for something that contradicts your own vision for your lifestyle, like military life, living in Africa as a missionary, or being under public scrutiny of political office, then seriously consider whether or not you're willing to sacrifice your lifestyle goals.

- **Role expectations:** Do you expect your wife to be a stay-at-home mom or a working woman? Is she willing to give up her career? Some women are more ambitious than their husbands and can emerge as the primary income earner. Are you comfortable with these roles? If your husband-to-be travels, will you be able to handle this? Would you have a problem with your husband working from home?

3) Principle of Prayer—*vv.* 12-15, 26-27, 52

In this chapter, we see that Abraham's servant prayed before meeting Rebekah. He prayed once he met her, and then he continued to pray for everything to work out well.

Whether a teenager, college student, employee, or a divorcee, specific prayer for a future boyfriend, girlfriend, or spouse is an excellent biblical principle to practice.

I recall praying with my adopted grandmother about finding the right girl for me. God had allowed me to date some incredible Christian women, but nothing worked out for a long- term relationship. They weren't God's best for me and neither was I God's best for them. So I prayed that if He wanted me to be in a relationship, He would have the woman pursue me. This was not from an ego perspective, but because I'm so dumb. I needed it to be obvious because I was done pursuing girls.

If you want to have a boyfriend, then a very practical and biblical approach is to have people praying for God's will for you in this situation. This group should include your parents. If your parents love you, whether they are followers of Christ or not, they will have better insight than most as to whom you should and shouldn't be dating because they usually know you better than anyone. This is true if you are in college or in the marketplace. Others in this praying group could be other close family members, one or a very few close friends, or it could be your youth group leader, pastor, or a trusted married couple. It is up to you how many people you want praying and speaking into your love life.

Do you have such a group of people praying for your dating life and future spouse? While in graduate school, members of my home church back in North Carolina were praying for me to meet the right girl and get married. My wife Brenda said she had a similar prayer support group back in her Maryland home church.

4) Principle of Timing—*v.*15

Before Abraham's servant finished praying, Rebekah, future bride of his master's son, arrives at the local well. The principle of timing can also be a little different.

Brenda arrived on the campus of my graduate school in my last semester before graduation. On our third date, God told me she was the one I was going to marry. No, I didn't tell her. But after five months of dating long distance, Brenda broke up with me with no explanation. That alone was devastating, but what was even more devastating than losing Brenda, was thinking I had missed hearing God correctly! About a year later, I ran into Brenda while visiting one of my best guy friends who attended the same grad school as Brenda. She wanted to get back together. I couldn't tell Brenda the things God had told me about her being the "one" because it would seem as though I was manipulating her. However, God told her the same thing. She shared this with me, so we began to date again. And in less than a year, we were married. *What I learned was that you can meet the right person, but it may not be the right time.*

5) Principle of Beauty—*v.*16

Beauty is in the eye of the beholder. The person you are dating or engaged to should be attractive to you. They may not be the most beautiful or handsome person in the world, but they should be attractive enough to you so you aren't breaking your neck looking at other people.

6) Principle of Virginity—v.16

This principle overlaps into the chapter on sex, but it is worth repeating. God is really big on the issue of virginity, because He views sexual intercourse as more than just a physical act. God designed sex is an act of worship! So, sexual purity is a vital aspect of worship or giving. God intended sexual intercourse to be one of the highest and most intimate acts of worship a couple can give together to Him. If you are familiar with the Old Testament, only animals with no blemish or flaws could be sacrificed to God as an act of worship. God views our sexual purity in a similar fashion.

For Teenagers and College Students:

I want you to know that God speaks to teenagers. You are important and have a purpose for being here, no matter what others may say.

Meet two biblical teenagers: Joseph and Mary. Joseph grew up in a step-family situation. His father blatantly showed his favoritism toward Joseph to his older stepbrothers. Driven by their jealousy, they attempted to gain their father's love, by selling Joseph into slavery when he was only seventeen!

Mary was about fourteen when she was told she had been chosen to be the mother of God's Son, Jesus Christ! WOW!! She was chosen by God to be the mother of Jesus because of her character and her virginity.

Joseph was discussed in the chapter about sex. He was possibly 17 years old and single when God first spoke to him. Do you remember how he dealt with the daily sexual harassment he encountered on his new job?

"Joseph was a strikingly handsome man (reminds me of me-just kidding). As time went on, his master's wife became infatuated with Joseph and one day said, 'Sleep with me.' He wouldn't do it. He said to his master's wife, 'Look, with me here, my master doesn't give a second thought to anything that goes on here—he's put me in charge of everything he owns. He treats me as an equal. The only thing he hasn't turned over to me is you. You are his wife, after all! How could I violate his trust and sin against God?' She pestered him day after day after day, but he stood his ground. He refused to go to bed with her." Genesis 39:6B-10, The Message

Some of you are thinking to yourself, "I blew that and I can never match up to Joseph or Mary. So I can never have this kind of intimacy with God and my future spouse." Not true because God is a God of grace.

7) Principle of Character—*vv.* 18-19

Character, or being a person who possesses a standard or code of ethics, is critical to being able to establish a long-term relationship or a mutually beneficial marriage. It is essential that you are able to trust the person you want to date or marry. Honesty issues such as cheating, even while you're dating, will only get worse in marriage.

In these verses, Rebekah offers to water Abraham's servant's ten camels. The average camel can drink twenty gallons of water at a time. So Rebekah could have drawn and carried as much as 200 gallons of water! Imagine having to lower, then, raise buckets full of water and then carry them to the camels to drink. Imagine the time that would have taken! Furthermore, camels are known to be mean animals. Rebekah demonstrates a servant's spirit. She has learned this from her family. So even though Rebekah doesn't go on a date with Isaac, her character tells Abraham's servant that Rebekah is a keeper!

8) Principle of Parental Consent—*vv.* 1-9, 28-52, 49

In the days before the Bible was written, and even, for centuries afterwards, it was almost impossible to get married without your parents' consent. The reason for this was because most marriages during this time were prearranged. The parents of both parties knew each other and planned much of their children's future.

As for those marriages that weren't prearranged, parental consent was often still required. Parental consent was usually a form of protection for the girl from a man of poor character. Usually, once married, the girl had very few rights and almost no help from parents. Parental consent also protected the boy. Though he didn't have to worry about abuse, he did have to worry about being *stuck* with a girl of poor character.

This is not the case today. It is not uncommon today for parents to have no input into whom their child marries.

When Brenda and I provide premarital counseling, we suggest, not demand, that if possible, both individuals get their parents' consent or blessing for their marriage. Why? We believe that if your parents love you, whether they are followers of Christ or not, God has given them an amazing ability to discern if the person you are dating or engaged to is a good match for you. It is certainly not required, but I would surely want my parents' blessing for the person I was planning to marry.

When I was twenty-four, I dated a beautiful model in the Maryland area.

When I entered a room with her on my arm, heads at the stuffy government parties in Washington turned. It wasn't long before I was in love with her. I got along well with her parents and her older sisters. My only problem with her was that she wasn't in love with me. She was *"in like"* with me. But I was determined to win her over! I brought her home to meet my mother and sister. They both gave me the thumbs down sign. It broke my heart, but I trusted them. Later, Mrs. Karolyn Chapman, wife of best-selling author, Dr. Gary Chapman, also spoke some profound words to me. She said in her beautiful North Carolina southern accent, *"Honey, it shouldn't be that hard."* When I heard her words, it clicked. I knew my Mom and Jean were right, so I broke up with her. It was difficult because she started crying. I hated that. We parted as good friends. Emotionally it was tough, but I had a peace in my heart, which is one of the fruits of the Holy Spirit.

9) Principle of God's Will—*vv.* 66-67

This may be the most significant of all the principles, yet I've never heard a sermon or a talk about practicing the principle of God's will in the context of friendship, dating, or marriage. And I have no idea why not. Let's look at the last two verses in Genesis 24:66-67:

"After the servant told Isaac the whole story of the trip, Isaac took Rebekah into the tent of his mother Sarah. He married Rebekah and she became his wife and he loved her...." The Message

The question I also ask those attending my *Looking for Mr. or Mrs. Right* seminars is "when did Isaac love Rebekah, before or after they were married?" Teenagers and older singles always appear to be shocked when they take a closer examination of the verse. Isaac loved Rebekah *after* he married her, *not before!* So Isaac didn't *fall in love* as much as he *learned to love.*

In fact, Rebekah was accepted because of Isaac's trust in his father's most trusted servant. WOW!!

Abraham, Isaac's father and his servant prayed for God's will regarding Isaac's wife-to-be. Isaac had nothing to do with it except to receive the blessing of the prayers of probably the two men he trusted the most!

All the other principles help you determine God's will for you. Again, if you want to read more on these biblical principles, they can be found in Dr. Gary Chapman's book, *The Marriage You Always Wanted.* Some additional comments and insights are from Dr. Shuler's 2005 study of Genesis 24.

I hope this chapter has been helpful for those of you who desire to find a godly boyfriend, girlfriend or spouse. Hopefully, this chapter has provided some biblical tools and some clarity.

SUMMARY POINTS

1. Remember, you are complete in Christ regardless of whether you are in any kind of relationship.

2. If you are seeking a boyfriend, girlfriend, or spouse, then *commitment* needs to be part of your vocabulary and lifestyle.

3. Biblical relationships are more about giving than getting. If you give, you'll actually receive more than you give.

4. Relationships are good things.

5. If you desire to be in a relationship, you need to be willing to accept constructive criticism from that special person in your life without becoming defensive.

6. Much of what you have already read in this book about friendship and dating will help you as you seek a boyfriend, girlfriend, or spouse.

7. If your parents love you, then they will be invaluable in assisting you in your pursuit for your significant other, regardless of whether your parents are followers of Christ.

8. Mentally process the nine principles.

ACTION POINTS

1. Are you seeking a boyfriend, girlfriend, or spouse? Why?

2. What does commitment look like to you? Why?

3. Are you ready to focus on giving to someone else first before receiving for yourself? Why or why not?

4. How do you think giving first will impact you and your future relationships? Why?

5. Do you have a handle on your selfishness? Why or why not? Do you even think you are selfish? Why?

6. Do you think you could handle dating or marrying someone who is more selfish than you? Why or why not?

7. Do you think you could tell another person that he or she is selfish? Why or why not?

8. What is your relationship with your parents? Why? Do you trust them? Why or why not?

9. If you don't have a good relationship with your parents, is there another older couple or person you can trust?

10. Apply the nine Principles.

Chapter Ten

Cultivating a Dating or Marriage Relationship That Lasts

"He answered, 'Haven't you read in your Bible that the Creator originally made man and woman for each other, male and female? And because of this, a man leaves father and mother and is firmly bonded to his wife, becoming one flesh—no longer two bodies but one.' Because God created this organic union of the two sexes, no one should desecrate His art by cutting them apart."
Matthew 19:4-6, The Message

What is the difference between this chapter and *Finding Mr. or Mrs. Right*? It is one thing to find the right person, but cultivating a lasting relationship even with the *right* person is quite another matter. Yet, there will be some overlap between that chapter and this one. Relationships are dances that are usually perfected over time—actually, a lifetime. Although they require consistent work, these lasting relationships are well worth learning how to dance.

Let's review some of the principles that we have covered so far. In cultivating a lasting dating or marriage relationship, you need to know you have healed from any past wounded relationships. You know the importance of self-worth. Knowing why your previous relationships didn't last is essential for a successful future relationship. And having a loving support group consisting of family and close friends is a critical foundation for having a future or maintaining a mutually beneficial relationship.
DESPERATION MAY LEAD TO DESTRUCTION

You may recall that it is necessary that when you are in a relationship that you continue being an individual. Some single guys say a common reason for breaking up with some girls is that the guys feel these girls are wanting every single minute of their free time. One guy recently said of a former girlfriend, "She simply took too much time."

I think it is crucial that the person you are dating wants you, but can function without you. An older girl who was a friend, but wouldn't date me, became a relationship mentor for me. I don't know why she wouldn't date me because I was really cute and funny back then. But she did tutor me in my relationships with girls. She once said, "You need to stop dating girls that need you and start dating the ones that want you. You are always rescuing some girl then you start dating her. You date these needy girls for the wrong reason, even though they make you *feel* good. Then you break up because the relationship drains you so much." She continued by explaining that needy people usually unintentionally create dysfunctional relationships that usually end badly. She suggested that I pursue girls who weren't needy. They didn't have to be with me 24/7. She said, "These girls are strong and can stand with you when the difficulties of life come." The same should be true for girls looking to cultivate a relationship with a guy.

Her advice was priceless because it changed the type of girl that I pursued. This characteristic was key in my pursuit of Brenda, my wife. In fact, it drew me to her.

Consider Investing in Your Relationship

After finding the right person, get confirmation, if possible, by those who love you such as family and close friends. If you are a Christ follower, then the Holy Spirit should also confirm with your spirit that this is the right person for you. Romans 8:16: says, *"For His Spirit joins our spirit to affirm that we are God's children (NLT)."* Peace, one of the fruits of the Holy Spirit (Galatians 5:22-23 is one aspect of confirmation that this is the right person for you.

Now that you are with the *right* person, consider investing in your relationship. We will spend time and money to invest in a car (the interest rate, where we can find the best deal, vehicle history reports, and so on) and other major decisions. We do the same for our apartment or house. But it appears people seldom invest in their relationships even though most people want their relationships to last forever.

Amazingly, couples will spend all kinds of money on the wedding, which is typically, a one-day event; but relatively little to any money on the quality of marriage, which is long-term.

A Good First Step

Once you have established whom the *right* person is, I'd recommend having a relationship assessment such as *Prepare/Enrich* that evaluates you as a couple in more than ten relationship areas such as: background (parents, upbringing, etc.), communication, conflict resolution, partner style and habits, financial management, leisure activities, sexual expectations, family and friends, relationship roles, relationship dynamics, commitment, abuse, personal stress profile, and spiritual beliefs. This survey evaluates couples' strengths, areas that may require possible growth, and overall satisfaction. One of the key components of this survey is its evaluation which reveals *idealistic distortion,* or as some counselors call it, "blind spots" or expectations in relationships. This is simply a reality check for individuals and couples.

What is so impactful about this survey is that it is an evaluation of the couples' answers to a variety of questions. It assists couples in seeing how they view the relationship individually and exposes possible trouble areas that many couples may easily overlook.

Want Your Relationship or Marriage to Last? Get Premarital Counseling

Another critical component for cultivating lasting relationships for couples is having premarital counseling. Research from the Administration of Children & Families discloses that premarital counseling can increase a couple's chances of staying married up to 70 percent! AMAZING!! This is a huge statistic when research documents that 65 percent of marriages today will end in divorce within the first five years!

Premarital counseling and the Prepare/Enrich Survey provide outside and non-emotional perspectives on relationships. These perspectives help most couples to more realistically assess their relationships. These tools require couples to ask and answer the *tough* questions many couples don't think of or are afraid to ask.

Attend a Marriage Conference/Retreat

You may say, "We're just dating. I ain't even thinking about getting married." I hear you, but a marriage conference such as **FamilyLife's** *Weekend to Remember Marriage Getaway,* our *BLR: Building Lasting Relationships Marriage Retreats/Seminars* or the DVD series, *The Art of Marriage* (www.familylife.com) will cause more of your relationship issues to surface and offer tools to help you work through your issues. A marriage-intensive weekend retreat creates opportunities to learn more about yourself and the person you are dating and possibly considering marrying. If you do go as a dating couple, commute or stay in separate rooms.

What if you don't want to take that person with you? Go by yourself, but if that person isn't willing to invest in your relationship, there may be a huge problem. However, I'm noticing more and more singles that aren't even in a relationship attending these conferences. When I ask them why they are coming, their overall response is, "I just want to know what to do in a relationship as well as what to look for in a potential spouse." I publically commend them. It is a wise investment to make. Attending one of these conferences or something similar is a must for engaged couples.

Family Litmus Test

When you are in a relationship that you believe has potential to become a lasting one, bring your potential life-long partner home. Let her meet all the crazy folks in your family (we all got 'em—the alcoholic uncle, the busybody aunt who often says the wrong thing at the wrong time, the grandfather who passes gas in public, etc.).

Observe how your significant other interacts with your family. Find out what your family thinks of your potential spouse. Don't easily dismiss their opinions. Then you visit her family. These visits will give you tremendous insight into each other as well as your potential future together. You need to know that you aren't just marrying the girl of your dreams. You are marrying the family too!

The Less Physical Before Marriage, the Better

If you have read the chapter on sex, you now know that the less physical you are with your partner the better potential for a lasting relationship. The physical can cloud either of you making clear decisions as well as being able to more objectively evaluate your relationship. The less physical you are in your relationship, the less likely you are to bond with the wrong person. You might get a guy in bed before marriage, but often your heart will still be empty.

And ladies, I don't intend to be rude, but this is what single and married women keep telling me in regards to premarital sex or living together, *"Giving men everything for free—women giving their bodies away outside of marriage—decreases a man's incentive for marriage."* As the old adage says, "If you're giving your milk away for free, there is no need for men to buy the cow!"

If A Christ Follower, Consider . . . .

If you are a Christ follower, I encourage you to consider someone who shares your faith if you are thinking of a long-term relationship or possibly marriage. One of our most intimate qualities tends to be our spiritual character. And the Bible speaks of not being unequally yoked, meaning tied to someone who isn't going the same direction as you.

According to *The Daily Beast* reporter, Nina Strochlic (*July 1, 2012*), "Differing religions are bound to get messy in a relationship, especially when one is as controversial as Tom Cruise's Scientology. Holmes's papers cite 'irreconcilable differences,' and *TMZ's* sources say the two couldn't see eye to eye on Suri's involvement in the church. Holmes was raised Catholic and converted to Scientology before marrying Cruise in 2006, but she's reportedly worried about their daughter's involvement in the religion. Suri, age 6, is now old enough to participate in what a *Village Voice* report describes as a Scientology practice called "sec checking," which is a security interrogation by an ethics officer of the church. The report also implies that Holmes didn't like what she saw of the religion over the past six years and has chosen the opportune moment to pull out."

If this report is true, then Holmes and Cruise violated the biblical principle in 2 Corinthians 6:14-15, which says,

> *"Do not be yoked together with unbelievers. For what do righteous and wickedness have in common? Or what fellowship can light have with darkness? What harmony is there between Christ and Belial? What does a believer have in common with an unbeliever?"* (NIV)

Katie Holmes and Tom Cruise had different religious beliefs, but married anyway. Holmes being brought up a Catholic wanted the same for her daughter. From a distance they seemed to be doing so well until the baby came and their different family values clashed.

Couples can learn an important principle that we may compromise initially in relationships, but our spiritual foundation may have a stronger influence than we realize. Don't ignore this truth if you want to have a long-lasting relationship or marriage.

The "C" Word

A key factor is *commitment* to the relationship. It isn't about emotion. It is about being in this relationship for the long haul, no matter what. I believe that *the more committed you are, the more compatible you'll be.* What I mean is that the more you work and serve in the relationship which is motivated by commitment, you'll discover that compatibility is easier and actually more of an attitude adjustment issue. When we are committed to a relationship, it makes it easier for our partner or spouse to be more patient with us and vice versa.

If you decide to get married, a critical element in commitment is eliminating divorce as an option for your marriage. Such an attitude drives you to talk about your issues and problems, which in reality are opportunities for you to grow closer as a couple once you learn how to communicate effectively, especially through conflict. Just remember when you are having conflict which is quite natural, the goal is never to win; but to gain understanding. If one of you wins, the couple loses. Often our cause for conflict is frustration. Once an individual understands the other's perspective, the frustration tends to dissipate. Usually when the frustration dissipates, the couple can often find agreement.

Show Me the Money

Another critical issue for couples is their money management. How do you and the person you are dating view money? Some people view money as a sign of power. For others, it provides security. Research says that money is one of the top three reasons couples divorce.

I believe that if you work hard for your money, make it work hard for you. Ben Steverman in the August 8, 2008 *BusinessWeek* edition wrote these tips for saving money:

- track every expense
- vacation in the off-season
- buy used
- eliminate investment charges and fees
- cut back on eating out
- downsize your car
- cut utility bills-especially electric
- don't have too much insurance
- find cheaper beverages to drink
- examine your phone service
- don't pay for premium cable
- drive less—consolidate trips
- use warehouse stores wisely
- lay down the law to your free-spending friends
- find free entertainment
- consider alternatives to gym memberships
- cut your own lawn

- be smart with credit cards

- annualize your expenses

- force yourself to save

- institute a waiting period before buying major purchases (maybe 48 hours)

- make sure you are deducting all business expenses and

- shop smart

Ben gives us quite the list, but the idea is to be more responsible with your money so you have more of it for a longer time and for emergencies.

This is so huge in relationships, especially marriages. Usually most couples consist of a saver and a spender. There is nothing wrong with this. In fact, it can be a wonderful built-in check and balance for a couple if they know or learn how to speak with each other about money. If not, look out for conflict.

It is frequently common for people who have divorced over money and remarry to insist on separate bank accounts, thinking that this will prevent money from ever being an issue again. A problem with this kind of thinking is that it becomes a hurdle against intimacy. Woundedness and trust are issues here.

Ideally, you may have different accounts, but both individuals should have access to all the accounts. Paying bills together is necessary. This can alleviate money arguments because it usually helps the couple see their individual priorities in spending, which are usually different. Typically, a couple is composed of a spender and a saver. Neither is wrong, it fact, this usually helps to give a couple balance in the area of finances. Of course, if Christ followers and realizing the money all belongs to God and you are just stewards, puts a different perspective on money as well.

If you are dating, I strongly suggest not putting your money together in one account.

When you are close to getting married, then debts and financial planning need to be discussed. Devise a plan created to eliminate debt and plan for wedding expenses, buying a home or other agreed-upon goals. In marriage, your spouse's debts become yours and vice versa. Again, I strongly recommend keeping separate accounts until marriage.

Keep Romance Alive!

For couples, whether married or not, once you become comfortable and familiar with each other, it is so easy to begin taking each other for granted. No matter how beautiful she is or how handsome he is, couples can eventually take each other for granted.

A frequent result of taking each other for granted can escalate into couples feeling disconnected. This can even be true of couples that are Christ followers. Couples may stop doing some activities they used to do together and may begin doing individual activities.

Couples need to keep the romance in their relationships because with jobs, children, hobbies, and familiarity, it is easy to eventually begin taking each other for granted.

For married couples, I recommend attending at least one marriage conference per year. It's like changing the oil in your car. If the oil in your car is never changed, the engine will eventually be destroyed. I think the same can be said of marriages.

These conferences are excellent reminders of what you should be doing even though you're already doing them. You never really stop learning about relationships in marriage. Marriage education can be preventive maintenance for divorce.

Another key for a successful serious dating relationship that may lead to marriage is praying with your spouse or the person you are dating. I recommend praying together consistently only when you are serious about the relationship. Building spiritual intimacy gives you a closeness, which helps couples when they experience conflict. Conflict is natural and if handled correctly leads couples to even more intimacy.

Correctly Handling Conflict Leads Couples to More Intimacy

Any two people (whether the same gender or not), who spend enough time with each other will usually experience conflict. Not only is conflict natural, but it's healthy and appropriate for most relationships. So conflict is reality. To avoid conflict is to attempt to avoid reality.

Thinking of conflict often scares individuals, even to point of avoiding conflict at all cost. Yet if you and the person you are dating desire to have a long-lasting and mutually beneficial relationship, then both of you must cultivate your ability to correctly handle conflict.

Unfortunately, I'm constantly counseling couples that never learned to effectively work through conflict even after twenty years of marriage. Often when couples don't learn to effectively communicate with each other during conflict while dating, they carry this problem into their marriage and they usually divorce. When couples that have children divorce, the divorce rate for their children increases dramatically according to the Administration for Children & Family. Their divorces typically impact their family usually for the next three to four generations! Not learning how to work through conflict while dating can be incredibly expensive in the context of emotional pain and your future family!

Another problem with not working through or avoiding conflict is that couples tend to enter marriage thinking that they really know each other and that their relationship is fine. But once the honeymoon is over and the blinders come off, couples are often shocked to realize they really don't know each other. Their avoidance of conflict has limited or kept them from seeing the actual person they married. They never learned about each other. It isn't uncommon for these folks to believe they have married the wrong person, but that may not be the root of the problem at all. They deceive themselves into thinking they are ready for marriage because they know each other so well; but they really don't. They may have been physically close (sex before marriage), but not so emotionally. *You have to talk about the hard stuff before marriage while you have leverage.*

Most couples usually have conflict because men and women are radically different. Men and women often use the same words, but are usually speaking a different language. We have to learn how to speak *Woman 101* and *Man 101*. But conflict isn't bad. In fact, it is actually good if it is handled correctly. If handled correctly, conflict leads to more emotional, intellectual, spiritual intimacy, which is usually expressed in sexual intimacy in marriage. This doesn't happen overnight. Learning to have a mutually beneficial resolution of conflict issues is a *dance that is perfected over time.* This is exactly why one-night stands and living together are detrimental to long-term relationships.

Transparency

Without being able to work through conflict, transparency may be out of the reach of some dating couples.

Transparency is indispensable because it lays the foundation for you as a couple becoming *best* friends. If you had a best friend in elementary, middle school, high school, or college, you typically told him everything. Can you imagine being in a dating relationship or marriage and not being able to talk about everything with your boyfriend or spouse? That would be tragic. I hear people say that the best marriages are the ones where the couple started out as best friends.

If this is the case, then transparency isn't optional!

Biblical Roles in a Marriage

Let me share with you a biblical passage written for married couples, but the principles can be beneficial to dating couples who are considering marriage. Ephesians 5:22-25 reads:

> *"Wives, understand and support your husbands in ways that show your support for Christ. The husband provides leadership to his wife the way Christ does to His church, not by domineering but by cherishing. So, just as the church submits to Christ as He exercises such leadership, wives should likewise submit to their husbands. Husbands, go all out in your love for your wives, exactly as Christ did for the church—a love marked by giving, not getting"* (The Message).

There is one principle for the male and one for the female. First of all, women do not have to submit to a man simply because he is a male. Women don't have to submit to men they don't even know. Biblical submission here is being taught only in the context of marriage. So what does this have to do with dating? I think this passage encourages gals to find guys whom they don't have a problem trusting so that they can support these significant men in their lives. When guys have the gal in their lives supporting them, they believe they can conquer the world! Their leadership begins to emerge.

The guy is to provide *servant-leadership* for the gal in his life. This isn't about a dictatorship. When this relationship functions as it should, submission and servant-leadership aren't issues. The relationship is like a finely tuned engine running without making sputtering noises like it is about to cut off.

Guys and ladies, submission is defined as a voluntary yielding. It doesn't mean that ladies have no input in decision- making, but the very opposite. Ladies, respect must be given and it also needs to be earned. *And respecting your man is like giving him oxygen to breathe.* He seldom will lead without it. So ladies, how you speak to your man in private and public? Also, the tone of your voice will be crucial in your relationship. You can speak life or destruction to him. Men, the same is true for you. Proverbs 15:4a states, *"The tongue that brings healing is a tree of life."* And guys if we want our ladies to follow us, we need to have a vision of where we are going. And they need to have input into this vision. Many women aren't following their husbands in marriage because the men aren't going anywhere. They don't have a vision.

Ladies, Jesus Christ gave His life for the Church. When you find a guy who is willing to give his life for you, more than likely, he will have little problem in living for you. And this is the guy you will have little trouble submitting to.

So when you are dating, evaluate your dates to see if they fall into this category. Are they more about giving than getting? Remember, long-lasting relationships are more about serving than getting, which is extremely counter-cultural in our "you deserve" mindset in society today.

Know Yourself and Don't Be Desperate

If you desire to be in a relationship or to take your current relationship to another level, possibly marriage, it is at times like these that you must be careful not to be so desperate that you'll do anything to end your singleness.

Don't get married in order to escape your shame of singleness, loneliness, boredom, parents, your financial situation, or other issues. And please don't **ignore God's warning** that you shouldn't get married. If you don't have a peace about it, don't get married.

Please don't ignore certain reoccurring behavior, any kind of abuse, fear of your significant other, or other warning signals. Don't do it. If your parents who love you or your close friends don't approve, they may be seeing a blind spot that you don't. Seriously consider their concerns or objections before entering a marriage you may regret.

Love gives, it doesn't demand. I've counseled too many people who rushed into marriage, ignoring God's warning that they shouldn't marry a particular person. And some married because they are people-pleasers and didn't want to offend anyone.

Become a Student of the Person You're Dating

One of the many principles I'm learning from my wife is to become a student of the person whom you are dating, or in my case, my spouse. For my fiftieth birthday, Brenda got all of my friends to chip in to pay for a trip for me to go to the U.S. Tennis Open in New York! I couldn't believe it! For years, she saw me compete in tennis tournaments and watch the U.S. Open religiously each year on TV with my girls. It has become a tradition in our home. When I asked her why she did this, she responded, "I wanted to make one of your lifetime dreams come true." She studied me. I never said anything about going because it was so unrealistic. She did this after nineteen years of marriage. I can never repay her, but I'm becoming a student of her.

Three Practices That Are Revolutionizing My Relationship

Reading and Applying God's Word Together

As a Christ follower, I've seen the power of God's Word in helping married couples overcome affairs. I've seen clients who have a drug problem restore their marriages by spending time in the Bible with their spouses. And I know that when Brenda and I spend time in the Bible it makes a positive difference in our relationship.

Praying Together as a Couple

Another practice that revolutionizes a relationship is praying with your spouse. I have couples that drive more than an hour for counseling. If they are Christ followers and I can get them to hold hands and pray together, most times, they can work out their difficulties. Brenda and I are both strong-willed and stubborn. When we pray together, it dulls the sharp edges of our relationship. We tend to become more sensitive and patient with each other.

Research reveals that couples that pray together have a better chance of staying married. Read the following research. In fact, there is so much research on prayer and its impact on marriage that another chapter could have been written on it.

- From the book, *Couples Who Pray*: *"Virtually every one of the categories measuring marital bliss escalated significantly when couples simply prayed together a lot versus prayed together sometimes. In some cases the swing was 15 to 30 percent."* (Source: www.coupleswhopray.com)

- A national research study (1980) cited in *Retrouvaille's International Handbook* established that married couples who attend church together weekly and read the bible or pray together daily have a divorce rate of *approximately 1 divorce in every 1,105 marriages*. (Source: http://www.retrouvaille.org/pages.php?page=1)

- In his book, *Faithful Attraction*, noted researcher Fr. Andrew Greeley reports that of all the factors known to contribute significantly to marital happiness, praying together as a couple is *"the most powerful correlate of marital happiness that we have yet discovered."*

Being a Pleasure to Be Married to . . .

Recently, I was scheduled to speak at a *FamilyLife Weekend to Remember Marriage Getaway*, but since I was tired, Chuck, the other male speaker substituted for one of my talks. I told Beth, his wife, who was sitting with me in the back of the ballroom at the Speakers' Table, "Your husband is a great guy. I can't believe he is doing that for me." She responded, "He's a pleasure to be married to." Her phrase blew me away!

Immediately, I couldn't help but wonder if Brenda thought that I was a pleasure to be married to. Sunday evening after the conference, she picked me up from the airport. On the drive home, I repeated the story, concluding it by asking her if I was a pleasure to be married to. She smiled and said I was okay or something to that affect. I determined to become a pleasure to be married to.

I began doing things around the house that I normally didn't do. Brenda would come into a room where I was and ask me, "Did you do . . .?" I would say, "Yes." Even when I felt she didn't do what I thought she agreed to do, I would do what needed to be done.

Now, please don't give me any credit. It was definitely the Holy Spirit motivating me and empowering me. For example, Brenda wanted to counsel a marriage couple in my office at home. One problem: it was a mess. When I write, I get messy. It took me 8 hours in one day to clean my office. She was supposed to fix the sprinkler. She didn't do it. Satan began telling me all kinds of lies. She actually forgot. So, I reminded her. It still didn't get done right away. Then she asked me to help her. I'm thinking, "I did my part. I cleaned my office." Immediately, the Holy Spirit asked me, "I thought you wanted to be a pleasure to be married to?" No longer could I be so petty to struggle with my perception of right and wrong or whose turn it is. Brenda really noticed. But it ain't easy. You must rely on the Holy Spirit.

Determine If This Relationship Is God's Will for Both of You

In finding Mr. or Mrs. Right, this principle of God's will is seen in Abraham's and his servant's prayers and God's response to their prayers for this relationship. In our culture today, Isaac accepts Rebekah as his wife before he loves her according to Genesis 24:67, which reads,

> *"Then Isaac took her into his mother Sarah's tent, and he took Rebekah, and she became his wife, and he loved her; thus Isaac was comforted after his mother's death."* (The Message)

Think about this. Isaac didn't date Rachel. He hadn't even seen Rachel. Is this counter-cultural or what? Isaac trusts his dad and his dad's number one servant—his support group for his marriage.

We can *fall in love* with anyone. What I seldom hear Christ followers talk about is, "Is it God's will for me to date or marry this person?" Knowing that the person you are dating and planning to marry or that the person you have married is in God's will for you will help you stay committed when you experience that God's perfect gift for you isn't perfect.

Does the person you're dating live at home? Have they ever lived away from home on their own? Why do you want to know? If living at home, he or she may not be as mature as you think. His or her parent(s) may allow him or her to be late with paying the rent if it has to be paid at all, may wash his or her clothes, do all the cooking, and so on. So you may be dating someone who looks like an adult and even acts like one away from home; but when the relationship begins to get serious, you find you are dating a glorified high school or college student who isn't ready to leave her nest.

What Are Their Priorities?

- What about shared values? Do they value kids, money, integrity, or other things you value?

- What are possible issues that may destroy your relationship or become a problem in your future marriage? For example, if one or both of you are always busy to be successful and can't spend quality time together, this could create tension in the relationship.

- What about your plans for having kids? An issue in some remarriages is that one individual already has children from a previous marriage and doesn't want any more kids, while the other individual doesn't have children and wants some. It isn't uncommon for one individual to lie or change his mind after you say, "I do."

SUMMARY POINTS

1. Just being in a relationship and cultivating that relationship to be a long-lasting one are two different issues.

2. Desperation tends to create dysfunctional relationships thus destroying your chances for a long-lasting dating or marriage relationship.

3. Investing in your dating or marriage relationship by taking a couple's profile survey, attending a marriage conference (even though not married), and having premarital counseling are indispensable components in cultivating a long-lasting dating or marriage relationship.

4. If you are in a serious dating relationship, meeting your boyfriend's family is a good litmus test. Remember, you're marrying the entire family.

5. The less physical you are in your relationship before marriage, the better it is for your marriage afterwards. And it lessens the couple's chances for having affairs.

6. Sharing the same faith is also critical to cultivating lasting relationships, which includes determining if it is God's will for you to marry the person whom you are presently dating.

7. Having an understanding of how both of you view money before marriage may help you avoid divorce.

8. Keep dating and keep romance alive in your relationship.

9. Transparency—being a student of the person that you are dating—and praying together as a couple are foundational to long-term dating and marriages.

10. Be a pleasure to date.

11. Praying with the person you are seriously dating or engaged to, will lower the chance of divorce if you get married and if you continue praying in your marriage.

ACTION POINTS

1. What non-negotiables ((i.e. kissing only if you are in a committed relationship or not dating other people when you are in a committed relationship) let you know you are committed to a relationship? Why?

2. Have you ever lost a relationship because you were needy? Do you think this will happen again? If not, what will be different the next time you are in a relationship?

3. How are you investing in your dating relationship? Are you experiencing the dividends from your investment? Why or why not?

4. If your dating relationship is serious, what do you think of introducing him to your family and visiting his family?

5. How do you know that you and the person you are dating are on the same page spiritually? Is this important to you? Why or why not?

6. Why do you think praying with the person you are seriously dating improves the relationship? Why do you think it helps couples avoid divorce?

7. If you are in a serious dating relationship, have the two of you discussed how you view money? Is one of you a spender and one of you a saver? What could be the benefit(s) of this for you as a couple?

8. How do you keep romance in your relationship? Does romance mean the something to you as it does to the person you are dating?

9. What does transparency look like to you and what does it mean to you?

10. Would the person you are dating say you are a pleasure to date? Why or why not?

11. How can you tell if you are a student of the person you are dating? Do you feel they are they a student of you? Why or why not?

Chapter Eleven

What the Church Can Do for Singles

*"We proclaim Him, admonishing every man (woman) and teaching
every man (woman) with all wisdom, so that we may present
everyman (woman) complete in Christ. For this purpose I also labor,
striving according to His power, which works mightily within me."*
Colossians 1:28-29

Initially, one purpose for writing this book was to benefit both secular and faith-based singles. But during my research, singles continually told me they felt the church, for the most part, was doing little to assist them in their journey. And they also felt the church often treated them as outsiders and not as inclusive members of their respective churches. Thus, I decided to focus on the church first.

So, I thought, who can best educate the church as to how to be more effective in serving singles, than singles? In this chapter, you'll read comments by singles of various ages expressing their thoughts on what the church can do for singles. Their names, ages, and relationship status will be listed before their comments.

Daniel, *15 (never married)*

I would love it if the church gave more sound Bible-based advice on dating and relationships, and in addition to that and with that information, have events or get-togethers where people of both genders can meet and get to know each other in a natural way that doesn't have to be romantic. I think that relationships come out of friendships, and sometimes people just want to be friends, but it seems that the culture that has been created is one where you can be totally cool to have friends of your same gender, but when it comes to people of the opposite gender, the sole reason you would ever want to talk or say hi to them is because you think the person is cute, and you want to date them. And while sometimes that may be the case, for the most part, what everyone really wants to do is get to know their brothers and sisters in Christ in a normal way.

I think this is very important because it is natural and healthy to have a diverse group of people to hang out and do life with, and get different perspectives on life, and have a community whom you know is there for you. And I think that my church has done a very good job of fostering this. When I first began to really become a part of my church community, I really felt that this was not the case. It seemed like if you were a boy, you hung out with boys exclusively, and if you were a girl the same thing, but over the past few years that culture has changed, and it has really become a welcoming place for everyone, and it feels like a family, which is what I think church should feel like.

Luke, *21 (never married)*

Our culture is flooding the minds of teenagers and young adults with ideas that they need to be in a relationship or they need to be having sex to be happy and that they are somehow a failure if they are not with someone. For most people, this is a problem of identity. We do not know who we really are and we constantly try to gain satisfaction through many things including relation- ships. We need the church to come alongside young adults and help us understand that we are far more than who we are or are not with. Our identity is not in someone else. *Our true identity* is in God our Father, the only one who can truly satisfy us and the only one that loves us unconditionally.

Catrina, *33 (never married)*

As a 33-year-old-single woman, I feel that the church can stop looking at us as if there is something wrong with being single. I always feel that many married couples look at singles as a group of individuals that need fixing and are not capable of "finding the one." I also wish the church would pray and nurture singles because it is very difficult being single in a world that caters to married people when all you want to do is be married. I know the church needs to be more understanding and willing to accommodate all people and take singleness for what it is: a gift. Instead, the church just sees it as a season of life and so often that season will last much longer for others not because something is wrong or this individual may not want to get married, but because the opportunity of marriage has yet to present itself as a tangible option.

Connor, *22 (never married)*

The church must rediscover the value of singleness as it has marriage. An over-emphasis on marriage in Christian circles has left singles feeling alone and incomplete.

Jean, *60 (divorced, single mom)*

As far as what the church can do for me: find physical activities for women only, as well co-ed physical activity groups for older single men and women; create women's reading groups for Christian books or books of the

Bible. Don't assume that single women have a need for men in every aspect of their activity. Sometimes having men around is more stressful than beneficial.

Patrick, *39 (nevermarried), LawProfessor*

Single adults who embrace Christianity want the same thing that everyone else of the faith wants: to unconditionally love and be loved like Jesus did. Being single is the optimal time when God is able to direct our focus primarily toward Him. This is an opportunity for churches to foster environments conducive to singles serving actively in all areas of ministry without limitation imposed by our marital status. As we search for God's chosen best, churches should also promote an atmosphere that acknowledges and encourages the pursuit of purpose, passion, and professional development. These are all critical areas of focus for single adults, as our primary purpose is to love God first and foremost. We are all *becoming . . ..*

Hillary, *31 (never married)*

I hesitated in contributing, because of my fragile heart. Having recently dated within my church community, suffering the pain of heartbreak, and now needing to move forward while existing within the same fellowship as a former boyfriend (I hate using the term "ex," although that's what he is), I have worried that bitterness, cynicism, or at the very least, hurt will color my view. Still, I have grown and healed in time, although not completely, and now having finally made it past the anniversary of our first date without much ado. I can be grateful I'm in a better place. I'm learning more than I could have imagined about my brokenness, a past that has colored my present more than I care to admit, and all the ways I would do this relationship over again—differently—if I could. I started seeing a counselor at church to help me process my wide array of emotions post-break- up. And certainly, as is what happens when you face pain head on, it forces the evaluation of long-held attitudes, the events that formed those, and the pain that's been buried for so long that you may not have even known was there. I sure didn't know, and my revelations have been unexpected. I've talked to friends, spent time in prayer, read books, and listened to audio books. I feel like I'm only at the tip of the iceberg of appropriately and maturely dealing with pain in a way that will allow me to be whole as a single person so that I can be a better contributor to a romantic relationship in the future.

If I took the time to write about the valuable personal lessons I'm learning, I'd have to write my own book! But I can say this: I have never encountered, in my lifetime of following Jesus and actively participating in church life, a straightforward approach to making sure we are healed (or at least healing) individuals in order to be able to date. We hear of personal character, rules for dating or not dating, the inevitable reminder to not have sex outside of marriage, the even worse reminder of how good sex is and how it's such a gift (do we really need to be told that?), and how we should "wait on God" for the right person. Check. Check. Check. And yet, nobody has said, "Hillary, you need to face your personal issues because of the significant impact they will have on the most important person in your life. You need to examine the unaddressed pain that causes your eating compulsion, constant comparison with others, ceaseless striving to be better. If you don't, you'll enter into a relationship with wrong ideas that will dictate your behavior in marriage, much to its detriment."

A lot of people complain that young adults within the church aren't dating enough. Well, I've come to realize that it's a good thing with so many broken, hurt people walking around with unaddressed issues who are unintentionally inflicting pain on those they date. What I wish is that instead of encouraging young men to ask out the ladies, spiritual leaders would first ask them, "Are you actively seeking to emotionally prepare yourself for relationships? Have you examined your life and heart for evidence of bondage, internal vows, shame, un-mourned grief, and if not, why not? The ladies are waiting, but they need a man who can face his own personal failings, not a boy who lacks depth. But this is not an excuse to not ask women out. Rather, it's advice so that you can ask them out even sooner."

In short, we all need to be in counseling. Seriously. Right now I'd say that there is little else that could make a guy more attractive than seeing a counselor.

Paul, *23 (never married)*

I do think the church should stop trying to suppress our biology. We are made and wired to have kids early on in life. But the church says, "Don't date till college; don't marry till after college, preferably when you are established in your field," and "don't have kids till like 3 or 4 year into your marriage." Most medical experts would agree, the later in life you have kids, the harder on the body it is, and if the church worked harder to convey realistic images of marriage and dating, that would be helpful.

Hephzibah, *46 (nevermarried)*

Many churches have done various things like dancing, hiking, even separate Bible studies for singles but none has been really positive for me. I guess I don't like to be separated from marrieds. I'm much more comfortable when I'm in midst of singles and marrieds. The chance to be introduced to someone and get to know him while with others is more likely in such a setting than when I'm in an all-singles crowd.

I personally feel very uncomfortable when I enter a place with only singles. I've gone to too many events like that to know how I feel. I go to these Christian-sponsored events assuming that all are Christians and assuming that all who attend a Church singles event are indeed singles. It has been a shocking disappointment to find out that's not always the case. I just wonder why some people bother to attend a Christian event when they are not single. More shocking has been to find out that many are not even Christian.

To observe the hungry eyes of our brothers has been very discouraging. I have very high moral expectations. That's maybe because I've been prey too often and have felt the sharp teeth of the wolves that had come covered in lamb's cloth.

Today I'm much more cautious. Not seeing a wedding ring doesn't necessarily mean he is single and hearing him quote Bible verses doesn't mean he is a born again Christian; Satan can quote them as well.

Adam, *33 (never married)*

I feel most supported by members of the church community who reach out by including me in dinners, potlucks, and chances to participate in their family's happenings. I'm often touched when a couple will take the time to invest in me; to show that I matter and am important. I don't often struggle with loneliness, but could easily see how this is such an effective way to "do life together" in a way that is very fulfilling. Even when I was in my early 20's and all my closest friends were getting married, I often felt so blessed when married friends would offer to care for me; I felt like one of the widows in the Bible, finding her needs met by the community of faith.

I suppose I appreciate it when members of the church attempt to provide helpful feedback—but the reality is many people view dating differently, so I often receive contradictory information. The most significant thing that's given me peace is remembering to listen for God's voice and leading. I was in a serious relationship, and even our wise counsel and premarital counselors couldn't really tell us if it was a "good thing" or not, which meant we just had to really listen to God. In His mercy, he made it very clear (to each of us separately) that "NO" was the answer. At that point we had no choice really but to be obedient. By His goodness we were able to part ways with only hearts of sadness and love, not harboring bitterness or anger.

I think it's important to ensure that those who are more introverted are still found and known and welcomed into the community. By creating men's and women's ministries for older folks, and the college and young people's ministries that exist at our church, I've been very pleased to know people with a heart for singles have a place to make sure that they're not walking the Christian road alone.

I've been very thankful for the Young People's ministry at our church. Sometimes I feel isolated in my unique story of being almost ready to wed and then hearing 'no' from God. But in that community there are others whose stories have been similar to mine. I'm so very grateful for that kinship that I feel with those others who uniquely understand my story up to this point.

Heidi, 53 (Divorced)

Ok, this 50 year-old single is out to speak out! I feel singles lack REAL support from the church because we really need to be embraced by the married couples and families. Part of the pain of singlehood is feeling isolated and alone. Even if we have many single friends, we seldom experience a sense of community. Being part of a family structure is nurturing and healing and makes us feel part of something larger than ourselves. We are told that we are part of the "family of God," but most churches segregate us into our own little groups or home-groups. It can be healing for us to be around children, young adults, and married couples. (This last statement may not be true for younger singles, but as people mature, they crave family situations more).

Secondly, some of us are *serious* believers, which means that we do not want to do things the world's way. If we did, we would still be out there, fishing in shark-infested waters. Many of us believe that the Lord is the best matchmaker; however with that said, if we are going to "date" in the church, we need to all be on the same page about things like sex before marriage, pornography, adultery, which are *not* Christian practices. After all, there is nothing worse than thinking the fish you caught is a live one, only to find a shark on the line.

Steve, 54 (divorced, single dad)

I'm concerned about the balance many adult Christian singles have. To me, too many seem to be content to stay in their 'stuff' and seem to almost expect to be 'fed'—as if simply showing up at church, Sunday school, bible study is somehow holding up their end of the deal. There is a strange comfort in the familiar, even if it is less than ideal or even dysfunctional. My take is God has not envisioned this in the design plan for the precious singles in His flock. Yes, He knows we will grapple with our stuff, but he also wants us to know and take comfort in the fact that He sent his Son to help share the burdens. He also knows there will never be a time when we become free of stuff or 'fixed'.

There are gifts of outreach, spiritual growth, relationship building with others both inside and outside the Christian community and inside and outside the singles community, that He wants us to activate concurrent with our healing and repair. These are not mutually exclusive or divergent. In fact, it seems to me Satan is at work in us when we think we must first reach a certain level of functionality or enlightenment before we can do God's work. God does not place that expectation on us. We do. I see that many singles are slow to evolve from their inward focus to an outward focus; slow to let Jesus share the burdens; slow to accept that we will never be unbroken and we are still loved and valued in our brokenness.

His plan does not dictate that there be a singles flock that grazes in some isolated, infertile field. We are a part of one big and treasured flock that includes all that believe in Him! In His view, the marrieds and singles in the flock are all unique and different but are together in His pasture!

Rachid, *48 (never married)*

The church could have more married couples walk alongside singles sharing their discernment or providing practical advice on dating and relationships; more teaching on certain topics from the pulpit. Singleness is a big issue for many Christians in our church and I believe as a whole in the body of Christ! I think (if I remember right) our senior pastor said that *40% of our congregation are singles*! It is a high percentage! I don't hear of too many marriages taking place each year in our church! I think somebody initiated a group for singles this year or maybe last year. Is that enough to see more marriages taking place in our church? I don't believe so!

I believe our pastor delivers one sermon per year for singles! Is that enough to encourage a culture encouraging marriages to take place? Obviously not! Maybe our senior pastor is blind to the power of the pulpit to encourage, emphasize and promote a culture of marriage! I am sure he feels the pain as well as a father and can relate and empathize with the singles because of his son, promoted as a youth pastor and yet single still (I think his son is probably in his early thirties). Even two of the women he ordained as associate pastors are singles as well. Maybe he didn't think of having a pastor specifically for the singles to disciple them, to train them and to encourage and prepare and equip them in practical ways on how to get married and to promote and encourage interactions between the singles toward that purpose! My church has fallen short of being proactive in this area even though the need is great! Maybe the leadership believes that single groups and cell groups are enough to generate more marriages in our congregation! The rate of marriage per year in our church and the still high number of singles in our church must wake them up to the truth, to the reality that it is not enough!

Why is this important? I believe that it is not God's will for his children to be single! He even said in His Word that "it is not good for a man [or woman] to be alone!" Loneliness is not a blessing! God's commission to Adam and Eve is to "be fruitful and multiply." This commission is still valid today! I believe there are only a few people in this world that have the same grace that Paul the Apostle had to be single and give himself completely to God's purposes! Even the other Apostles had wives (1 Corinthians 9:5: *Don't we have the right to take a believing wife along with us, as do the other apostles and the Lord's brothers and Cephas?*). Children are a blessing from The Lord (Psalm 127:3) and I do believe that His will is to bless His children with the joy of having children.

Why then do so many not get married and don't have this joy of having children? Is it a lack of faith? Is it a lack of discipleship on how to date successfully as a Christian? Is it a lack of leadership from the church to be proactive in promoting and encouraging and creating a culture of "marriage" within the church? Is it a lack of skills on how to date as a Christian? Is there maybe some generational curse or some word curse that have been pronounced by parents that needs to be broken in order to see God's will to take place? Maybe the answer is all of the above; maybe the answer is one of the above. Maybe the answer is simply not God's timing yet. God did say that without faith, it is impossible to please Him! Maybe the answer is simply our fault for not being proactive in prayer and actions to make it happen! Is it too late, even if it is our fault or maybe the church leadership's fault? No, a thousand times, *no!* I do believe also that even if we "missed" God's best for our lives for one reason or another, since Our God is a Redeeming God, if we don't give up and "stir ourselves in God," God can still help us overcome our barren past and give us a soul-mate because His will is that "it is not good for a man [or woman] to be alone!"

Prophetic words have affected me sometimes in a positive way but in the case of marriage, they have so far affected me in a negative way. Well, the evangelical churches don't have this problem, but the Charismatic Church has to deal also with "prophetic word." The questions are many: 1) How to fight the good fight of faith successfully to make His promises come true in our lives? 2) How to make sure that "this prophetic word" is a true word, a true promise from God? 3) Is there a guarantee when God makes you a promise or can the person say no to God, even though she knows God's will? What do you do in this situation? Do you wait like Abraham for God's will to be done, for his or her will to line up with God's will? Is it a sin or a lack of faith to move on and not wait? There needs to be some training in this area as well.

Summary

Many of these comments from singles are cries for help. Writing this book reminded me of when I first heard their need. I was the closing keynote speaker for Family Week in the Denver area many years ago. This closing event was a Sunday evening at a mega church. I was told that there were 3,000 people in the audience.

I'd struggled all week trying to hear from God as to what to say. I actually went into the pulpit not knowing what I was going to say. The Holy Spirit led me to speak to the singles first. As I spoke, I noticed a group of 400-500 singles sitting in a certain section.

When I finished the sermon, these singles mobbed me. They were saying, "No one ever speaks to us in a sermon." They shared their struggles with sex purity; as singles never been married; single moms and dads; some shared their struggles with their gender identity; their painful loneliness; and other issues that were heart-felt. I answered as many of their questions as possible.

I was physically whisked away from the crowd by one of the event organizers who wanted to have dinner with me. Although I resisted, I was strongly advised to go. I felt I could have done so much more even though I didn't know what that was. If I had had thought of it, I would have given the single's leader my number and returned to talk, listen and love them.

Now, I hope I can help with this book and by meeting singles and senior pastors across the country to do what?

I'm not sure pastors and their staffs are hearing their numerous and complex needs and issues.

As a former pastor, the last thing I want to do is offend pastors. I know how easy it is to develop tunnel vision and unintentionally overlook a group with whom you may not be familiar or comfortable.

My prayer is that this chapter will be a tremendous blessing and opportunity for pastors to give and learn from singles in their church, if they are not already doing this. I also pray that pastors won't be defensive, but prayerfully begin asking singles in their churches, "What should be some of our first steps to serve singles in our church?" This sampling of singles sharing their various issues and concerns calls for churches to begin integrating, equipping in biblical and practical relationship principles, as well as protecting singles from wolves in sheep's clothing.

Every church is different and so are the singles attending each group. Some singles want Bible studies specifically for singles and others don't. So, as in all ministries, not everyone will be satisfied. Ministries aren't perfect just as people aren't. But this doesn't excuse our churches from making a concerted effort to serve and offer healing to the often-neglected members of the Body of Christ. We must all be prayerful and proactive.

SUMMARY POINTS

1. From singles who regularly attend church, it is their perspective (in most cases) that the church does little to specifically meet their needs whether teenagers or singles in their sixties.

2. Most single churchgoers feel their churches treat them like outsiders. Singles feel tolerated, certainly not celebrated, by their churches.

3. Churches need to stop viewing singles as abnormal simply because they are single.

4. Many singles feel there is a double standard for them versus married couples. For example, if a single has issues and wants counseling, particularly in the area of relationships, they are often told to pray and wait for God's timing. Yet, counseling for married couples is a priority in most churches.

5. The church needs to create "safe communities" for singles, not separating them by gender (all guys versus all girls).

6. Church should feel like family for everyone. Many singles feel isolated and alone.

7. The church should pray for its singles.

8. Being single should not be viewed as a *season of life*; but as a gift to the church.

9. It would be wonderful according to older singles if the church could provide physical activities.

10. Don't assume that singles need or want cross-gender interaction in every aspect of their lives.

11. The church should encourage the pursuit of purpose, passion, and professional development.

12. Many singles want to be integrated into the mainstream of church life with married couples and families.

13. Some churches are doing an outstanding job of integrating into the mainstream of church life and supporting their singles.

14. Singles should take some responsibility in initiating friendships at church.

15. Singles need help with maintaining biblical principles of no sex before marriage, avoiding pornography, and other behaviors that are not biblical.

16. Churches should have married couples available to mentor those singles who would like the experience of being with such a couple.

17. Singles are a higher percentage of most church populations than most pastors realize.

18. The church needs to be proactive in its ministry to singles.

19. There needs to be clear biblical teaching on singleness (including God's will and God's Grace). Many singles feel God wants them married. Yet, in an age with most married at the ages of 14-18, Jesus Christ was still single at 33—making Him a "really old" single.

ACTION POINTS

1. To the Senior Pastor and Singles' Pastor, how many times a year is a sermon preached for singles?

2. If you never preach a sermon for singles, why do you think you don't? What are you communicating to your singles by not preaching a sermon regarding being single? Is this what you want to communicate to the singles in your church? Why or why not?

3. The church needs to provide more biblically based advice on dating and relationships for singles as well as get-togethers to take the pressure off dating, yet providing opportunities for singles to meet.

4. The church needs to provide realistic picture (good, bad & ugly of marriage & why many marriages are failing) of dating and marriage.

5. How do you help singles who are Christ followers experience their identity in Christ without being preachy or making these singles feel guilty?

6. As a church and church staff, are you praying for the singles attending your church? If not, why not? If yes, what are you praying for your singles other than for them to get married?

7. As a church are you nurturing and helping your wounded singles to heal? Why or why not?

8. How is your church protecting singles from each other and wolves in sheep's clothing?

Endnotes

Chapter Seven

1. Dr. Tom Lickona, Development Psychologist and Director of the Center for the4th & 5th Rs, wrote article entitled *10 Emotional Dangers of Premature Sexual Involvement.* http://www2.cortland.edu/dotAsset/199337.pdf

2. Sexual Revolution: http://james-a-watkins.hubpages.com/hub/Sexual-Revolution

3. Dr. Helen Fisher, Kissing's Effect on the Brain: http://www.youtube.com/watch?v=dSPypODYvg4&feature=related

4. The Witherspoon Institute, *The Social Costs of Pornography* (2010)

5. Quentin McCall: http://quentinmccall.com/overcomingsexualsoulties/

Chapter Eight

1. Single Mother Statistics: October 13, 2012; *http://singlemotherguide.com/single-mother-statistics/*

2. *Modern Life Rough on Men by Dr. Sanjay Gupta, August 18, 2011, CNN Health - http://thechart.blogs.cnn.com/2011/08/18/modern-life-rough-on-men/*

3. These Fast Facts were written by Eli J. Finkel, Paul W. Eastwick, Benjamin R. Karney, Harry T. Reis and Susan Sprecher in their article, *Dating in a Digital World* in the September/October 2012 issue of *Scientific American Mind,* pgs. 26-33.

Chapter Ten

1. Focus on the Family: Marriage and Relationships http://www.focusonthefamily.com/marriage/strengthening_your_marriage/ commitment.aspx

2. Couple Prayer Series: www.coupleprayer.org

About the Author
Dr. Clarence Shuler

Clarence is husband to Brenda, father to three young adult daughters (he's the minority in their sorority), author, marriage counselor, speaker, and life and relationship coach. Clarence is President/CEO of *BLR: Building Lasting Relationships*. For nearly 30 years, Brenda and he have conducted marriage, men's, women's, and singles' seminars (United States & internationally). They're members of *FamilyLife's* Weekend to Remember Marriage Speaker Team and have also taught *Managing Marriage/Family & Ministry* for The Billy Graham Schools of Evangelism. Their relationship expertise also helps military marriages, especially in the area of overcoming affairs and surviving deployment. Clarence has assisted the Administration for Children & Families in its National African American Healthy Marriage Initiative. He's a certified Marriage Educator.

As a Life & Relationship Coach, executives experience fulfillment in their personal/professional lives. He's been featured several times in *Essence Magazine, Discipleship Journal, Black Enterprise* and other magazines as well as radio. He's authored six books, including *Keeping Your Wife Your Best Friend. Winning the Race to Unity* is used by colleges/graduate schools as a textbook, inspiring Wheaton College's first ever *Civil Rights Movement Conference!* A few of his cultural diversity clients: War College of U.S. Air Force, U.S. Army Equal Opportunity Advisors (Europe-based), Mississippi Valley State University, plus numerous churches, Christian universities & organizations. Clarence is a founding member of the Coalition for Black Marriages/Families. *Winning the Race to Unity* is also a resource for the 2011 diversity movie, *The Grace Card.* Clarence has spent the last few years speaking to singles on college campuses, in churches, and men's groups.

Clarence also is a Chapel Speaker for NFL teams.

Dr. Shuler's (a.k.a. *"The Love Doctor"*) Contact Information:

E-mail Address: clarencefs@gmail.com
Twitter: @clarenceshuler
Website: www.clarenceshuler.com
Facebook Community Page: Building Lasting Relationships
For Speaking Engagements: Please call 719-282-1340

About the Contributing Editor
Myrna Gutierrez

Myrna has appeared on local and national media including *CNN, C-SPAN*, and *NPR*. She has also been published in national and local newspapers and magazines. Her media experience spans producing TV for which she received a local Emmy Award and several other media recognitions.

A native resident of Los Angeles, Gutierrez graduated with a Bachelor of Arts degree from the University of Southern California (USC) and is a former member of the USC Alumni Board of Governors. Ms. Gutierrez was also named among Hispanic Business Magazine's 100 Most Influential Hispanics.

Recognizing the need for a singles forum, Gutierrez hosts a blog, singlesoutloud.blogspot.com where single women contribute stories about their adventures, issues, advice and other relevant topics to encourage singles.

Contact information: Singlesoutloud@gmail.com

More Down-to-Earth Insights from Dr. Clarence Shuler

Winning the Race to Unity
Dr. Clarence Shuler
ISBN- 10: 0-8024-8159-0
Also available on Kindle

Winning the Race to Unity is thorough, insightful, provocative and distinctly Christian. Clarence Shuler has given us an excellent resource to stimulate, guide and stretch us in our interracial relationships, so we as Christ's followers can lead the way instead of always trying to catch up. This book is to be read, discussed, prayed over and acted upon. I highly recommend it.

Randy Alcorn, author of *Heaven* and *The Purity Principle*

Dr. Jeffrey Shears
Dr. Clarence Shuler
ISBN: 978-146622553-

It is not difficult to be a biological father, but it is extremely difficult to be a successful father. All of us had fathers: some good, some great, some absent, and some abusive. I've never met a man who wanted to be a bad father. Most of us would like to be loving, kind, supportive, and good role models for our children. But most of us need help to make that desire a reality. In **What All Dads Should Know**, Drs. Shears and Shuler offer such help. The book is readable and practical. I highly recommend it to all fathers.

Gary Chapman, Ph.D., Author of *The Five Love Languages*

213

Your Wife Can Be Your Best Friend
Dr. Clarence Shuler
ISBN: 9781470020170
Also Available on
Kindle

In these pages, Clarence engages our minds and hearts . . . he shows us how to nurture the relationship with our life partner and identifies what it will take for her to be our best friend. This book is a valuable resource and a treasured tool to move us from self-centeredness to self-sacrifice.

Dr. Crawford Loritts, Jr.,
Senior Pastor Fellowship Bible Church

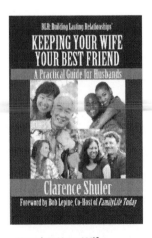

Keeping Your Wife Your Best Friend
Dr. Clarence Shuler
ISBN-13: 978-1491237731

In these pages, you'll find practical insights on how to make your marriage the kind of relationship that honors Christ and brings fulfillment to your life. The author, Clarence Shuler is the kind of mentor you want. He is honest. Real. Transparent. He's made his share of mistakes, just like the rest of us. But when he trips, he gets back in the game. He learns from his mistakes and from the rich wisdom he has found in God's word. There is hope for one of our greatest challenges just ahead.

Bob Lepine, Co-Host, *FamilyLife Today*

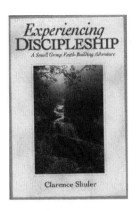

Experiencing Discipleship
Dr. Clarence Shuler
ISBN: 0-7644-2406-8

These 10 fun and engaging small group study sessions are designed to equip Christ followers with basic biblical principles that will result in a solid and mature faith. Through Bible-based discipleship, you'll grow deeper and stronger in your faith as you interact with others in a caring small group community setting.

A great group resource that also includes a personal through-the-week study option to help participants go deeper in God's Word.

An easy to follow and lead format that includes a unique *Faith-Building Adventure* action challenge in each session.

Soon to be released: ***The Discipleship Challenge***

These books are available on **www.clarenceshuler.com**

** One third of the profits from ***Single and Free to Be Me*** will help students attending Moody Bible Institute and help with research at Hampton University's National Center for American Marriage and Parenting. **Books purchased from Dr. Shuler's website will provide more money to students at both institutions.**

BUILDING LASTING RELATIONSHIPS PUBLISHING
www.clarenceshuler.com clarencefs@gmail.com
Twitter: @clarenceshuler
Facebook: Building Lasting Relationships Community Page
Clarence and Brenda Shuler

*For Speaking Engagements Call: 719-282-1340